Transformative Pastoral Leadership
in the Black Church

Black Religion / Womanist Thought / Social Justice
Series Editors Dwight N. Hopkins and Linda E. Thomas
Published by Palgrave

Transformative Pastoral Leadership in the Black Church

Jeffery L. Tribble, Sr.

palgrave
macmillan

BX
8468
.T75
2005

First published in 2005 by
PALGRAVE MACMILLAN™
175 Fifth Avenue, New York, N.Y. 10010 and
Houndmills, Basingstoke, Hampshire, England RG21 6XS
Companies and representatives throughout the world.

PALGRAVE MACMILLAN is the global academic imprint of the Palgrave Macmillan division of St. Martin's Press, LLC and of Palgrave Macmillan Ltd. Macmillan® is a registered trademark in the United States, United Kingdom and other countries. Palgrave is a registered trademark in the European Union and other countries.

ISBN 1–4039–6608–7

Library of Congress Cataloging-in-Publication Data

Tribble, Jeffery L.
    Transformative pastoral leadership in the Black church / Jeffery L. Tribble, Sr.
        p. cm.
    Includes bibliographical references and index.
    ISBN 1–4039–6608–7
    1. Christian Methodist Episcopal Church—Clergy—Case studies.
2. Pastoral theology—Christian Methodist Episcopal Church—Case studies. 3. Christian sociology—Christian Methodist Episcopal Church—Case studies. 4. African American women clergy—Case studies.
5. African American clergy—Case studies. I. Title.

BX8468.T75 2005
262'.14783—dc22   2004060231

A catalogue record for this book is available from the British Library.

Design by Newgen Imaging Systems (P) Ltd., Chennai, India.

First edition: July 2005

10 9 8 7 6 5 4 3 2 1

Printed in the United States of America.

Dedicated to Cherlyn and Jeffery Jr.
For your love, sacrifices, encouragement, and support

Contents

Series Editor's Preface

Jeffery Tribble has given us a book that, if taken seriously, can help the black church transition into the challenging demands of the twenty-first century. Tribble confronts head on the daunting calling of how to make black pastors become transformed leaders so that they, in turn, can foster the transforming agency of church members in society. Tribble, with a critical and self-critical mind, acknowledges that many black churches are not equipped to realize salvation and liberation in what he calls a post–Civil Rights, post-Christian, and post-industrial urban America. To tackle this problem, Tribble performed field work among a male- and a female-led black congregation. The reader of this book enjoys theoretical, methodological, and practical insights from an author who knows both the written texts of scholarly approaches to black churches and the living texts of what really goes on in these ebony ecclesial formations. Finally, we have a work that provides a plan for implementing salvation and liberation.

Tribble's excellent work broadens further the scholarly interests of the Black Religion/Womanist Thought/Social Justice Series. The series will continue to publish both authored and edited manuscripts that have depth, breadth, and theoretical edge and will address both academic and non-specialist audiences. It will produce works engaging any dimension of black religion or womanist thought as they pertain to social justice. Womanist thought is a new approach in the study of African American women's perspectives. The series will include a variety of African American religious expressions. By this we mean traditions such as Protestant and Catholic Christianity, Islam, Judaism, Humanism, African diasporic practices, religion and gender, religion and black gays/lesbians, ecological justice issues, African American religiosity and its relation to African religions, new black religious movements (e.g. Daddy Grace, Father Divine, or the Nation of Islam), or religious dimensions in African American "secular" experiences (such as the spiritual aspects of aesthetic efforts like the Harlem

Renaissance and literary giants such as James Baldwin, or the religious fervor of the black consciousness movement, or the religion of compassion in black women's club movement).

Dwight N. Hopkins, University of Chicago Divinity School
Linda E. Thomas, Lutheran School of Theology at Chicago

Acknowledgments

I am deeply grateful for the contributions of many persons who have helped me to bring this work to publication. I am indebted to the guidance and encouragement given by Linda J. Vogel, Margaret Ann Crain, Aldon Morris, and Mary Pattillo during my earlier work on this project in the Joint Ph.D. Program of Northwestern University and Garrett-Evangelical Theological Seminary. In particular, I cannot imagine how I would have persevered with a project on "spiritual pastoral leadership" without the guidance of Linda, who served as "midwife" for the birth of my research and writing. As a graduate advisor throughout my program, she traveled with me in a relationship of care and prayerful concern. Linda did not try to shape me in her own scholarly image, but encouraged me to seek out the resources and people who would help me in my own transformational journey.

In addition, I must acknowledge the contributions of other colleagues who generously offered their critique at various stages of the writing process. These persons included Dale Andrews, who serves on the faculty of Louisville Presbyterian Theological Seminary, as well as Larry Murphy and Jim Poling, my colleagues on the faculty of Garrett-Evangelical Theological Seminary. Jack Seymour, academic dean, provided the space for me to complete the research while beginning my journey as faculty member and administrator. Janet Allen, formerly an administrative assistant in church relations, was a great help in transcribing all of my interview tapes. Finally, through Garrett-Evangelical's Connecting the Seminary and Congregations Lilly foundation grant, I received financial assistance for travel, qualitative analysis software, and tape transcription.

My vision for researching the perspectives of leaders at various levels of the Christian Methodist Episcopal (CME) Church would not have been realized without the explicit consent of the congregations, clergy, and laity who are my "coresearchers." Because of our agreement to shield the identity of persons participating in this human subjects' research, I cannot name them in writing. However, using the pseudonyms that I have given them, I must express my gratitude for the ministers who were most responsible for my obtaining consent to do research in the two congregations: Bishop Isaiah Douglas, Presiding Elder Coleman Crider, Rev. Walter Harrison, and Dr. Carol Evans. No less important to this research was the cooperation of the officers and members of Christopher Temple and Isaiah-Matthews who warmly received me and shared their ministry experiences and perspectives of pastoral leadership and congregational ministry. I hope that I have been a good steward of their trust.

Originally, my research design called for more extensive comparative interviews with clergy of the African Methodist Episcopal (AME) and African Methodist Episcopal Zion (AME Zion) Churches. However due to the limitations of time, it was necessary to funnel the research down from the more ambitious study of "Pastoral Leadership in the Black Methodist Church" to the more manageable comparison of a male and female pastor of the CME Church. Using the pseudonyms that I have given them, I must still express my gratitude for the insights of Bishop James Norman and Rev. Michael Linton of the AME Zion Church as well as Rev. Benjamin Richards of the AME Church. Because of the depth of their knowledge of their churches, they have strengthened my knowledge of the praxis of pastoral leadership in the other black Methodist itinerant systems.

My "fantasy" of a broad ranging conversation on the subject, "The Quest for Transformative Pastoral Leadership in the Black Church" was carried out on a modest scale through the resources of the Center for the Church and the Black Experience at Garrett-Evangelical Theological Seminary. The presentations of Robert Franklin and Cheryl Townsend Gilkes especially challenged and expanded my thinking during the revision of my earlier drafts on this subject. With the cooperation of my colleague in congregational studies, Margaret Ann Crain, participation in this conference was a requirement for our Methods of Research in Congregations course. As a result, I acknowledge with gratitude the direct critique of several of our graduate students: JoAnn Deasy, Lorenzo Fincher, Christina Itson, Un Chu Kim, Christina Manabat, Mikyong Park, and Elizabeth VerHage.

My desire to see this research published was facilitated by the recommendations of the editors of this series on Black Religion/Womanist Thought/Social Justice: Dwight N. Hopkins and Linda E. Thomas. It was a pleasure working with them and it is really an honor for my work to be associated with them. The editorial staff of Palgrave MacMillan, has greatly improved the form of this work.

I must acknowledge with gratitude the support of my family and church family. My wife, Rev. Cherlyn W. Tribble continually encouraged me, saying, "You can do it!" while bearing with the inevitable family sacrifices involved in research and writing this book. Our son, Jeffery Jr., also was a great encourager and source of support. The members of my family of origin—my Mom, Mildred Tribble, sisters, Cecilia Tribble-Holmes and Sheree Tribble-Boyd, and brother, Rev. Dr. Sherman R. Tribble—and my parents by marriage—Alexander Washington, Jr. and Jacqueline E. Washington were all part of my support. My late father, Willie R. Tribble, still serves inspiration and example. I am thankful that my family, close friends, and Martin Temple AME Zion Church family kept me grounded in humility, love, and in the values that define what is first in my life.

Finally, I give God thanks for ultimately giving me guidance, grace, favor, healing, strength, resources, and opportunities for me to offer this book as a contribution to the church and the academy.

Introduction

Some of our churches are on life support systems. They are clinically dead. . . . We need to reevaluate the church as leaders. . . . We must ask the question, "Is your church a transforming church?" Not a transformed church for this implies a finished product. . . . Are you a transforming leader or are we stuck in tradition? In Matthew 7 Jesus said, "By their fruits you will know them." A good tree will bring forth good fruit. You will see the evidence of a transforming leader by how they make a difference.

—Bishop Douglas of the Christian Methodist Episcopal Church[1]

At the outset of my plans to conduct field research on "Pastoral Leadership in the Black Methodist Church," I was pleasantly surprised to discover the focus on transforming leadership in the Christian Methodist Episcopal (CME) Church. I had been welcomed by Bishop Douglas to visit the Tri-State Annual Conference of the CME Church in the summer of 2000 as a part of my comparative study of a selected male pastor and a female pastor ministering within the contexts of their congregations, communities, and the CME denomination. Although I had come to the conference with an interest in exploring the role of church leadership (bishops, presiding elders, pastors, and laity) in fostering transformation as well as in conserving tradition within the systems and structures of the CME Church, I did not expect the practical questions of church leaders and denominational officials to so nearly coincide with many of my own research concerns.

However, in 1998, the chief ruling body of the CME Church, the General Conference, adopted as their quadrennial theme, "A Transformed Church: Living in Hope for the Life of the World." Thus, at all levels of the Church—whether General Conference, Annual Conference, District Conference, or Local Church—the planned focus for this four-year period was on explicating the need for educating and mentoring transforming leadership in such a way that these leaders would then have the spiritual and practical wisdom necessary to change individuals, congregations, and communities. Thus, a serendipitous discovery (or act of providence) was that my interest in researching transformative pastoral leadership in the black church occurred at the time when the CME Church was focusing on this practical concern.

The vignette placed at beginning of this introduction is an excerpt from the communion message shared by Bishop Douglas in his Tri-State Annual Conference in the summer of 2000. The concept of a transforming leader is contrasted with a leader "stuck in tradition." Though we might say that the concept of a transforming leader is an elusive one related to the complexities of leadership in the black church, Bishop Douglas reminds us that the evidence or indicators of persons being transforming leaders is "how they make a difference."

Although I had come to this conference with a central question in mind, Bishop Douglas's message and my participation in the rest of the conference helped me to continue my work of framing basic questions for my study. Thus, I began my field research in November 2000 with the following set of questions: What is the role of pastoral leadership (also bishops, presiding elders, and lay leaders) in fostering transformation as well as in conserving tradition within the systems and structures of black Methodist churches? What practical wisdom, qualities of leadership, skills, and experiences are necessary for the praxis of faithful and effective leadership in black churches? How do black Methodist churches educate and mentor clergy for effective pastoral leadership? How do pastoral leaders in black churches help their congregations fulfill their historic mission of effectively responding to the social crises of urban America? Finally, how can the praxis of pastoral leadership be transformed so that congregations better fulfill their mission in oppressed local communities?

These and other related questions guided my sampling process of the activities, accounts, and archives of the work of these congregational leaders within the context of their communities and denomination over the course of approximately one year. After my initial research in August 2000 at the Tri-State Annual Conference, my participant observation at Christopher Temple and Isaiah-Matthews continued on the first Sunday of November 2000.[2] I ended my active participant observation in their activities after being present for Easter Services, April 2001. My last interviews were completed in August 2001. Though my direct observation of pastoral leadership in my two congregational sites was limited to a six-month period (November 2000–April 2001), my analysis of their ministries is over the course of their pastoral tenure from the time of my research back to the time of their respective appointments.

The premise of this research is that a new vision of pastoral leadership in the black church is needed at the outset of the twenty-first century. My vision is that "transformative pastoral leadership in the black church" is needed to transform individuals, churches, and society. This new vision is needed because many denominational black churches do not have the capacity to empower persons and communities for salvation and liberation. This vision grows, not only out of my love for the church, but out of my theological commitment to the mission of the church in the world. In particular, I am committed to the classical mission of the church, that of "making disciples" of all cultures, as well as to the conviction that the black church continues to have a special calling to be an instrument of survival, elevation, and liberation of its people. In a new urban context, that I describe as post–civil rights, post-Christian, and postindustrial city, new strategies of transformation are needed.

Central to this work is the conviction that we must learn about the subject of transformative pastoral leadership in the black church not only from scholars who have written about related subject areas, but also from living people who have much to teach us. In particular, I advocate for a gendered perspective of leadership in the black church. I have chosen an exemplary female pastor as well as an exemplary male pastor to feature in this study. Though the pastoral office is my primary focus, I expand my view of the pastoral vocation to include laity with leadership roles as well presiding elders and bishops. Thus, the whole hierarchical structure of leadership in this black Methodist context—bishop, presiding elder, pastor, and lay leader—is a focus of my exploration. Thus, the gender tensions that are present in the black church because of the ambivalence over the roles of women at all levels of this black Methodist church are seen in this study.

Chapter 1, The Quest for Transformative Pastoral Leadership in the black church, introduces this study as an explicit interpretive dialogue between me and others. W. E. B. Du Bois's vision of the "Negro minister," that of one who is an intellectual and moral leader, ethically astute, spiritually grounded, and practically trained, is set as a classical touchstone for this. As in the past, the black community is in need of leadership that is committed not only to the future salvation of black people, but also to present salvation (i.e., the quest for freedom, healing, and wholeness) as well. However, Du Bois and other more contemporary voices, like Cheryl Townsend Gilkes, remind us of the central and indispensable role of black women to the health and leadership of institutions in the black community. At the heart of this chapter, I introduce my emerging concept of transformative pastoral leadership in the black church and how my approach to studying pastoral leadership grows out of my own journey in the praxis of pastoral leadership. I close this introductory chapter by introducing the pastoral leaders whose ministries in the contexts of congregation, community, and denomination provide the primary data for this work.

Chapter 2, "God Did It": A Tale of a Male Pastor in a Transforming Traditional black church, is a narrative of the experiences of Rev. Walter Harrison over the course of his fifteen-year ministry at Christopher Temple CME Church. Through my eyes, "God Did It" is a witness to God's transforming grace by this pastor and people. The basic story line is of the ministry praxis of Rev. Harrison, a student of the CME Church itinerant system, who was educated and mentored in the living tradition of the black preacher. His vision of "salvation, education, and liberation" resonated with congregational leaders and members with whom he made the "dream work through team work." Through his ministry, he not only fosters continuity with the black church traditions but also creates innovative ministries for the present circumstances.

Chapter 3, "God of a Second Chance," A Tale of a Female Pastor in a Transforming Merged Mission Church, is a narrative of the experiences of Dr. Carol Evans over the course of her seven-year pastoral tenure at Isaiah-Matthews CME Church. "God of a Second Chance" in my eyes is a witness to the radical transforming grace of God who not only forgives people, but also offers a new start for a merged congregation in a changing community. The basic story line is that of the "blessed burdens" of a black woman pastor in the CME Church. This female pastor, despite the ecclesial patriarchy of her church, entered the system, learned to "manage the messes," proved herself capable as a leader, and nurtured "partners in stewardship." She works in this context of urban crisis to transform attitudes and behaviors by building up the people's self-esteem. The result is not only the renovation of a burned-out facility and numerical membership growth, but also the work of building what I describe as a community of survival, healing, and wholeness. By "keeping it real," she and others move toward greater healing and wholeness.

Chapter 4, Emerging Strategies of Transformative Pastoral Leadership in the black church, discusses the common urban context for black urban religion, which I describe as post–civil rights, post-Christian, and postindustrial city. The two "tales of transformation" are compared, contrasting the different resources, structures of leadership, and congregational cultures. Because of their different situations as well as their different gifts and graces for ministry, Rev. Harrison and Dr. Evans develop different adaptive strategies as the means of transforming their congregations. These strategies are then analyzed to summarize what I have begun to learn about the emerging concept of transformative pastoral leadership in the black church.

Chapter 5, Independent Black Methodist Systems as Contexts of Transformative Pastoral Leadership, explores the question of how black Methodist denominational systems can be irrelevant to, a hindrance to, or a supportive context for the work of transformative pastoral leadership. This study of the possibilities, problems, principles, processes, and practices of transformative pastoral leadership was first inspired by my reading of Warren's *Purpose Driven Church*. It is widely used as a congregational developmental resource. However, Warren dismisses denominational churches that rotate pastors as a context for the study of pastoral leadership. Warren writes:

> Can you imagine what the kids would be like in a family where they got a new daddy every two or three years? They would most likely have serious emotional problems. In the same way, the longevity of the leadership is a critical factor for the health and growth of a church family. . . . Churches that rotate pastors every few years will never experience consistent growth. I believe that this is one reason for the decline of some denominations. By intentionally limiting the tenure of pastors in a local congregation, they create "lame duck" ministers.[3]

Frankly, I did not enter this study expecting to disprove this theory of the problematic of getting a "new daddy" or a "new mommy" every few years. However, I did see a need for studying how health and growth was possible in an itinerant system of ministry where pastors are moved from time to time. Evangelism and church growth in itinerant context are not the only mission concerns in this study. I have chosen the independent black Methodist context as a focus because of their explicit historic mission "to lift the downtrodden" and "to set the captive free" as a particular mission growing out of the black experience in America. This particular mission priority of the black church is seen in tension with the universal mission of "saving souls."

Chapter 5, explores how transformative ministry is possible in the itinerant context because of visionary leadership. There are tensions because of the hierarchical structure of leadership as well as because of the natural tendency to not want to deal with complex issues of change. This chapter takes on the pertinent question of the upward mobility of black women in this black Methodist context. The book closes by exploring the implications of a model for fostering movements of social reform. I suggest that this might be used as a framework for creating communities of transformative pastoral leaders who have the character, courage, compassion, competence, and commitment to make a difference in the lives of people, churches, and communities.

The Quest for Transformative Pastoral Leadership in the Black Church

The Negro minister needs to know and do more than preach and pray. He must be possessed of public spirit and have the capacity to cooperate in educational and other social movements which promise present as well as prospective salvation. He must fit himself to preach and also practice the scripture that hath the promise of the life that now is as well as that which is to come.

—*Du Bois*, The Negro Church

On February 8, 2003, talk show host Tavis Smiley convened a conference that was called "The Black Church: Relevant, Repressive, or Reborn?"[1] Some of the most trusted and best-known spiritual leaders of the black church[2] serving in the church and academy were invited to participate.[3] I learned about the conference via e-mail messages sent in advance to make sure that the word was spread about this important interpretive dialogue. Has the black church, "our refuge in times of trouble" abdicated its responsibility on the most critical issues of our time? Does the black church have any response to the issues of gang violence, HIV/AIDS, or U.S. policy toward Iraq? Many Americans tuned in to this critical discussion within the black community, which was aired on C-SPAN. Undoubtedly, this telecast provoked numerous conversations as blacks talked among themselves in black churches, around seminary lunch tables, in barbershops, and in beauty parlors across the country.

In my mind's eye, I envision another conference, perhaps more ambitious in some ways than the one that Smiley convened. In my fantasy, I am the convener of this conference. I moderate the discussion.

I report the discoveries of this set of conversations to the world. The chosen medium of dissemination is this book.

The writing of a book is always a communal affair. In some ways, this book presents snapshots of the black church today. The central question that is debated and discussed is "What form of leadership is needed for these critical times in the life of the black community?" Many people in the black community would respond that one of the crucial arenas of leadership in our community is the vocation of pastoral leadership. Even though, as I explain later, the pastoral vocation is embodied by some spiritual leaders who are not serving in the pastoral office, the work of those spiritual leaders serving in the pastoral office *is* central and indispensable to all who work toward the health of the black church and the black communities. Nevertheless, recognizing that much is wrong in the black church and black community, I think there needs to be further dialogue about the transformation of people, churches, and communities. The black church that has been vaunted as a "refuge in times of trouble" for its people is itself in trouble.

With this as a working assumption, I entitle my conference "The Quest for Transformative Pastoral Leadership in the Black Church." All of the invited participants at this large circular table share three important assumptions. First, they care about the health of the black church. Second, they believe that the black church has a critical role to play in the black community given its track record of being the dominant social institution in our community. Third, they believe that the rise and fall of that church depends on its leadership.

Like Smiley I have invited persons who are capable of articulating the crises that we now face and also the diversity of our community's thinking on the issues. Prominent pastors, bishops, denominational leaders, black theologians and womanist theologians, sociologists, community activists, and civil rights leaders are all invited to represent communal perspectives. Gendered perspectives are evident in the variety of the panelists' presentations.

There would be some differences in my conference. First, I would bring to the table the voices of representative leaders from the past, as well as the present. Second, I would not limit my invitation of pastors to those who oversee large churches. The voice of the pastor in small struggling churches must be heard as well. Third, I would also invite representatives of the views of the people in the pews. Trustees, stewards, Christian educators, pastors' spouses, prayer warriors, and Sunday School teachers must sit at the table as well. Dedicated matriarchs and patriarchs with limited formal schooling would also be invited to speak because of their practical wisdom. Last, I would have an active voice at the table, shaping this communal discussion and guiding it forward in a respectful and constructive manner.

This book is, in some sense, my living out of this fantasy. From my perspective, the subject that I am trying to understand is a concept that I call, "transformative pastoral leadership in the black church." The problem of generating theories to better understand transformative pastoral leadership in the black church rests on the general principle that leadership does not occur in a vacuum; it always occurs in a community, in a group, in a social–historical context. I envision myself as being in relationship with a community of knowledgeable persons with whom I am trying to generate greater understanding of wisdom that is all a part of us, and yet beyond us. These "knowers"—female and male clergy, lay church leaders, theologians, sociologists, scholars of the black church in the past and present—are connected by their common concern for discovering truth about the black church and its ministry to the world. None of us is, in the final analysis, "experts" passing down knowledge to "amateurs." We all have a stake in the black church and bring valuable knowledge to the table.[4] Moreover, the life of the world beyond the sacred walls of our institutions is at stake, and many are languishing who are within the membership.

If such a discussion were to occur, I am sure that it would be a noisy one. Egos would clash. Temperatures would rise. Some "expert" would try to show his or her "knowledge" while some layperson would shake his or her head and say, "You don't know what you're talking about!" If some of the brothers were indifferent to women's perspectives, one of the sisters (or a sensitive brother) would rise up and remind us, "If it wasn't for the women, you wouldn't have a church!"[5] At the end of the discussion, there would probably not be any neat "prescription" to solve all of the problems. However, we would probably leave with more insight, hope, and appreciation of our mutual struggles. We would have increased resolve to use some of what we have learned to make a difference.

This book is the external product of this inner vision. In this chapter, our journey begins with a historical perspective, a classical sociological view of the black Christian minister articulated by W. E. B. Du Bois. This represents almost a core vision of the educated black "public theologian" who is fit to lead in the classical dual mission of salvation and liberation. Writing in conversation with Burns's idea of "transforming leadership,"[6] Franklin develops a cultural understanding of transformative leadership in his concept of the "public theologian."

Franklin's twenty-first-century vision of black pastoral leadership is of the public theologian who is an anointed spiritual guide, a grassroots intellectual, a civic enabler, a steward of community development, a cultural celebrant, a family facilitator, and a technologically literate visionary.[7] Franklin's model is a helpful ideal of the kind of pastoral leadership needed in the black community, but I hope to add additional substance to the ongoing conversation through my own tales of transformation, strategies for change, and concept of transformative pastoral leadership in the black church.

Recognizing that there have been many changes in the situation of the black church, I give a brief assessment of those changes that have brought us to the present critical moment. Because a central focus of this text is challenging the assumed "males only" nature of black pastoral leadership, I continue by introducing gendered perspectives of this quest. Then, at the heart of this chapter, I introduce my concept of transformative pastoral leadership in the black church. In my view, transformation can be construed in many ways and understood from a variety of perspectives. Hence, I describe these multiple modes and the bodies of literature that shape my own perspective on this concept. Acknowledging that the discoveries of this qualitative research are shaped by who I am, I help the reader to know who I am in my discussion of "the researcher as research instrument," as well as in my description of my praxis of pastoral leadership. Finally, I close by introducing the pastoral leaders who are central to my study.

Historical and Present Perspectives of the Quest

At the start of the twentieth century, W. E. B. Du Bois's vision of pastoral ministry was indicative of the historically prominent role of black Christian pastors in mobilizing people for mission in the public arena as well as in maintaining and developing their congregations. Linking race and religion, Du Bois calls for intellectual and moral leadership in the pulpit because of the dominant role the black church played in the lives of blacks, whether or not they were members of the institutional church. He is concerned with the qualities, the practices, and the training that will enable the black pastor to be a catalyst for present and future salvation in a context of continued racial oppression. He calls for a trained ministry that is "dominantly ethical and spiritual" as well as moral and intellectual. Building upon the academic foundation of "broad culture and thorough scholarship,"

Du Bois recommends that theological training be "practical" because the race needs "good, educated . . . leadership in all that pertains to race development."[8]

Du Bois's core vision of the black pastor as someone equipped to lead in the crucial matters of present and future salvation is a helpful one. It is, however, dated: we have witnessed since that time important changes in black churches and communities. These changes include the transformation of the Negro Church to the Black Church;[9] the urban migrations of blacks from the South to the North and now back to the South; the rapid expansion of a new black middle class; the development of black secular institutions, and the rise of competing black religions;[10] and some limited acceptance of women as preachers and pastors in the historically black denominations as well as the acceptance of black women as preachers in predominantly white denominations.[11] Scholars of the African American experience have recognized pastoral leadership as critical in the history of African Americans because of the uniquely dominant role of the black church in black communities.[12] Although black secular organizations created in the twentieth century have lessened the dominance of the black church, there is still not a complete differentiation among the spheres of religions, education, politics, and economics in the black community. Hence, clergy and other members of the black church exercise a great deal of influence in institutions and political processes as they work through the black secular institutions.[13]

Gendered Perspectives of Leadership in Church and Community

All too often when the black community seeks the leadership that is needed in crisis, its quest for transformative leadership is focused on male ministers. Du Bois's description of the Negro minister in *The Negro Church* is exclusively male as one would expect given the limitations placed on women in American society a hundred years ago. This is not to say that he was not keenly aware of the crucial influence of black women who, despite simultaneous structures of inequity based on race, gender, and class, contributed to the emancipation of all women and hence to the realization of American democracy. In *The Gift of Black Folk*, he devotes an entire chapter to analyzing the key influences of black women, many of whom were poor and uneducated but who "rose out of the black mass of slaves not only to guide their own folk but to influence the nation."[14]

Du Bois writes of black women's influence in economics, showing white women the way toward an economically independent womanhood. In 1910, half of black women over the age of ten worked outside the home, compared with one-fifth of white women. Many of these black women had only the beginnings of an education, with 40 percent of those over sixteen unable to write.[15] Du Bois lauds these women, who were working as farm laborers, farmers, teachers, washerwomen, and in the trades, as "a group of workers, fighting for their daily bread like men; independent and approaching economic freedom."[16] He further argues that Sojourner Truth's "Ain't I a Woman" speech, delivered at the second National Woman Suffrage Convention, provided direction and inspiration for white women's rebuttal of the usual sentimental arguments against women working outside the home.[17]

The historic work of black women in the ongoing struggle for total freedom should not be forgotten. Harriet Tubman is often cited as "the Moses of her people" because of her journeying back and forth between free and slave states leading hundreds of black fugitives to freedom. Du Bois also cites the less well-known example of Mammy Pheasants, a shrewd businesswoman who was a conspirator in and benefactor to John Brown's revolt at Harper's Ferry in 1858.[18]

Perhaps most pertinent to this present work is Du Bois's insight into the effectiveness of black women in terms of the social uplift of people through their personal contact with the downtrodden of society. Not so much through the giving of money, but by giving their personal service, black women then and now serve society through their churches, social clubs, missionary societies, and sororities, ministering to all sorts of needs. They work to visit people in prison, help in hospitals, teach children, distribute charity and relief, and sustain outreach to orphans and the elderly. To the extent that these social needs do not become a drain on the broader society, this little known work provides an essential safety net of social services.[19] Engaging in preaching and pulpit leadership was rarely an option for women as a mechanism of social uplift, but the practices of ordinary black women working with the downtrodden through personal contact demonstrated their "public spirit" as well as their practice of the scriptures preached by black male preachers.

Gilkes builds upon this theme to demonstrate the primary and indispensable role of black women in church and community. Chiding those ignorant of the leadership of black women in the past and those who are blind to their transformative leadership even today, Gilkes asks, "Why do we ignore the legacy and lessons of black women in our quest to discover transformative pastoral leadership in the black church?"[20] She argues that black women need to be placed in the foreground of studies of the black church and community because of their "agency, centrality, importance, and indispensability to their churches and communities."[21]

To take seriously the indispensable role of women in religion, we must begin to examine the inherent gender tensions, conflict, and ambivalence toward, women's experiences and women's roles. Gilkes writes:

> Taking seriously the social fact of gendered antagonism in religion means always addressing the patterns and processes that women and men construct as they go about the routine of sacred work. Black women and men share a religious life but often disagree about how that life should be organized and the relative importance of women's roles to that life. Black men and women agree on the necessity of opposing racial oppression, but they often disagree over the degree to which the patriarchy that is normative in the dominant society should be reproduced in their lives.[22]

As I develop my concept of transformative pastoral leadership in the black church, I attempt to bring the experiences, voices, and wisdom of black women, clergy and lay, into this critical dialogue. In both of my research settings, the pastors are interested in fighting the twin evils that one of the featured pastors in this study calls "racial and sexual apartheid."

The Concept of Transformative Pastoral Leadership

A new vision of black pastoral leadership is needed at the outset of the twenty-first century, a time when many denominational black congregations are struggling to fulfill their traditional priestly and prophetic functions in communities that really need the spiritual and social services that these congregations provide. As Lincoln and Mamiya explain in their discussion of the dialectical model of the black church, the priestly function involves worship and maintaining the spiritual life of the membership. The prophetic function, although it includes the classical notion of pronouncing the radical word of God's judgment, also includes the church's involvement in the political concerns and activities of the broader community.[23] Furthermore, in a complex time of rapid changes, which scholars can describe only by a series of adjectives preceded by "post" (e.g., post–civil rights, post–black power, post-industrial City, post-modern, and post-Christian), the mission and practices within the black church movement need critical assessment and renewed vision.

At the start of the twenty-first century, the black church is being transformed by internal and external forces. As in the past, the social crises in the black community place special burdens on the black church. Furthermore, respected observers of American congregational life believe that it is far more challenging to be an effective pastor today than it was in the past. Believing that there are many discontinuities with the experience of pastors and congregations from fifty years ago, Schaller writes:

> It was far easier to be an effective parish pastor in the 1950s than in the 1990s. One part of the explanation for that statement is the increased competition for new members. Another is the distrust of institutions. A third has been the erosion of denominational identities by the success of ecumenism and the attractiveness of the large nondenominational congregations. A fourth is the skill required to choose wisely from among that exploding abundance of resources now available to pastors and congregations. Perhaps the most important single factor is the rising level of expectations people bring to church. The emergence of the consumer-driven economy . . . has raised the level of expectations people bring when they shop for . . . a new church home.[24]

Andrews puts this situation of discontinuity with the past situation of the black church in the social context of the black community as he argues that the black church has failed to come to grips with the extent that it has been impacted by American individualism. Even while seeking to work toward the espoused goals of the transformation of souls as well as of society, there is fragmentation. Precisely because of the gains of the civil rights movement, we are a fragmented community in which critical areas of our community, such as poor urban youth, young adults, and successful middle-class blacks often feel that the black church is irrelevant to their struggles. This impacts the mission and message of the black church. Andrews writes:

> The question becomes, How does the church shape itself, its message, and its mission? The predominant refuge image in black churches has failed to sustain effective social reform even within the black community itself. The circumstances of fragmentation require attention to corporate

and cultural identity, as well as values and needs, in the quest for liberation from racial oppression in all its sociopolitical and economic forms. Neither the immediacy of survivalism nor essentialized political notions of blackness can alone comprise adequately the central pattern of liberation in the ecclesiology of black churches today.[25]

Today, as in the past, the black church must continue its tradition of adaptation to its new circumstances, while remaining rooted in the grace of God. In a similar call for transformation of the church a missiology scholar writes: "The contemporary world challenges us to practice a 'transformational hermeneutics,'[26] a theological response which transforms us first before we involve ourselves in mission to the world."[27]

Hence, the thesis of this work is that transformative pastoral leaders are needed to cooperate with God's work of transforming the Church, the people of God, in light of the perspectives of the past and the challenges of the present and future. This is essential if the black church is to effectively fulfill its mission in the world—an age of crisis and rapid change. By transformative pastoral leadership, I mean spiritual leaders who are intentionally engaged in the work of transforming persons, churches, and communities.

Spiritual leaders are women and men called of God within the context of their faith communities to lead the people of God in the pastoral vocation of priestly and prophetic ministry. Though some women and men are called by God and sacredly set apart to serve in the pastoral office, I believe that the pastoral vocation is in some sense shared by laywomen and by men as well. Harris writes helpfully of the ministry of people called by God to make a difference in the world:

> The pastoral vocation, as the phrase suggests, is a call to, and a demand for, a particular way of living. The particularity can be summed up in the word, "pastoral" which implies a caring for, and relationship to, persons, and an active and practical engagement to the work of Christian ministry. We are called to care: for ourselves, for one another, for the earth which is our home. We are called to take seriously our relation to God, and to all God's creatures, both within and beyond the church.[28]

Those who are appointed to the pastoral office embody the pastoral vocation in a special way, strengthening the people of God through the Word and the administration of the Sacraments. Their identity as pastors is a reminder to everyone that "God is the source and the strength of their life." By their calling, gifts and graces, education, and preparation, they are chosen to speak to the faith community and for the faith community. They uniquely represent their faith community in the broader church and world.

Although my concept of transformative pastoral leadership is centered on the pastoral office, I think that a healthy tension of the essential ministry of laity and clergy can be held together by this notion of a shared pastoral vocation. This, I believe, can be done without undermining the needed spiritual authority of clergy as overseers, builders, and leaders of God's people.[29] Laywomen and laymen are empowered by the Spirit to be hearers, believers, and doers of God's Word.[30] Together, clergy and laity must seek God's vision of transformation of people, their church, and their communities.[31] Transformative pastoral leaders must cease the "over under games" in which women and men are made to feel as though they are "just laity"—implying they are ignorant, lacking training and knowledge, and without power.

Transformative pastoral leaders tend to "the soul of a congregation" while building the congregation's capacity to address the concerns of the broader community. We can say that congregations have "a soul" in the sense that there is an enduring character to them over time even as people come and go. Other terms used to express this idea are "the personality of a congregation," "the identity of a congregation," or "the culture of a congregation." Of the soul of a congregation Frank writes:

> But congregations as intergenerational communities that stay together over time have their own corporate being, their own unique ways of expressing themselves and living in their world. They spin a rich and complex narrative; they make symbols; they weave a fabric of relationships; they carry out practices of worship, fellowship, using the cultural materials available to them.[32]

Too often, pastors come into churches trying to transform the congregation without understanding them. By failing to cultivate a disposition of paying attention to the particular congregations that they serve, making keen observations, asking questions, and gaining the trust of members of the church and community, they create unnecessary problems because of attempting to spend authority that they have not yet earned. Changes may be in order, but openings for ministry will grow out of their sensitive engagement with the congregation.[33] By taking the long view of respecting the soul of the congregation, allies may be discovered to help in making changes that would otherwise provoke unnecessary resistance. As in a marriage, you cannot make people change. But, you can interact with them in such a way that people choose for themselves the path of change. Leading in this manner, transformative pastoral leadership is a "dance" between leaders and followers or "a call and response" that involves both continuity and change.

Transformative pastoral leaders are open to being continually transformed themselves as they understand the interdependence of their ongoing growth and development as spiritual leaders and the transformation of individuals, churches, and communities. Transformation of persons and groups has many modes or forms. The many modes of transformation include dimensions that are spiritual, mental, physical, emotional, social, and political. Transformation is not simply change; it is a process of growth and development in a particular direction. From the perspective of Christian theology, the direction of transformation that we seek in persons and society is toward the kingdom of God manifested "on earth as it is in heaven."

Transformative pastoral leadership in the black church is a visionary concept that I seek to recognize and understand. Like all other concepts, it is a designation that we give to "something" that we perceive is a part of our social reality or is an ideal that we conceive in our social world. Yet, I believe that the concept of transformative pastoral leadership in the black church can be grounded in the social–historical–religious experiences of pastoral leaders and other church leaders. By engaging pastoral leaders and their followers in their social context, theories of a more effective praxis of ministry can be understood. The social context of the black church is the African American experience, which must be analyzed from the perspective of race, gender, and class.

The Meaning of Multiple Modes of Transformation

My understanding of the meaning of transformation is influenced by insights from my field research and several bodies of literature: evangelism, adult transformative education, congregational studies, and sociology of the black church. The literature of evangelism construes spiritual transformation of persons by conversion to faith in God through Jesus Christ. An evangelical theological framework envisions not only the prospect of changed lives by conversion to Jesus Christ, but also a call to lifelong growth and development as people of faith in mission in the world. Today's practices of evangelism must be joined with nurture. By construing evangelism more broadly (not simply leading an individual in praying a "sinner's prayer") in terms of a "set of loving, intentional activities governed by the goal of initiating persons into Christian discipleship in response to the reign of God,"[34] the evangelist can lay the foundation not only for assimilation into the community that shares the experience of conversion, but also for a moral vision that is communal as well as personal.

Though evangelicalism has often lost its way in holding in dialectical tension the complementary poles of "conversion" and "social engagement," it does not follow that evangelical commitment today necessarily undermines the communal value of social freedom. As we see in our tales of transformation, black Methodists are attempting to retrieve the Wesleyan synthesis of evangelism, nurture, church reform, and social responsibility.[35]

Though disciples may be of all ages, I have focused on the formation processes of adults in the context of church and society. In teaching and learning communities, adult transformative learning—growth and development of one's thinking processes and shifts in one's perspective—is the consequence of a faith development process that is cognitive, affective, and behavioral. Hence, transformation from the adult transformative educational perspective embraces changes in thinking, attitudes, relationships, and behavior.

The study of transformation from a congregational studies perspective asks questions of how faith communities interact with the larger social world. Viewing urban congregations as open systems, these congregations may reflect, resist, or influence urban transformations and other changes in the world. Finally, the sociological study of the black church intersects somewhat with the congregational studies perspective in its concern for understanding the church's response to societal changes and in its participation in movements of social change. Rather than prescribing one dimension of transformation as being indicative of effective transformative pastoral leadership in these contexts, I have chosen a more open-ended approach, seeking to describe and explain the modes of transformation wherever they are evident in these contexts.

The Researcher as Research Instrument

Because this study is an explicit interpretive dialogue between myself and the people studied, it is essential that I acknowledge my relationship to this study. In my qualitative research design, I understand myself to be the research instrument. As such, I have attempted to be keenly aware of how I have affected the course of the study throughout. For the reader to enter into this conversation, they must know something of who I am to critically judge the merits of this discussion.

As is more fully explained in appendix A: Research Method, I conducted field research simultaneously comparing and contrasting the activities, accounts, and archives related to pastoral leadership in two CME (Christian Methodist Episcopal) congregations over the course of a year. I acknowledge my own subjectivity as I worked in these social settings. My unique capacities were actively utilized to plan and conduct the field research and to reconstruct and represent these particular arenas of social interaction in new ways. In my preparation for this work, I sought to develop my spiritual, intellectual, and emotional capacities to be present with others in ways that are faithful to who I am and true to my research aims. The partial, situated, and subjective insights of this study express the relationship between me and persons in these faith communities, whom I seek to honor and empower as agents-subjects in a relationship of shared praxis.[36]

In the succeeding chapters, the perspectives of my research partners will be described and explicated; yet, who I am, the questions that are important to me, my presentation of self to others, where I situate myself in the field, and my ability to creatively revise my research strategies in the field are reflected in this work. Furthermore, various perceptions affecting my reception by the congregants were created as this African American male was introduced to congregants as "a fellow AME Zion pastor who is completing his doctorate at Northwestern University and is a professor at Garrett-Evangelical Theological Seminary using our church as a model for studying pastoral leadership." Whether perceived as expert, critic, pastor, professor, friend, or fellow traveler in the Christian journey of learning and discipleship, my presence was interpreted and people responded to my inquiries in light of their interpretation of who I am and my research aims. The reader of this book likewise must know the personal history that has shaped this research.

Praxis of Pastoral Leadership as Primary Source of Reflection

After receiving my seminary degree, I served as an associate minister at Martin Temple AME Zion Church in Chicago. A year later, I was assigned to my first pastorate, a small membership church in Gary, Indiana. Six years later, I was assigned a slightly larger membership pastorate in Chicago. These ten years of being engaged full time in the praxis of pastoral leadership[37] provided a range of ministry experiences and interactions. I use the term "praxis of pastoral leadership" to denote the ideal of an active, reflective, and creative ministry that holds in tension the theories and practices of ministry. In addition to serving as pastor in these churches and communities, I served in a variety of denominational leadership positions on the district conference, annual conference, and Episcopal district levels.

After becoming a candidate for the Ph.D., I accepted a faculty and administrative position at Garrett-Evangelical Theological Seminary. Choosing to contribute to the church and the society as a teacher, minister, and scholar, I am developing a ministry between the practice of ministry in the Church and teaching and research in the area of the practice of congregational leadership. Thus, I am a Christian pastor and theological educator whose ecclesial context is the black Methodist tradition and community of the Christian Church.

I must acknowledge that my initial research plans did not include a gendered perspective on leadership in the church and community. However, my experiences in the church as well as in the academy have helped me work on my own blindness to the system of privilege that I enjoy as an educated male minister in the black church that is at the same time a system of disadvantage to similarly educated women in ministry. My transition from my Gary appointment to my Chicago appointment provided a set of eye-opening experiences for me.

My transition from pastoring in Gary to Chicago was an abrupt one, occurring within the week after the annual conference where the bishop announces pastoral appointments. I received my seventh consecutive appointment to the Gary congregation at the annual conference. A friend of mine, a female pastor, was assigned to succeed the outgoing male pastor of the Chicago congregation. In an unusual series of events, this female pastor chose not to receive the bishop's appointment. Our bishop, choosing to exercise his prerogative to change appointments in the interim of the annual conference due to the necessity of filling both pastoral charges, elected to change my appointment to the Chicago congregation. At the same time, another female minister with a seminary degree was assigned to succeed me at the Gary church.

I was really surprised at the level of resistance that my successor received going into the Gary church. After all, she had been warmly received by the women of the congregation two years in a row as a Women's Day preacher! I feel that part of her troubles was related to the congregation's shock at losing their pastor who had reported the previous Wednesday after the annual conference for the prayer meeting only to discover a new pastor in the pulpit the next Sunday morning. However, I also felt that some of the congregation's resistance was due to the fact that my successor was a woman. Some of the same people that I had come to know as "good people" supportive of my ministry showed an ugly side to my successor.

Meanwhile, as I entered my new pastorate in Chicago, one of the members confided soon after meeting me that she was "so glad" that I was appointed. She had heard that a woman had been sent by the bishop. This influential church leader of some forty years said that if "that woman" had come to pastor, she would have left the church. She was determined to leave the church inspite of having not met the woman pastor who had been assigned!

I had served along side of this particular pastor as an associate and knew her to be a wonderfully competent minister. She was recovering from a rough time in her first pastorate. Before jumping into a new pastorate, she needed space to heal. Only later would I learn of the high rate of women leaving the pastorate due to the tensions and resistance that they experience. Naively I thought that if any female could succeed, this one could because she was so well qualified. In addition to her having a Master of Divinity degree, she also had a Master of Social Work degree. Thus, she brought to her pastoral ministry administrative and counseling skills that greatly exceeded my own skills.

Nonetheless, I was greeted warmly by my new congregation from the beginning. Working with the people, we developed our mission, vision statement, and action plans. In a few short years, we were blessed to experience significant spiritual revitalization and to accomplish needed renovations and repairs to a facility nearly a hundred years old.

During this period, I was well aware that I could not have accomplished much of anything without the support of gifted and committed women of the church. Yes, there were a "few good men" who provided great support. Yet, "if it wasn't for the women" I would not have dared to initiate some of the plans that we accomplished together. These women did more than simply "pay, pray, and obey." Some of these women were well educated and had proven to be visionary leaders and managers in their work settings. Other women and men, though lacking higher education, were persons whose leadership in various projects proved indispensable.

Comparing my experience of pastoral leadership with my sister colleagues, I began to question why my experience was vastly different. Whereas my two seminary trained sisters in ministry, both mentored alongside of me in the same local church, "caught hell" in their pastorates, I was being told by my presiding elder that he was recommending me as a candidate for "a first church in the denomination."

Relating that set of experiences to a black female classmate of mine in doctoral program (an ordained minister in the AME [African Methodist Episcopal] Church) some time later, she confronted me saying, "And what did *you* do to *prepare* the congregation to receive a woman as a pastor?" My only defense was that I had welcomed women to my pulpit to preach (on Women's Day and Missionary Sunday) and that I provided opportunities for the women who had answered the call to the preaching ministry (including my own wife) in my pastoral charge. I also thought I had modeled acceptance of women preachers through my public interactions with them.

However, my classmate's rebuke initiated my to reflection on these experiences. Only then did I begin to see how I had only provided token access to the pulpit that I controlled by allowing women to preach on Women's Day and Missionary Sunday. Like most of my male counterparts, when I invited someone else to preach, it was usually the pastor of a church at least the size of mine who could bring a choir and members to help raise an offering to help us meet our budget for the special occasion. I thought my reasons were sound spiritually (I wanted someone who was a proven preacher) and economically (I wanted someone who could help us to meet our budget). I was yet to reflect on why there were few women pastors in significant pulpits that I could invite to preach, despite the swelling number of women passing conference courses of study and earning seminary degrees.

When one of the persons on my dissertation committee suggested that I broaden my study of pastoral leadership to compare the experiences of a female pastor with a male pastor, it made sense. Why would I think it sufficient to research and write about "Pastoral Leadership in the Black Methodist Church" and leave the experiences of female ministers in the margins of my study? Why should I be satisfied with the progress of women in ministry as a part of the AME Zion Church in which Julia Foote was the first woman ordained to the ministry in 1894?[38] Furthermore, in the struggle for increased lay representation at the General Conference, the highest law-making body of my denomination, Miss Fannie Van Bronk was one of the first women duly elected as a delegate in 1892.[39] Why has the AME Zion Church, known as "The Freedom Church" because of its history of fighting against racial injustice led by members such as Sojourner Truth and Harriet Tubman, not also been a leader to empower women to work alongside of men in ministry? What personal responsibility did I have in dealing with this issue?

As I was preparing to leave my Chicago congregation to join the faculty of Garrett-Evangelical, I attempted to make a better transition for the sake of the congregation and for the sake of my successor. As it became known that I was leaving the church, two influential ministers asked me if the bishop was going to allow me to recommend my successor. After much prayer and consultation with other persons whom I respected, I decided to recommend a woman in the ministry, whom I knew to be well qualified to serve. In the interim of my recommendation and the bishop's actual appointment, my classmate's question continued to convict me: "And, what did *you* do to *prepare* the congregation to receive a woman?"

This time, I had the opportunity of better preparing the church for my transition from pastor to faculty member. One of the things that I did was a series of sermons on my departure and the necessity of them receiving the spiritual leader that the bishop chose to send. This time, I told them, that, from my vantage point, it was quite possible that the next pastor could be a woman. I talked about the increasing number of women acknowledging a call to the ministry and the increasing number of women who were working toward acceptance by obtaining full ordination credentialing as well as seminary training.

I preached about the struggle for gender justice in the African American church and refuted the moral, political, economic, and cultural dimensions of this struggle.[40] I concluded my message with the passage that so many women have had to stand on in defense of their preaching the gospel of Jesus Christ. In Acts 5: 33–39, the apostles themselves were being challenged for preaching the gospel. In defense of Peter and the other the apostles, Gamaliel, a respected teacher of the law urged the following:

> So in the present case, I tell you, keep away from these men and let them alone; because if this plan or this undertaking be of human origin, it will fail; but if it is of God, you will not be able to overthrow them—in that case you may even be found fighting against God![41]

The apostles continued to preach and succeeded, although it was "not without a struggle."[42] Though flogged on that occasion and persecuted, they succeeded despite the odds. In the same way, women, called by God, will have struggles, but they have succeeded when at least some of their detractors "let them alone." Five years later, I am pleased that the woman pastor sent by the bishop to succeed me in the Chicago congregation is faring well working with God and the people of God.

These are some of the experiences on my own journey of healing from my own sexism. I have discovered that healing not only takes time; it takes work. For me, this work includes my advocacy for the acceptance of qualified female clergy at all levels of the church through my research and writing as well as by my teaching and mentoring of female and male clergy.

Thus, reflection on my personal experiences in the black church and professional experience as a pastor and theological educator are sources for this research study.[43] I am following a practice–theory–practice model of research and reflection where I name my congregational studies as practical theology.[44] In this model, practical questions are generated from present crises in ministry. Many of the research questions are practical questions that arise from my experience as a pastor and leader in my denomination. My studies have provided theoretical frameworks to think about these questions and to generate new questions. These questions have been framed and reframed during the course of field research of pastoral leadership of two pastors in the context of their congregations, communities, and denomination.

Thus, the praxis of pastoral ministry, particularly as it is practiced in the black Methodist tradition, is my first source of reflection. I continue my reflection from my location within the field of the theory and practice of ministry. Before moving to the heart of this study, the two tales of transformation found in chapters 2 and 3, let me introduce you to the pastors and congregations that graciously consented to be partners with me in our quest for transformative pastoral leadership.

A Description of Pastoral Leaders Studied

Rev. Walter Harrison is the pastor of Christopher Temple, a well-established congregation of over 3,000 members in a solid black middle-class community of a northern U.S. city. In the tradition of the Methodist traveling ministry, this full-time pastor had been appointed by bishops to six previous pastoral assignments in his first seventeen years of pastoral ministry. After a pattern of moving with his wife and children to serve churches for no more than three years at a time, Harrison was appointed to Christopher Temple, a leading church of his denomination. At the time of this research, this denominational leader and community activist had served as pastor of Christopher Temple for fifteen years. Over his pastoral tenure, the membership grew from 1,200 members on roll with about 400 active to 3,000 members on roll with about 2,000 active. With a theological commitment to church growth and to developing leaders, Harrison received at least a hundred new members into the CME Church in each of the last twenty years of his ministry and helped twenty-five men and women develop their ministry as clergy in the CME Church.

Besides this record of evangelistic growth and leadership development, Christopher Temple emerged as an interesting case of the transformation of a traditional denominational church in the wake of the civil rights and black power movements under the leadership of Rev. Harrison, who was greatly influenced by these social movements. He began his pastoral ministry in the late 1960s, completed his seminary education in the early 1970s, and has been a community activist and national leader of Operation P.U.S.H. (People United to Save Humanity).[45]

Rev. Dr. Carol Evans is one of those persons received under Rev. Harrison's ministry who grew as a minister in the CME Church at Christopher Temple. She was appointed by Bishop Isaiah Douglas to serve as pastor of the Isaiah-Matthews Temple church, two fledgling congregations merged into one at the time of her appointment. She convinced her congregation, her bishop, and a bank that she could capably lead a quarter of a million dollar renovation of their burned out church facility. Under her leadership, the congregation has grown from 31 on roll to over 200. Dr. Evans wrote her Doctor of Ministry project to develop a methodology for renovating her facility and redeveloping the ministry. Despite the growth and development of the congregation, Isaiah-Matthews cannot afford to employ Dr. Evans as a full-time minister. Thus, she is a bi-vocational pastor, maintaining a full-time secular position. Rev. Dr. Evans emerges in my study as an interesting case of the challenges posed by the growing presence of gifted, committed, well-trained female clergy in the black church, which is still dominated by male clergy leadership. Like many other clergywomen, she has carved out ministry as a "second career" independent of her first husband, who was a minister before his death.[46]

Though recently married, Evans was single during the time of my participant observation. Because of her Pentecostal background in ministry, she also illustrates how some black Methodists are reclaiming the Holiness-Pentecostal heritage, long neglected in denominations formed in the Wesleyan theological tradition.[47]

Appendix B: Clergy Interviews, gives background descriptive data on Rev. Harrison and Dr. Evans as well as the other clergy participants. All but one of the clergy interviewed (an associate minister of Christopher Temple) has achieved at least one graduate degree in theology. A bias of this study is that of the importance of a theologically educated ministry for my concept of transformative pastoral leadership in the black church. The category, "years in the traveling ministry" may be roughly equated to the number of years of service as an ordained minister. Thus, the reflections of these ministers are grounded in many years of ministerial praxis in the black Methodist context. Dr. Evans is, unfortunately, the only female clergy included in my research design. Her experiences, perspectives, and style of leadership are not meant to be representative of all women. However, in this study of transformative pastoral leadership in the black church, her voice is a minority voice that is given "equal" status to the male pastor in this study, Rev. Harrison.

Appendix C: Lay Leader Interviews, gives background descriptive data on the laypersons interviewed in this study. Six in-depth-taped interviews were done with leaders in each of the congregations. In some instances, husbands and wives were interviewed together with the goal of gaining a gendered perspective of Dr. Evans's ministry at Isaiah-Matthews. The church membership of the person interviewed, whether he belongs to Isaiah-Matthews or Christopher Temple is noted. All bear significant leadership responsibilities in their respective churches and are deeply involved in the life of their congregations. These lay leaders interact with their pastor through their manifold ministries as stewards, trustees, missionaries, Christian educators, evangelists, prayer leaders, and so on.

One important contrast in the characteristics of the lay leaders between the churches should be noted. On the whole, the leadership of the Christopher Temple members has a higher level of formal education. Whereas I have expressed my bias in my selection of educated clergy, I do not have that same bias with respect to the lay leadership. Some of the greatest insights were given by persons like Mrs. Cora Nolan, an eighty-one-year-old housewife with a tenth-grade education and Mr. Manford Billings, an eighty-year retired janitor with one year of college education. Nevertheless, formal education brings with it a set of skills and perspectives that may enhance transformative pastoral leadership. More importantly, however, we shall see in chapter 3 that Dr. Evans's efforts toward transformation were hampered by her work with what she calls "baby Christians."

Thus, these contrasting cases of pastoral leadership provided fruitful settings to analyze transformative pastoral leadership in the flow of congregational life. By generating theories of the praxis of pastoral leadership through the method of comparative analysis, it is possible to facilitate a conversation between particular cases and more general theories of behavior. I invite you to enter this conversation through the tales of transformation in the next two chapters.

2

"God Did It": A Tale of a Male Pastor in a Transforming Traditional Church

The gifts he gave were that some would be apostles, some prophets, some evangelists, some pastors and teachers to equip the saints for the work of ministry, for building up the body of Christ.

—*Ephesians 4: 11–12 NRSV*

High and lifted up above street corner sights and sounds at the gateway to the black middle-class community of Middleton[1] are carefully spaced posters on all sides of a yet undeveloped 275 foot by 245 foot corner property. The words proclaimed by these posters, "God Did It," are obviously intended to invite religious reflection by the thousands who daily pass by this commercial intersection adjacent to an expressway. This property acquisition is the site of Christopher Temple CME Church's yet unrealized dream of commercial development, affordable apartment rental, and a senior citizen high rise. It is one tangible expression of the belief that the black church continues their classic dual mission of autonomous African American worship and social service within the black community. I believe that this concern for the religious and secular welfare of the black community is within the best tradition of black religion.[2]

In the social context of Christopher Temple's black middle-class community, community economic development and other efforts to make the black community a better place to live may be interpreted as an evangelistic sign, a holistic way of building a new community ordered by principles of love and justice. As the pastor, Rev. Walter Harrison, Sr. says, "I am now clear that the black church must do the community development in our community. . . . We must teach spiritual development and economic development unapologetically!" This pastor is inspired by his U.S. Congressman who reportedly said, with regard to public investment dollars, "we can't be satisfied until the East Side looks like the West Side," a thinly veiled reference to inequities of public funding along racial and ethnic boundaries.[3] Pastor Harrison says, "It took a lot of prayer and about 5 years of hard work, but we got it. . . . You see the signs that we put on the property which say, 'God Did It.' "

Constance Harrison, Rev. Harrison's wife of twenty-seven years, says, it is an effort "to turn a negative into a positive" for the benefit of generations to come. Of her husband's motivation for the signs she says,

> I believe the reason my husband had that sign posted was because he wanted people to know that Christopher Temple stands as a beacon of light. He wanted people to know that there was no way in the world that man could take credit for what God did in terms of how this property became available through the prayers of the church, the fasting and through the conversation, wanting something positive to happen on that corner for the children, the next generation. . . . It's a reaffirmation of what God is doing in our lives, not only because of that building, the brick and mortar, but in our lives, spiritually, God is doing it.

Through my eyes, "God Did It" is a witness to God's transforming grace by this pastor and people. "God Did It" is an expression of Christopher Temple's theological belief that God is at work in the world, that they are called to be instruments of God's work, and that God is deserving of "the glory" and credit as they engage in the practices of religious and social ministry. With Rev. Walter Harrison at the helm of this ministry, "God Did It" can also be taken as an icon representing the "transformative pastoral leadership" over his fifteen-year pastoral tenure.

Transforming a Traditional Established Church

In the fifteen years since Rev. Walter Harrison was appointed as pastor, members and nonmembers alike have witnessed many changes— testimony to the growth and development of Christopher Temple. There are now three regular worship services, where there had been only the one traditional 10:45 a.m. Sunday worship. One of these is a Saturday "come as you are" worship service where the homeless are bused in from various shelters for worship, food, and clothing ministries. The Sunday worship services "with all the instruments going"—Hammond organ, two electric pianos, lead guitar, bass guitar, and full drum set—do not look like a customary Methodist worship service; demonstrative praise and worship is the emphasis throughout. These worship services are broadcast on two television stations. When Harrison arrived in 1986, there were about 1,200 members on roll with 400 active. Now, there are 3,000 members on roll with about 2,000 active. Of these new members, a significant number are men reached through a male emphasis ministry, Harrison's response to what he sees as systemic racist oppression of black men.

Members who had grown used to simply reading Bible passages from the hymnal are now active Bible students. Harrison preaches and teaches the Bible from a black historical and cultural perspective, an interpretive approach, which he feels is crucial to liberating black people in a racist society. This Afrocentric approach to preaching and teaching the scriptures was accompanied by Harrison replacing Eurocentric art (e.g., pictures of a white Jesus) with Afro-Asiatic depictions of Jesus and the disciples soon after his arrival.

Now, a full-time office staff, ministerial staff, and a team of volunteer leaders share the leadership, management, and administration of this ministry. This shift from church leadership being "a one man show" to a broad-based team of trained congregational leaders is seen as a significant shift from the past. This is part of the church's vision of generating leadership for church and society, a vision, which is supported through significant scholarship support, which the church provides for college students and ministers who pursue theological training in seminaries. Christopher Temple's One Church One School Program[4] links their church with local public schools in a collaborative effort to save children by helping them to value life and learning.

While the congregation's progress is not the result of the pastor's singular efforts, I would assert that pastoral leadership is decisive for the transformation of Christopher Temple from a traditional middle-class church to what it is today. The congregation's mission has emerged from a fifteen-year relationship of pastor and people at this particular time and place. Rev. Harrison came to Christopher Temple with a unique vision of the untapped potential of the black church to respond to the needs of its race.

A product of the social movements of the late 1960s and early 1970s, Harrison was educated and mentored in the tradition of the black

Methodist preacher in the CME Church. Harrison came to Christopher Temple looking for leaders to carry out his vision of transforming the church. Existing leaders found in Harrison a pastoral leader whose vision, of projecting the CME civic presence through evangelistic and social ministry, was what was needed at this time and place.

A Student of the Black Methodist System

Traditionally, the pastors of "flagship churches" in the black Methodist tradition, like Christopher Temple, are appointed because of a favorable relationship with a bishop who judges that they have the requisite "gifts and graces" to maintain that congregation for the denomination. Few CME churches have the resources to support a full-time pastor. As Bishop Douglas laments, "It takes a real good church [to provide for a full-time pastor and their family] and you don't have that many really good churches."

In response to my question of how he rose through the ranks from his pastoral appointment to his present appointment as pastor of Christopher Temple, a leading church in the denomination, Rev. Harrison replied, "I give God all of the glory, praise, and credit and also being a student of the system itself." He is saying, in effect, "God Did It"—ultimate credit belongs to God. But, he acknowledges that his rising through the ranks is not only a spiritual matter but a political one as well. Ministers who really understand "the system" of the black Methodist church and choose to compete as "players" take risks and receive rewards based on their knowledge of how to play "the game." Gleaning insights from various interviews with ministers who have received successively larger churches, it might be said that they "display their wares" in the "market" so that they might choose the "paths" of service at various levels of the denomination and thus have the best opportunities for use of their ministerial talents.

Some ministers, functioning in this competitive political system, do little that could be recognized as transforming persons or communities. How Harrison manages to do transformative ministry in the context of the Methodist system of governance is the subject of this chapter. But, first, defining the key concept of the traveling Methodist ministry is essential.

The Traveling Ministry in the CME Tradition

All Christians are increasingly recognized as "ministers," because of their baptism and gifts for service in the church and in the world. But, certain persons are set apart by the church as ordained ministers. The CME Church, a church "set up" on December 16, 1870, by astute ex-slave preachers working with leaders of the Methodist Episcopal Church South, has a system of ministry that is adapted from its Methodist traditions in light of the circumstances of the black experience in America.[5]

The roots of the pattern of ministry in the Methodist tradition go back to the early 100s CE, when it is clear that, typically, three orders of Christian ministry were recognized: deacons, priests (termed "presbyters" or "elders" in some Christian traditions), and bishops. Methodists, inheriting this pattern from the Church of England, prefer to call their second order, "elder" and to view bishops as a higher degree of elder rather than as a separate order of ministry. The CME Church follows the historic practice of the office of the Methodist deacons being a probationary office for those preparing for the office of elder. Elders are ordained to preach and administer the sacraments of baptism and Holy Communion.[6]

In this system of ministry, a distinctive innovation of Methodists is the itinerant or traveling ministry. This method of deploying ordained ministers proved to be a fruitful strategy for reaching an expanding American frontier in the 1800s. The practices of itinerant ministry have evolved somewhat in relationship to the changing society and the necessities of the church's mission of spreading the gospel. Campbell explains:

> One historic characteristic of the Methodist office of elders is their *itinerant ministry*. This originally meant that the elders traveled about from place to place, preaching in a different location from day to day as they followed large circuits. In American episcopal Methodist churches, the circuits have been reduced to the point that congregations expect the same pastor from week to week. Itinerancy still refers to the distinctly Methodist manner of appointing elders, where bishops in consultation with churches and "Presiding Elders" (AME, AMEZ, CME) [the black controlled African Methodist Episcopal, African Methodist Episcopal Zion, and Christian Methodist Episcopal denominations] or "District Superintendents" (UM) [United Methodist Church] assign elders to their pastoral charges. The Methodist itinerancy gave Methodists as a whole an advantage in evangelization through the 1800's, by allowing a particular flexibility in following the expanding American frontier.[7]

Thus, ordained Methodist preachers become members of a "traveling connection" and are in an accountable relationship with other ministers in their given annual conference over which their presiding bishop has oversight. As members of this "traveling connection," preachers are annually appointed to pastoral charges by the bishop. Frequent "moving" of preachers—changing their appointments to different pastoral charges—became characteristic of Methodism as bishops used their "godly judgment" of sending preachers to each pastoral charge as they judged best suited for the interests of the connection.

In this system of the traveling ministry of the CME Church, Rev. Harrison was appointed to six different charges in six different cities over his first fifteen years of pastoral ministry. His seventh pastorate, the Christopher Temple CME Church is one of the sites for this study of transformative pastoral leadership. Christopher Temple has become a place where his unique calling in ministry could be fulfilled in that context. How he got there is our next subject.

Rising through the Ranks of the System

Rev. Harrison is known by his members as a man of vision. In his mind's eye he has pictures of a preferred future. His recollection of a long-standing vision of ministry in the itinerant system in response to my question of how he was appointed to Christopher Temple is revealing. Rev. Harrison says:

> I always had a vision of our church growth, that the church could and should grow numerically, quantitatively, but also qualitatively. The quality of the ministry itself, its music, its ministries, its office staff, the way we serve our people could be certainly improved and I felt that if I had opportunities to do that and was in an area where there was people, flesh and blood people, I would have the opportunity to add souls to the church and see it grow.

This statement suggests to me a person who believed that his vision of ministry could be realized if he had opportunities to pastor in contexts with a sizable unchurched population and where there were resources to support his vision of his unique calling. His first appointment, which paid about $25 per week, may have qualified as a place to add souls to the church, but it certainly was not enough to support a family. Likewise, it did not have paid staff and ministries that he envisioned one day having as a pastor in the CME Church. When he asked his bishop, his "father in the ministry," why he was sent to such a place, his bishop responded, "Son that is why I sent you there because you have the skills and you have the gifts. Whatever you want, you have the skills and gifts to build that church to the level that you are capable of doing."

Rev. Harrison, in starting "at the bottom," was introduced to the "law of sacrifice" related to leadership in the black church and in other settings as well. Sacrifice is inherent in true leadership: a leader must "give up to go up." Whether he realized it or not at the time, sacrifice is required time after time for leaders. Of this principle, Maxwell writes, "Often, the greater the calling, the greater the sacrifice required."[8]

Some persons would merely "pay their dues" laboring without a vision of growth and development. In addition to the sacrifice involved in his decision to obtain an undergraduate degree in sociology and a Master of Divinity degree, Rev. Harrison became a student of "the system." His theorizing about his rise through the ranks is based upon his analysis of the Episcopal form of government in the CME Church, a tradition in which black bishops yield considerable authority over ministers through their power to ordain and appoint their preachers. In response to my asking what he meant by being a "student to the system" Rev. Harrison replied:

> Well, basically, I think that you have to know that a church is spiritual but also made up of human beings. As a political system, ours is an Episcopal form of government, so therefore you want to study the system so that you are able to put your best foot forward at all times. You want to be able to get the attention of the leaders to let them know, "I'm ready to play the game. I'm ready to enter the fray. I'm prepared. I have gifts and graces that will allow for me to serve the church well." Pretty much like you would say a football player, who works himself up from the minor leagues to the major leagues, and wants to let the coach know, "I'm the guy that can handle that appointment. I'm the guy that can get it done for you."

Functioning in a system that he sees as both spiritual and political, Rev. Harrison makes the following points about his rising through the ranks of the church. He has been intentional about studying the CME system from a spiritual as well as a political point of view. It is not uncommon for ministers to portray themselves in the best possible manner in front of the leaders who can open doors of opportunities— bishops, presiding elders, and leading pastors. It is important to prepare oneself to be productive in many aspects of ministry. An aspiring CME minister should demonstrate his or her willingness to help his or her bishop fulfill the bishop's visions as well as their own.

As Harrison says, let them know, "I'm the guy that that can get it done for you." His commitment to the denomination by being present for connectional meetings, paying registration and offerings, and being willing to serve on denominational committees without compensation is not incidental to the politics of being a leader in the denomination. By so doing, Harrison says, "not only was I counted, I was weighed!"

Lest one get the impression that the church is all about politics, Rev. Harrison also notes the spiritual dimensions of being appointed to greater positions in the church. He believes it is essential to display Christian character, showing that a minister is a credible person, one of integrity, one who loves the Lord and the church. Most importantly, one must keep the biblical idea of servant leadership in view. Leadership in the church is for the glory of God and the benefit of God's people, not for personal gain. In his concluding remarks, Harrison says:

> I've been willing to do that and because I see the larger picture. It's about my serving the Lord. And the Book says, "He who is great among us should be a servant,"[9] not who's popular, not who's well known, not who has prestige, but he who serves. So, anywhere I've been able to serve I think things like that get you ready. I think things like that are noticed by real spiritual leaders.

By real spiritual leaders, Rev. Harrison certainly has in mind persons of similar values and vision, including Episcopal leaders who, seeing his readiness to "get the job done for them" would be willing to appoint him to serve in successively greater leadership roles. Bishop Isaiah Douglas proved to be an episcopal mentor that Rev. Harrison needed to navigate the competitive system and serve effectively in it.

Following established tradition, Bishop Douglas says that he brought Rev. Harrison along with him as he himself was appointed to different episcopal areas. His testimony is consistent with Rev. Harrison's discussion. Discussing CME epicsopal traditions, Bishop Douglas said:

> Traditionally, when bishops transfer[10] they bring with them [pastors that will be a part of their leadership team] . . . Rev. Harrison, when I was in another episcopal district . . . I took him to that district with me and when I came here [another episcopal district covering a different geographical area] I brought him here . . . It's just the nature of the itinerant Methodist ministry. The bishop makes the appointment. Usually, if you make bishop you've had a number of people who've demonstrated an interest in you and your ministry. They have proven their commitment to the church where they're serving and if they need

an appointment, as far as possible, you try to provide for them. I mean, this is the nature of the Episcopal ministry.

Bishop Douglas hastens to add that it would be unwise for a bishop to appoint a pastor to a major church on the basis of relationships alone. Other considerations include his assessment of the gifts and graces of the candidate and the personality of the congregation. According to Bishop Douglas, a pastor can be a success in one congregation and a failure in another because the personality of the congregation is not compatible with the man or woman sent to pastor that congregation. In the best episcopal appointments, the personality of the congregation is a good "match" for the person sent. What is commonly known as "the godly judgment of the bishop" includes some assessment of the appropriateness of the match. Because of the limited number of pastoral appointments that provide the material resources for full-time ministry, the pastors of these "flagship churches" also bear the major responsibility for raising the budget of the denomination and are "leading pastors in the denomination." They are expected to support the work of their bishop and denomination with their presence at connectional meetings and their financial support of connectional initiatives. Thus, a mutuality of interests is found in these pastoral appointments, which call for bishops to carefully weigh relationships as well as results.

In fact, the relationship between Bishop Douglas and Rev. Harrison would prove especially helpful in Rev. Harrison's efforts to transform Christopher Temple. Conflict and some internal political struggles were experienced in the process of change and innovation. Laypeople also study the system and know the political nature of the church. Some, disgruntled by the changes, wrote anonymous letters of complaint to the bishop during the early days of his pastoral tenure. Because of his confidence in the ministry of Rev. Harrison and because letters of complaint were unsigned, Bishop Douglas threw the letters of complaint away.

Yet, in the worst case scenario, powerful church officers could have derailed the changes. Of the reality of these power struggles, Bishop Miller of the AME Zion Church writes:

> I can remember . . . how some ministers I knew literally cried, had near heart failures, blood pressure, and ulcers, as side effects, resulting from the lingering and contagious disease called: "powerful trustees." Most of these trustees were inherited by the incoming pastor and had been on the board so long until their influence outweighed any new arrival's prestige or long time pastor's ingenuity. . . . This may sound like a fairy

> tale and untruthful, but it is an established fact, that the trustees, not all of them, in most charges, have been the "Bosses" and at times told the Bishop what to do regarding their local church. They have made it clear . . . that if their demands were not met they gave the ultimatum: either do what we ask or we will do our worst; which meant no assessments, no acceptance of a pastor which could result, as it has done, in a division of the membership, a split church, or a destroyed one.[11]

In this instance at Christopher Temple, Bishop Douglas expressed his confidence in the leadership of Rev. Harrison while asserting that people who did not have the courage to even sign their letters did not deserve an audience for their complaints. Furthermore, Rev. Harrison had to exercise wisdom and skill in dealing with these conflicts and power struggles.

Mentored in the Tradition of the Black Preacher

Across from Rev. Harrison's office is a bulletin board with his picture on the cover of a CME publication with the caption, "The CME Preacher: Prophet, Priest, and Pastor." Not coincidentally, Christopher Temple's January 14, 2001 bulletin gives a similar description of one described by Rev. Harrison as "a profound, prepared preacher":

Happy Birthday
Rev. Dr. Martin Luther King, Jr.
Preacher, Prophet, Freedom Fighter

Sunday worship services on that day were merely the kickoff for an extensive birthday celebration the following day that was King's birthday. An interdenominational ministerial alliance service would honor female and male community leaders whose contributions merited recognition as "keepers of the dream." These dream keeper role models would then present scholarships to college students. Climaxing that service, the guest preacher exhorted the congregation to undergo a moral and ethical examination as he preached on the ethical principles of Gandhi, the Indian leader who was inspired by Dr. King's principles of creative nonviolence.

During the day, a "Dreamkeeper's Workshop" was held for about 100 youth of the church and community. A Howard University Professor of African American History worked with the young people to help them develop ideas about what they thought King would say today about education, teen pregnancy, electing qualified political officials, and fostering a culture of respect. Explaining the power of culture, the professor told the group that "the world that we make is the world that we leave to succeeding generations." The workshop was concluded with a practical list of things for the youth to do: serving, working, and studying.

Rev. Harrison attended a portion of this workshop, jotting down notes of the perspectives shared by the youth in the dialogue. Asked to give remarks at the end of the event, Harrison used this opportunity to continue the theme of being a dreamer and dream keeper, which was the focus of the previous day's sermon:

> It does not matter where you are from. Your dream is where you are going. . . . My dream is that you will lead your family, your school, your community to racial unity to exemplify the principles of non-violence . . . Malcolm X once said, "Education is the passport to the future." Look into the mirror! *You* are the leader that you've been looking for! Say, "I am Dr. Martin Luther King, Jr. The dream lives on in me!"

Rev. Harrison entered the traveling ministry of the CME Church in 1968, the year of Dr. King's assassination. Mentored in the CME Church and in the tradition of the black preacher in America, Rev. Harrison's development as a minister was profoundly impacted by the lessons of the civil rights movement and black power movement. Of his experience of being mentored in this environment Harrison said:

> All of that was a part of the culture and milieu, late 60's, early 70's that impacted me to say this: this is some institution, the black church and the black preacher. We need to bring excellence, commitment, courage, compassion and a sense of history and belonging to try to pass it on to the next generation. Pass it on also to the church so that the black church is saved by its black parishioners in light of what it really is. I don't think that black people fully . . . see the black church in light of its history and in light of its potential. Not fully, because it's a tremendous, tremendous [institution], the contribution it has made, and the potential, yet unrealized potential.

Bishop Douglas's appointment of Rev. Harrison to Christopher Temple brought to the pastorate one mentored in the context of these social movements, believing that through the ongoing transformation of the black church, it might more fully realize its potential to transform individuals, families, and communities. A description of this mentoring yields insights into the development of this preacher and furthers our understanding of how to foster the development of other ministers for transformative pastoral leadership.

A Male Pastor's Mentoring Environment

Asked about the mentoring relationships in his ministry, Rev. Harrison discussed the role of Sunday School teachers, pastors within and beyond the CME Church, presiding elders, bishops, community activists, and black seminary professors in fostering his development. Reference was made to the interplay between himself and the social–political environment and the power of mentors that were guides to him on his ministerial journey. Mentoring is a transformational journey that takes place in environments where people live, supporting and challenging their development. In the context of caring relationships, mentors gain trust, provide support, issue challenges, and offer vision to persons on their life journey.[12] As we will see, lessons learned from these mentoring relationships are imbedded in Rev. Harrison's ministry praxis.

Asked the question, "tell me about the mentoring relationships in your ministry" Rev. Harrison said:

> Oh, it's so important. I've had it in my life. J. Claude Allen was my father in the ministry[13] back in the ministry back in the early 60's, mid 60's, 70's. Matter of fact, he was able to be a guest at my graduation . . . from seminary. I was able to get him recognized there. . . . By 1975 or 1976 he had passed.[14] But, an indelible impression. Always, "my son" and gave me tremendous advice. He taught me the importance of tithing. He taught me the importance, I really see it now, of having strong leaders around because he had such strong pastors around. He was an expansionist, a church builder, a financier, and was always compassionate. . . . These were lifelong friends. So, I was mentored by that.

An "indelible impression" remains twenty-five years after the passing of Rev. Harrison's mentor—his father in the ministry. It is clear in this example that a mentor concerned about the development of the protégé is the concept Harrison has in mind here. It is not the type of mentor often discussed in the business world who may only help one move up the corporate ladder without personal attention to the development of that person.[15] In this instance, a special relationship existed between

Rev. Harrison and a bishop who demonstrated his personal interest in Harrison's development by attending his graduation from seminary. Concepts central to Harrison's praxis of ministry such as the importance of tithing and of developing strong leaders around him were learned. Perhaps of greater importance is seeing, within the bishop, ways of love and compassion toward the poor.

As Rev. Harrison was at the beginning of his ministerial vocation, he looked to his father in the ministry as a nurturer of his own dreams, gaining from him a self-image crucial to the formation of his own identity and aspirations.[16] Once, he may have looked at all bishops as "gods." But, he grew to be able to look at this bishop as "friend." Another late bishop, the late Bishop Cummings spent time teaching him "what it meant to pastor, what it meant to prepare messages, what it meant to get into the heart of the city . . . how to work in the community."

Bishop Douglas is credited as a mentor who imparted practical wisdom regarding pastoral work. Rev. Harrison says:

> Bishop Isaiah Douglas has been my mentor in light of just strong pastoral work. How do you capture their hearts? What do you do to make the families of a church feel close to you? How are you there for them in times of trouble as well as triumph so that you're there at the critical time? You're there at baptisms, the happy times, you're there at marriages, you're there at the deaths, you're there at the hospitals. How do you take them communion? I take them communion on first Sundays. I learned that from him. [Bishop Douglas taught me] "Go on Sundays when the families are still there and go into the hospitals on Sundays because the family is going to be gathered. They'll see you walking in and count the number of people in the room and for each number you get a point. Let the people see you. Wait and delay your supper. Have your family wait. Be off on Monday . . . Go on holidays, because you can take the next day off while the people are going to work, but you can go on a holiday and spend a few hours in the morning. Then go [home to be with your family] in the afternoon and enjoy that game with your family." I learned that from him.

Embedded within this advice is one mentor's theory of one of the ways that a pastor gains legitimate authority within a congregation. All Methodist preachers have experienced the lag time between the bishop's appointment and the people's allowing her or him to "be the pastor." Pastoral authority must be earned. One of the ways to earn authority is by demonstrating sacrificial dedication to "being there" during significant life transitions, "times of trouble as well as triumph."

Some have put it simply: "people must know that you care before they care how much you know."

Unfortunately, some pastors neglect this principle. Not moving beyond the tradition of being "the Sunday Preacher"[17] some pastors fail to adequately demonstrate personal concern for the well-being of individuals and families in their flock. They may have great preaching ability, vision for the church and race, and leadership ability, but their pastoral authority may be hampered by underestimating the relationship between strong pastoral work and strong leadership. This certainly does not mean that senior pastors should do all the visitation of members; but, they will certainly make sure that the visitation gets done and find appropriate ways of personally connecting with others in time of trial.

In addition to his exposure to powerful church leaders who took a strong interest in his development, black professors in seminary also had a strong impact. Rev. Harrison went to seminary in the early 1970s when the first generation of black theologians was laying the foundations for the academic formulations of black theology. Through his black professors, he was exposed to the writings of James Cone, J. Deotis Roberts, Gayraud Wilmore, and the late Joseph A. Johnson, Jr., a teacher, theologian, and bishop of the CME Church. Of Bishop Johnson's influence on his thinking Rev. Harrison says:

> Bishop Joseph Johnson of our church wrote *The Soul of a Black Preacher*, still a classic. He was one of the first up front black theologians that I met that had an impact and understood. Preaching in his African regalia, sharing, knowing the Greek and knowing the Hebrew and throwing that out and sharing. . . . He shared with us who the black preacher was.

Of the experience of black seminarians in the late 1960s and early 1970s when Rev. Harrison matriculated in a predominantly white seminary, Bishop Johnson wrote:

> The young black seminary student today has been introduced into a whole new experience—one fashioned by the late Martin Luther King, Jr., but clarified and profoundly interpreted by Frantz Fanon, Malcolm X, Stokely Carmichael, and Ron Karenga. The young black seminary student today has been tried by every conceivable ordeal that sadistic racial minds can devise; from the fire hoses to vicious dogs, from tear gas to electric animal prods. They have matched wits with the white racist of the power structure and are helping to pull down the system

of segregation and discrimination. They have no objection to the combination of such words as "black and power," "black and theology," "black and church," "black and Christ," "black and God.". . . . They are not shocked nor are they discouraged if the term Black Power seems to offend or frighten white or black Americans. To these young blacks, Black Power means consciousness and solidarity. It means the amassing by black people of the economic, political, and judicial control necessary to define their own goals and share in the decisions that determine their faith.[18]

As we continue our discussion of this pastor's mentoring environment, this passage enlarges our vision of the ecological environment in which this pastor was mentored by seminary professors. General systems theory, first developed by naturalists to explain growth and change in nature, is also a helpful tool for understanding the invisible forces influencing human development as well. Mentors are only a part of the system of forces that are barriers to or incentives for growth. As individuals change, their environments may change as well in response to internal and external factors in the systems or the smaller subsystems within these larger systems.[19]

Thus, Harrison's system of education in seminary was radically affected by the context of struggle to challenge the racist power structures, to transform the consciousness of black minds, and to determine blacks' economic, political, and legal destinies. Subsequent to this, other movements to empower blacks and people of color such as Rev. Jesse Jackson's runs for the presidency in 1984 and 1988 also involved Rev. Harrison in voter registration, voter education, and political campaigns to elect public officials. Taught by Rev. Willie Barrow, the female chairman of Operation P.U.S.H., about the importance of fighting the institutional sins of racism, sexism, and economic exploitation of communities, Rev. Harrison worked with other ministers as a part of the movement to negotiate covenants so that blacks could get a larger slice of the economic pie. The above sketch of Pastor Harrison's mentoring environment is intended to hint at his own transformation. Of this transformation Daloz writes:

In any case, it seems apparent that the transformation we are concerned with can be understood as having something to do with a radical change in vision, with perception shifts from smaller to larger systems. . . . Thus, when we speak of the environment in which mentors and students work, we are speaking of a *perceived environment*, one that includes the student's view of parents, spouse, children, "significant others," and the mentor—as well as ideas, memories, dreams, values, external events, old patterns, and new information.[20]

Educated and mentored in this environment over the years to understand the interconnected beliefs and practices of the priestly and prophetic functions of the black preacher, Rev. Harrison has embodied a culturally shaped understanding of ministry in the black church, rooted in the social movements of the 1960s and early 1970s. Like other pastors representing the civil rights and black power generation consciousness, Rev. Harrison successfully recruited persons who helped him transform Christopher Temple in light of lessons from these movements.[21] Mentored in the tradition of the black Methodist preacher, I would assert that Rev. Harrison has worked with laity and other ministers to foster a congregational environment where youth, college students, young ministers, and members can be mentored in the ongoing freedom movement first fostered by independent black Methodist churches.

Congregational Culture as Environment for Political Action

Just prior to the fall elections of 2000, the closest presidential election year in our nation's history, Rev. Harrison and Christopher Temple hosted a "Gospel Get out the Vote Rally." The purpose of this rally was to educate the community residents and to motivate them to vote. If this was not a church led by a pastor mentored in the tradition of the black preacher, it might seem strange to witness this mixture of praise, prayer, and partisan racial politics. The pulpit, often reserved for the sacred task of preaching, was freely offered to political leaders to educate congregants on political matters judged relevant to the interests of the black community.

Christopher Temple choirs rocked the house with their powerful opening song: "Clap Your Hands and Say Amen" Gospel music's great, Albertina Walker, was a featured soloist who found a way to encourage people to vote during her singing. Ad-libbing the lyrics at one point, she inserted the political exhortation that, "I've just come by to say we need to get out and vote!" She didn't linger in this mode for long.

One of her gospel songs that she performed that afternoon, "I Can Go to God in Prayer" may have seemed to indicate what others have called, "the other worldly" character of religion. However, this event is more indicative of the dialectical character of the black church, which may hold in creative tension polar opposites such as the priestly and prophetic roles of the preacher, the other worldly and this worldly dimensions of ministry, the universal and particular missional orientations of the church, the communal and privatistic response to member and non-member concerns, political resistance and accommodation, the charismatic and bureaucratic organizational styles of leadership, and the sexual politics of male–female relationships.[22] Clearly, Albertina Walker, Christopher Temple choir members, and other singers and musicians were present to bring the spiritual energy of the black church into this social–political communal event.

In what I saw as a significant symbolic gesture, Rev. Harrison invited the "the ministers of the community and their wives" to sit on the "first few rows to my right." Politicians were invited to sit on the first few pews to his left. During Christopher Temple's regular worship services church trustees and stewards sit on the first few pews to his right and the stewardesses, clad in their white dresses and hats, sit in the first few pews to his left. But, for this communal event, the spiritual leaders of the community were at Harris's right and the political leaders of the community were at his left.

There are those in the black church, clergy and lay, who do not think it appropriate for politicians to speak from the pulpit. In this view, the pulpit is reserved for preaching. The church, they would say, is not the place for politics. Clearly, this is not Rev. Harrison's perspective as several black and white Democratic politicians—a U.S. Congressman, States Attorney, State Comptroller, State Senators, and Judges of the Appellate and Circuit Courts—were invited to speak from the pulpit.

In a community in which black voters are overwhelmingly Democratic, this political voter education rally became a Democratic Party Voter Rally. Republican candidates may have been invited, but they were not present on that day. People were told *why* they should turn out and vote and *why* they should vote for particular candidates. This was clearly racial partisan politics. The black church was the place for voter education and voter motivation.

Despite the fact that the state attorney was not on the ballot in the ensuing election, he was introduced to speak by Rev. Harrison with the exhortation, "Give Him a hand!" His message to this community included his avowed commitment to go after gang leaders and drug dealers, to recruit a diverse workforce for his office, and to encourage citizens to identify young people who can be turned around before their problems with the law become too serious. Of the critical nature of black people voting in this election, one politician intoned:

> God has placed us in this position. The election will come down to the black community. The battle ground is in 6 critical states. . . . A lot of black folk live there. Now, you can't scare us into voting. We've already survived Nixon, Reagan, and Bush. Our survival does not rest in the hands of the one in the White House. Our survival is in the hands of the Lord. I used to talk about black power in my younger days. . . . I now know what black power is. It's about an election where there is a possibility of three-four powerful committee chairmanships at stake. . . . The next president will appoint hundreds of federal judges and likely appoint the next justices to the Supreme Court. We need to put some people on the Supreme Court that look like us and think like us. The Black Church, Christians must lead the way. It is our Christian responsibility. . . . Each of you needs to reach out to your friends, relatives, neighbors and make sure that they vote. . . . And II Chronicle 7: 14 says (he pauses, allowing his black church audience to shout out the familiar scripture) "*If my people* who are called by *my name* will humble themselves and pray and seek and seek *my face, then* I will hear from heaven, and will forgive their sin and heal their land!"

In this event, elements of black congregational culture—the songs, the prayers, the call and response interaction, the Christian imagery, and theological rhetoric—were effectively used as a strategy for social action.[23] Rather than being an opiate of the people, black religion at Christopher Temple is a cultural resource for black politics.[24] The message within this black church is clear that Christians ought to pray, but prayer is only part of the Christian responsibility. Prayer is a partner of political action to promote the values and vision of people with whom God is concerned. Furthermore, Rev. Harrison and his congregation are seen here fostering an environment where electoral politics is perceived as an arena where God is active and God's people should be active.

The Tradition of Struggle Celebrated

A more than thirty-year tradition of Christopher Temple's jointly celebrating Thanksgiving service with a sister AME Zion Church was conceived this year, by the two pastors, as an opportunity for "thanking God for our struggle." Christopher Temple's regular worship services valorize black history and the wisdom of African American people nurturing youth and other members to better understand the connections between their past, present, and future. Yet, this special service is a particularly rich example of how Rev. Harrison, mentored in the tradition of the black preacher, in turn fosters with his congregational leaders an environment where the personal and collective struggles of a people are interpreted in sacred context.

At the heart of the service is a sermon in which Rev. Harrison and an AME Zion pastor, Rev. Michael Linton, each expound on three points of an interconnected sermon, "Thanking God for Our Struggle." This sermon is indicative of a reading of the Bible and of American society that is common in the black independent church movements from the nineteenth century to the present. Mainstream black Baptists and Methodists are a part of this tradition. Of this establishment of the so-called black canon and black hermeneutical principle Wimbush writes:

> This reading of the Bible among African-Americans extends at least from the nineteenth century up to the present. It has historically reflected and shaped the ethos and thinking of the majority of African Americans. If the period of enslavement (certainly eighteenth century through emancipation) represents the classical period, the nineteenth century represents the period of self-conscious articulation, consolidation, and institutionalization. Frederick Douglass and David Walker stand as eloquent examples of nineteenth century biblical interpreters who took the hermeneutical principle of the kinship of humanity under the sovereignty of God and applied it to the emancipation agenda.[25]

This biblically derived ideal of the kinship of all of humanity under the sovereignty of God is the theological foundation of black peoples' religious and social struggle for equal citizenship in a racist society. It is at the heart of the mission of independent black churches such as the CME, AME Zion, AME, and black Baptist Churches. It is this struggle for freedom and equality, which both Rev. Harrison and Rev. Linton feel obligated to continue through pastoral leadership in the black church.

The scriptures chosen for the sermon were Genesis 32: 24, 28 and Roman 5: 1–5. I quote and comment extensively on Rev. Harrison's part of this "tag-team" sermon, because I find it a striking example of these black Methodist pastors' reading of the Bible, their theological–social–historical understanding of the black church, and their hermeneutical framework for the mission of the black church.

Illuminating the culturally shaped roles of the black preacher, Rev. Harrison was presented by Rev. Linton as a minister who stands in the tradition of "one of the premier preachers and leaders, and teachers and activists in our community." Rev. Harrison was assigned to expound the first three points of the message: the political, educational, and religious dimensions of our struggle. "Bringing it home," Rev. Linton expounded upon the final points of the message: the social legacy of racism and the impact of government policies on black family life today, the black church role in birthing economic institutions, and the historic struggles of blacks in the courts and criminal justice systems.

A preacher-teacher of the scriptures, Rev. Harrison opens the sermon laying biblical exegetical foundations for his preaching. Commenting on the context of his sermon text Harrison says:

> Genesis the book of beginnings . . . [Genesis is] the first book of the Pentateuch, the first five books of the Bible, like the five sided building in the capitol, the pentagon . . . Genesis is the first book in the Bible, but not necessarily the oldest book which scholars agree is the book of Job.

Emphasizing his oft-stated capsule summary of the mission of the black church he says, "We are twice blessed to be God's instruments of salvation, education, and liberation."

Harrison continues, "We give God thanks for our struggles, for our hurts, for our pain, for our tribulation." Noting the recent passing of Rev. Hosea Williams, one of the leaders of the civil rights movement, he honors him (along with King, Ralph Abernethy, Rosa Parks, and many other men *and women*) as "leaders . . . apostles of nonviolent social action." Bloody Sunday is a struggle that led to the passage of the Voting Rights Act and other freedoms. Harrison connects this past struggle to the present political struggle to elect the next president saying:

> And because of the struggle for the Voting Rights Act, just enough of us went to the polls to put an election on hold all over the nation and today *God* has America on hold. Wait Bush, not yet! Wait Gore, not yet! I [God] put power in the hands of some children who been struggling. . . . We had enough to hold the election up and it does not yet appear what God is going to do!

This gives some insight into Harrison's theology of liberation. God is involved in politics on the side of the oppressed: "some children who been struggling." God gives power to fight for freedom today just as God did for African Americans to fight for independence in the revolutionary war, for physical emancipation from slavery, and for the end of legal segregation in the civil rights movement. Harrison does not attempt to foretell victory for those who struggled in their efforts to get Vice-President Gore elected to the presidency. With the election over, his troops have fought to educate their constituents about what is at stake in the election and to get out the vote. With the outcome of the presidential election hinging on the legal challenges of Bush versus Gore, Harrison asserts that God is still involved in human history: "it does not yet appear what God is going to do!"

I see enthusiastic applause, laughter, shouts, head-nodding, and verbal responses throughout the congregation. This pulpit social analysis is well received here. Harrison's humorous rhetoric is appreciated: "Whoever is elected will be from a state with the letter T [Texas or Tennessee] and he has four letters in his name and he'll be a white man (laughter from congregation), but *we'll still have to struggle!*" Furthermore, Harrison tells the people to stay involved in the political process beyond Election Day. Giving the central proposition of the sermon, Harrison roars, "There's a blessing in the struggle!"

The "struggle" is not only collective; it is personal as well. Harrison continues:

> Some of you struggled to get out here today. Some of you struggled to get up today. Some of you struggle in life and some of us try to avoid the struggles, but I want you to know that there is a blessing in the struggle! We glory in the struggle because of what it produces in us. The Holy Ghost is given for us in the struggle!

Drawing upon the wisdom of Frederick Douglas who said, "there is no progress without a struggle," Harrison concedes many of us "try to avoid the struggle of marching and voting and studying and fighting for our liberation." Including in his portrait, the contributions of women: "Harriet Tubman and Sojourner Truth . . . there have been men and women in the struggle."

Harrison reminded the young people of the fact that blacks had to struggle for the right to get an education:

> It was against the law, *young people, I'm glad you're here*, to teach black folk how to read. If you were caught trying to read, they might punish you, whip you, even kill you because they knew that reading, freedom, knowledge, would give you *power.*

Commenting on an anti-intellectual bent in contemporary black youth culture, Harrison argues from racial–cultural historical sources against this:

> They have a new game today . . . they try to tell you, "Don't get an education because you might sound or act white." Let me tell you, we [African people] are the fathers and mothers of education. We taught the Greeks and the Romans from our libraries in Timbuktu.

Significantly, the black church was central to that educational struggle. As Harrison continues with the story:

> The Black Church, oh I love it, that's why we're here in it today. We were worship houses on Sunday but turned that same building into a school house on Monday and taught the 3-R's coming out of slavery, reading, writing, and arithmetic. *It was a struggle!* And out of those little grammar schools, we then developed elementary, then high schools, and eventually Livingstone College and Miles, and Lane, and Howard, Spellman.[26] Every significant black college can be traced back to the black church!

To the applause and shouts in the congregation to this "telling of the story" with respect to the black experience in America, Harrison continues, "We struggled and built our own institutions . . . and then had the nerve to say, 'we've got our own but we know that we ought to have the right to go to Harvard and the University of Tennessee, and U.I.C. [University of Illinois at Chicago]' and now we struggle and those doors also opened, *but it was a struggle! . . . That's why we love education is because it was a struggle!*"

Of the black religious struggle necessitating holistic forms of ministry addressing body, mind, and spirit, Harrison intones:

> We struggled to worship God in our own manner. We struggled to have a holistic gospel and not a schizophrenic gospel. . . . We're proud of the black church because it represents a whole gospel. . . . They were trying to give us a gospel that was heavenly minded, but no earthly good! It was a gospel, "by and by, when you die, you'll get some pie in the sky." . . . In the struggle, we had some songs that represent that whole gospel and not that schizophrenic gospel. . . . We struggled so that black theology began to emerge even before it was called black theology. We sang in the brush harbor, "everybody talking bout heaven ain't gwine [going] there!" Because when Jesus comes into your heart, you'll recognize that all men and women are equal and ought to be set free. . . . We had

trouble, but then they sang, "I'm so glad that trouble don't last always!" They created the spirituals children, the songs of liberation. . . . Yes, we want God's kingdom to come on earth just as it is in heaven. . . . Yes, we want to go to heaven by and by when we die, but we also need a gospel that gives us something sound on the ground while we're still around. That's the holistic gospel! *We struggled till we got a gospel that made sense, a gospel that fixed us up, a gospel that picked us up, a gospel that lifted us up, a gospel that dressed us up, a gospel that educated us, a gospel that emancipated us. That's why we gather today to give God thanks for the struggle!*

Examining Rev. Harrison's sermonic celebration of the tradition of black struggle through preaching, we see further evidence of how he is trying to mentor others in the living tradition of the black church being at the heart of black communal struggle. In fact, it is in this tradition of ongoing struggle that transformation is possible.

Making the Dream Work through Team Work

Arriving at Christopher Temple as a student of the Methodist system mentored in the tradition of the black preacher, Rev. Harrison also understood that the transformative potential of the black church could only be realized through a disciplined process of congregational leadership development. As Jesus embarked on his ministerial career recruiting the first disciples, Rev. Harrison embarked on his pastorate recruiting and training the leadership.

Priority of Making Disciples and Leadership Development

Of his early days at Christopher Temple, Mrs. Janice Parker recalls:

When Rev. Harrison came to the church, he seemed to have been looking for leaders and searching out for other leaders. I saw also how he was trying to transform the church. I was eager myself for that to happen. Prior to him coming, I think I had a desire that we would be more of an outreach church and maybe more socially involved and just some other things from association with my other colleagues and talking with them. And so there were some things that I hoped would happen in my church.

According to Mrs. Parker, one of Rev. Harrison's early priorities was identifying leaders to carry out the vision of transforming this traditional established church. A lifelong member of Christopher Temple, Mrs. Parker was baptized there when she was six-months old. Nurtured by former pastors as a youth, she recalls telling her grandmother that a former pastor's preaching was so clear that she could outline the sermon and follow what he was saying. As a young adult leader, she had various leadership roles and participated in different leadership training initiatives. Yet, she acknowledges barriers in her faith developmental process as a young adult. Other developmental tasks, namely, establishing herself in her profession, predominated. She says,

> I think at the time, I was more of a young adult and not giving as much attention and time to the church, even though I was coming to the church and I don't think I was as active as maybe I could have been . . . I was more into my profession and climbing the ladder in my profession.

Now, a retired educator, she is a key leader at Christopher Temple. Although she says that her spiritual growth and development as a church leader went to a new level under Rev. Harrison's ministry, Mrs. Parker is one example of the fact that Rev. Harrison inherited Christian leaders nurtured by former pastors. She and other members bought into his leadership, in part, because he embodied the vision they were longing for: a church involved in community outreach and social ministries.

Asked how he presently manages the strenuous demands of being a leading pastor in his denomination and a community leader, Rev. Harrison points to the priorities established at the beginning of his pastorate:

> I think the key is developing good leaders around you, the Jesus model. Three years pour yourself into your leaders. The first five years here I did nothing but pour myself into the leaders of this church. I did not do a lot of district and annual that I did not have to do. And I did nothing in the city. I refused to serve on any committees in the city. . . . It was five years before I was willing to take on a position of leadership in an community organization that I had been associated with for almost 20 years when I arrived here because I understood that the local church had to be very, very strong. The vision that I had of church growth and leadership could only be accomplished if I spent quality and quantity time training leaders, empowering, equipping and discipling them so that they could make good decisions in my absence, so that my job, in fact,

would lessen. My job would get easier through the years not harder. My job is actually a lot easier now than it was when I initially began this ministry in 1986. And such was my plan.

Disciplining himself to "say no" to church leaders and political leaders who would involve him in urgent activities, he deemed it more important to stick to his five-year plan of developing strong leaders around him. Working first with his officers, Rev. Harrison began his transformative work by empowering his officers and members through Bible study and membership classes that he taught. Officers were told to attend membership classes even if they had been members of the CME Church all of their lives. This process helped to solidify his leadership so they would be spiritually able to lead others in the church. Later, he would accept more invitations to serve in the broader church and society.

Mrs. Parker says that this helped her not only to assume the leadership of the influential steward board, but as a public school principal, she invited members of her staff to pray with her before school. All of this prayer and Bible study, implemented by Rev. Harrison, helped her to understand this big picture of making Christian disciples while dealing with the raw realities of church organizational politics. As she passes the baton of leadership to other church leaders she continues to emphasize this conviction. Mrs. Parker says:

> I don't think that I would have been looking at it from the bigger picture, the bigger goal, had I not gone through all of this teaching and training and bible study and witnessing. I believe that and everyone that followed me in these various leadership roles, I've always shared with them that the most important thing is to stay prayed up, to study, stay in bible study. . . . Otherwise, things happen that literally will blow you out of the water because a lot of times people don't realize that the same dynamics that go on in any other organization, the politics, the other kinds of things, they go in the church also.

Mrs. Parker's professional training as educator and administrator is valuable in helping the church advance their mission, "the bigger picture, the bigger goal," only because her skills are placed in service of this mission and she herself is committed to this mission. Moreover, leading the church volunteers presents a special challenge when the central task is making Christian disciples. Asked about the differences between her experience of leadership of a public school and her church leadership, Mrs. Parker comments:

> In many areas they are very similar. The differences I find are just like, I remember one time, Pastor said to me, "Sister, you know these people are volunteers.". . . And I was thinking, "They're not doing their job like in the school system. I can bring the teacher in and we go over what they're not doing, what you should be doing, there's a plan for how you can improve, if you don't this. . . ." The whole point is to help them to grow so that you have more and more who can witness and who can disciple and bring others in. You have to keep in mind because it's not about, "Well, this person doesn't do the job so I'll get somebody else to do this job." Even if you did that, you can't forget about this person because . . . ultimately, the thing is their souls more than it is this building, or this operation, or this organization.

Viewing church leadership from the "bigger picture" missional perspective of making disciples does not mean that business and organizational perspectives are not important, however. The light bills must be paid, the church must operate smoothly, and peoples' many problems must be dealt with. Although Mrs. Parker had a strong church background, she feels she had to grow in her faith to handle the business of the church keeping the "ultimate" spiritual goals in view.

Change does not come easy in the church. Making ministry a priority instead of traditional activities like fund-raising is not easy. The testimony of Mrs. Cora Nolan, an eighty-year-old woman, who is the president of the stewardess board and regularly attends Christopher Temple's daily 6 a.m. prayer services, is significant. She recalls the struggle of instituting a tithing emphasis. Asked what advice she would give a new pastor wanting to change a church from a fund-raising church to a tithing church Mrs. Nolan recalls:

> Pastor Harrison came into a church that had dinners, bake sales and things like that. He just kept saying, "If you tithe, then you don't have to be tithing and tired because you tired when you're not able to come up to the service, you're down in the kitchen cooking that particular Sunday trying to get the dinner ready for when the service is over, so the dinner will be ready for the people after church. . . . If you just go there and take that money that you're putting in there and put it into an envelope and tithe you can sit up and hear the service and everything else (laughing)." You still have some people that will never tithe, but that's between them and God. . . . They say I'm crazy because I come for the 8:00 service, I stay for the 10:45 service, and if there's something in the afternoon, I stay for that. It's my joy.

Even now, there are those who grumble and complain. Yet, because of her credibility as a "mother of the church" she is a leader who effectively deflects and defuses criticism of the pastor. Of her exchange with a man upset with the pastor Mrs. Nolan recalls:

> I was telling a man that worked here at one time that he was all upset. . . . I said, "Excuse me. Can you do what pastor do? Can you visit the sick? Can you bury the dead? Can you fool with a thousand people?" [He answered] "No." [She said] Then, stop complaining. . . . Pastor got all these people under his wings and everyday, I'm sure there is something that *somebody* don't like!

Administration in an Era of Declining Denominationalism

Administering a growing church requires Rev. Harrison to work with and train many teams of leaders. Because of the number of ministries, Harrison has created his own executive council with representatives from the board of stewards, the board of trustees, the board of Christian education, officers of major ministries, and different departments. Setting policies and procedures in accordance with the guidelines of the Book of Discipline of the CME Church, the executive council talks about upcoming events on the church calendar, projects that the church is involved in, ministry needs and anything else related to the overall operation and management of the church. Day-to-day management, supervision issues, hiring of staff, and other decisions are shared with Rev. Harrison by members of the executive council. Strategically coordinating the ministries in this manner, operational planning is done by the appropriate group, whether by the trustee board, steward board, board of Christian education, or ministry group.

This representative group sets the agenda for the monthly meeting of the church conference in which Harrison gathers all of the leaders for mandatory leadership training and implementation of the agenda set by the executive council. At one of these church conferences in 2001, the theme of the leadership training was "Proud to be C.M.E." Rev. Harrison used some of his time to keep before the new and old leaders alike the basic history of the denomination, the definition of each element of their name, and the structure of conferences in order of authority from the local level to the highest connectional level. Nonetheless, he is well aware that he is operating in a consumer culture and not a church culture. Accordingly, his approach is of making a case for *why* one can be proud to be a CME rather than simply stressing denominational loyalty.

Simply put, one can be proud to be a CME because of what God has produced through the CME Church in the past and what God produces in and through the CME Church today. Denominational schools that have trained CME leaders and persons that are not CME are one thing that he will not allow members to forget. When he brings in ministers educated at Interdenominational Theological Center/Phillips School of Theology in Atlanta, he stresses his belief in "an educated ministry" and suggests that you can judge that members' denominational assessments are well spent as they see, for themselves, the quality of minister produced there.

However, on a local level, members can be Proud to be CME because of the miracles that God has done at the congregational level. On the cover of the leadership training booklet for the March church conference we read:

> "PROUD TO BE C.M.E." The Christian Methodist Episcopal Church was founded December 15–16, 1870 in Jackson, Tennessee with Bishop William Henry Miles elected as our first Bishop. It is our goal to share Christ and to teach every member how to become a faithful, fruitful, positive, tithing (time, talent, treasure) member of the Christopher Temple C.M.E. Church. Why do we call our church "God's Miracle Church—Reaching and Teaching for Jesus?" From 1986, since Pastor Harrison was assigned by Bishop Isaiah Douglas to serve as Pastor, we've never had a month where a soul wasn't saved, a person didn't join, and a rededication to Christ and Church wasn't made. This is a "Modern Day Miracle of the Holy Spirit" because of the Power and Favor of God upon our church. . . . We are called by God now to become servant-leaders of Jesus Christ as we move to achieve the goal of 5,000 active, positive, attending weekly, tithing, mature disciples of Jesus Christ, who are loyal, obedient, blessed and faithful members of Christopher Temple C.M.E. Church.

Harrison is said to be "legendary" for his resourcefulness in bringing in renowned persons to train his leaders and expose his congregation to influential religious, political, educational, and business leaders. However on this night, Rev. Harrison conducts the training on the topic of servant leadership. He says this is a "new paradigm" in the CME Church, one that produces Christian church leaders that are "approachable." Utilizing a teaching method of dialogue, he applies a principle that he says he learned from one of his seminary professors, namely that "There is wisdom of God that comes from God through pastors, but there is also a wisdom that comes from God from leaders in the pew. It's a two way street."

The real paradigm shift that should be noted here is the shift from a clerical model of congregational leadership to an ecclesial model of congregational leadership. The leadership for the priestly and prophetic functions of ministry is the vocation of the whole people of God rather than the sole province of an ordained minister. Of this change from the more typical style of ministry in the black church where "you don't do nothing without the pastor's OK" Mrs. Parker says:

> The other [transformation] is this more broad based leadership. It's not a one man show. It's more open. More people have the opportunity for input and to take on leadership roles. Then, they are trained for that. You're not expected to just come in. Now, we have all kinds of leadership training activities throughout the year. We now are having specific leadership training time right before our church conference. Pastor Harrison has just brought in different persons to train the leaders. It's a whole change in terms of building leaders and building broad based leadership. To me, that's a change.

It is only through this cultivating excellence in ministry by training and releasing lay and clergy leaders for ministry that denominational churches like Christopher Temple can hope to attract and continually develop people in today's changing consumer culture.

Addressing the Crisis of Leadership in Society

One of the things that impressed Rev. Harrison about the leadership of Rosa Parks and Dr. King was what they accomplished at such a young age. Thus, the conviction grew within him that leaders must be developed and that they must be developed from their youth. Commenting on this ministry theme, Mrs. Parker says:

> Developing leadership for the African American community is key because one of the things that he believes is that there is a great need for leaders of integrity in every facet of our society. The problems we are having are related to a crisis in leadership and that leadership is not something that just appears, like we're looking for another Dr. Martin

Luther King to drop out of the sky and that doesn't happen. Leaders are developed and they are developed from early on. Yes, that is his belief and that is why we've always had some kind of either after school program or summer program for youth.

One of Christopher Temple's responses to this crisis is their summer Freedom School. A concept developed by Marian Wright Edelman, this program includes an extensive black literacy component, conflict resolution, and social action. Following Rev. Harrison's belief that the root of societal problems is spiritual, Christopher Temple has added a spiritual development component as well. The teaching for this program is done by college students, who receive intensive training at Alex Haley's farm in Tennessee. Volunteers are used, including senior citizens, to assist in other areas. Community people—bank presidents, congressman, ministers, doctors, ministers, grocery store owners—come in to read for ten to fifteen minutes to inspire and share with the young people.

An innovative program addressing the crisis of young black male leadership development is implemented through the Christian Methodist Men of Christopher Temple. Hundreds of young men from the church and from neighborhood public schools gather monthly for a "Man-Boy Breakfast." It is an all male function with many functions including exposing boys and men to prominent role models from all walks of life, rewarding academic achievement through a "pay for A's" program, and awarding college scholarships. After the breakfast, men and boys will take off for a game of basketball at a local high school rented by the church.

Christopher Temple's One Church One School Program, a focused response to the complex social problems created in public schools by our drug culture, absentee fathers, dysfunctional families of all income classes, inadequate moral education, and immoral media influences, works with local schools to support a positive environment where children can learn well. Working in various capacities, such as hall monitors or tutors, people of good will volunteer to help children have a moral thermometer and encourage children who do not have a parent or grandparent to give them support.

The mission of saving boys and girls is crucial, but strengthening women and men to work to save communities is crucial as well. Guy Roberson, president of the Christian Men, was influenced by Rev. Harrison to leave corporate America to pursue his own company. He says he was challenged by his pastor who said to him, "Why should corporate America have all of our best minds?" Commenting on his changing vocations from corporate employee to general contractor, Mr. Roberson says:

> The churches are strong. They've been here and they'll continue to be here, but what happened to our grocery stores, our gas stations, and all of the other things? We need to have more of an entrepreneurial spirit. College is great. Corporate America is great. I did both and now I traded in my three pieces for overalls and trucks. But, I own my own company. I work for me. . . . I got to college and then I went to grad school per se in Corporate America and let them train you, understand white American and do these things and do that, but I think at some point black men need to come back out and save our communities and build back up our communities.

Because people cannot simply lament the unfinished business of the human struggle for justice and equality or wait for some great individual to emerge, communities of faith must accept the challenge of developing ethical leaders committed to the common good of society. Although the particular challenges of their own racial and ethnic communities are pressing, in our interconnected world, race-transcending leaders are crucial for church and society. Of this crisis of leadership, Cornel West says:

> Quality leadership is neither the product of one great individual nor the result of odd historical accident. Rather, it comes from deeply bred traditions and communities that shape and mold talented and gifted persons. Without a vibrant tradition of resistance passed on to new generations, there can be no nurturing of a collective and critical consciousness—only professional conscientiousness survives. Where there is no vital community to hold up precious ethical and religious ideals, there can be no coming to a moral commitment—only personal accomplishment is applauded.[27]

The fruit of Christopher Temple's long-term commitment to being a community that passes on the tradition of resistance to talented and gifted persons is seen in Mrs. Cynthia Walker-Simpson. A twenty-nine-year-old bank vice-president with degrees in engineering and law, this product of the youth ministry sees her responsibility of giving back to others through her leadership of the college ministry. Asked to give a sense of how Christopher Temple's youth ministry contributed to her development, Mrs. Walker-Simpson says:

> I've been a member from the very beginning. I started those growing
> stages of even reading in Sunday School. . . . Pretty much throughout
> my childhood up until my late teens every social activity was through
> the church. My best friends were here, my mentors were here. I think of
> this church, specifically, as being my village, because often times when
> you live in a big city, you may not be as familiar with your neighbors as
> maybe you should be, but, at Christopher Temple, this has been my
> village. As a result of that, I am a product of many different people
> contributing to my development.

Through her church, she says that she felt that through the empowerment of God and her church family, she drew on her roots whenever she
felt intimidated or devastated by the challenges of growing up. When
her adopted mother died, her Sunday School teacher bought her a win-
ter coat and her youth sponsor bought school clothes. The church stood
behind her as she pursued higher education, providing book money and
scholarships from undergraduate school through law school.

Yet, the struggle for human equality continues. Despite her education,
she encounters racist attitudes today. Of the prejudicial attitudes that
she has faced, Mrs. Walker-Simpson says:

> In corporate America, just never really feeling like the status quo applies
> to you. It's as if when coming into an organization—as opposed to them
> assuming that I had the ability to do my job as my white counterpart,
> having to feel like more is expected for me to prove my abilities. . . .
> I remember when I just found out that I was expecting, an older white
> gentleman who worked there probably 30 years just assumed that I was
> not married. He asked me how I was going to do my job with a small
> child, you live too far and who's going to take care, just assuming that
> I was in a home without a husband. That kind of stuff. Assuming that
> I lived in the projects. . . . That is ridiculous in the year 2000 I think.

Addressing the struggles of women gifted for leadership, Rev. Harrison
promotes lay- and clergywomen under the banner of fighting "racial
and sexual apartheid." Of his effectiveness as a faithful pastor, I think
that it cannot be understood outside of an inner logic where God's grace
is credited as inspiring human innovation and responsibility. We might
simply say, "God Did It." Moreover, one of the women whose pastoral
ministry was launched from his ministry at Christopher Temple is
Dr. Carol Evans. Her ministry is the subject of the next chapter.

3

"God of a Second Chance": A Tale of a Female Pastor in a Transforming Merged Mission Church

In the last days it will be, God declares, that I will pour out my Spirit upon all flesh, and your sons and your daughters shall prophesy, and your young men shall see visions, and your old men shall dream dreams. Even upon my slaves, both men and women, I will pour out my Spirit; and they shall prophesy.

—Acts 2: 17–18 NRSV

Developing a New Congregation in a Redeveloping Community

Heralding the public and private sector partnerships that drive the forces of gentrification are city government signs: "Neighborhoods Alive Redevelopment Area." These signs and other visible changes mark the "good news" of neighborhood revitalization. Indeed, a drive through this community reveals the work of tearing down old structures and building up new or rehabilitated structures. During the spring of 2001, a huge crane sat idle next to an empty sixteen-story public housing building within walking distance of Isaiah-Matthews Christian Methodist Episcopal Church. This building and other high-rise projects, which have long concentrated black human poverty, crime, blight, and misery, are being aggressively demolished across the nation. Observers are left to presume that evacuated residents have moved to affordable housing, which their government has promised is available in scattered sites throughout the metropolitan area.

On another abandoned building in the vicinity is the sign, "Pioneer Park Place: Quality New Homes starting at $205,000."

Since 1930, blacks have constituted 95 percent of the population of Pioneer Park as whites fled to areas made safe from black migration by restrictive covenants that legally prevented black home ownership. Over the years, the racial separation produced by racially restrictive covenants allowed patterns of municipal neglect, poorly maintained streets, and deterioration of housing in this culturally rich area adorned by many old mansions. New housing development in the 1950s for Pioneer Park consisted of blocks of high-rise public housing. By 1990, Pioneer Park was 99 percent black with more than half of the families headed by females caring for children under eighteen. With more than a third of the residents unemployed, two-thirds of the families lived below the poverty line. In census tracts adjacent to the one in which Isaiah-Matthews lies, poverty averaged 86 percent in high-rise public housing units. Teenage crime, drug abuse, and sexually transmitted diseases were rampant. Like other black ghettos, congregations and a few community groups were left to improve the quality of life along with a handful of anchoring social institutions.[1]

So, the present neighborhood revitalization, which promises to attract members of the new black middle class and others with sufficiently high income, seems like a "second chance" for a troubled community. Asked whether gentrification represents a threat or opportunity, Mary Duncan, a community resident and lay leader at Isaiah-Matthews, frets whether her family will be able to afford to stay in the neighborhood. Asked a similar question, Dr. Carol Evans, the pastor of Isaiah-Matthews, is optimistic about the possibilities of ministry in a mixed income neighborhood. In particular, she looks forward to African Americans moving in "who have decent incomes." Community redevelopment is embraced as a sign that Isaiah-Matthews's efforts to renovate a burned out church structure will be worth the struggle.

Due to demolition of adjacent housing, the newly renovated structure of Isaiah-Matthews sits alone on one side of this street in this revitalizing neighborhood. Like the surrounding neighborhood, this faith community is also undergoing transformation. Old structures of thought and behavior are being challenged while new structures of thinking and behavior are being established. At the helm of the renovation of the structure and building of the faith community is a charismatic black woman who has shouldered the blessed burdens of pastoral leadership in a changing community.

Burdens of a Woman Pastor in the Christian Methodist Episcopal Church

On my initial visit to Isaiah-Matthews on the first Sunday of November in 2001, I was favorably impressed with the renovation of this eighty-year-old structure, which was the home of Christopher Temple until they moved to their present Middleton site in the 1960s. Dr. Evans's "first class" stamp is all over the renovation. It is intimate and beautiful, quite functional for ministry to serve the membership and community. A sun-lit sanctuary offers an aesthetically pleasing environment for worship. A transparent pulpit is the sacred desk for the proclamation of divine messages by a human messenger, who insists on "keeping it real" with herself and her parishioners. Two very fine musical instruments especially suited for black gospel music (a digital Kurzweil piano and C-3 Hammond organ) signal readiness for diverse cultural expressions of black sacred music.

On the other side of a one-way mirror behind the pulpit is the pastor's well-decorated office and bath. Above the pastor's office is a comfortable lounge to provide hospitality for visiting preachers and other special guests. The lower level features a furnished kitchen, a lower multipurpose area for dining and teaching, and offices for administration and for storage. Indeed, the building is resurrected from its ruined condition that was caused by an electrical fire several years earlier.

On my first visit, about forty-five people were present for morning worship. Men make up about half of the adults attending. Children and youth are about one-fourth of the congregation. At this service, the choir stand is empty. Two skilled gospel musicians play the organ for successive sections of the three-hour worship experience, providing nearly incessant organ background throughout the prayers, scripture readings, communion rituals, and the preaching celebration. One of the songs that brought the congregation enthusiastically to its feet was the traditional gospel song led by Dr. Evans in a call and response fashion just prior to her sermon:

> Glory, glory, hallelujah (entire verse sung by Evans)
> Since I laid, I laid, I laid my burdens down
> Glory, glory, hallelujah
> Since I laid, I laid, I laid my burdens down
>
> My burden down (Evans leads chorus)
> My burden down (congregation responds)

My burden down (Evans)
My burden down (congregation responds)
Since I laid, I laid, I laid my burdens down (Evans)
My burden down (Evans)
My burden down (congregation)
My burden down, Lord (Evans)
Since I laid, I laid, I laid my burdens down (Evans)

In the ensuing sermonic prayer, Dr. Evans draws strength from her own spiritual roots saying, "Lord, bless this tired, Mississippi woman." Implicit in this plea to the Almighty is a reminder of her own roots of southern poverty and her relationship with people who grow weary on the journey of life and long for new hope and strength. A quality most often praised by Dr. Evans's church members is what Bob Aikens calls her "relateability," that is to say, her ability to relate to people of all ages, levels of education, and economic class. At home speaking the vernacular of different segments of the black community as well as articulately speaking Standard English, Pastor Evans is perceived as "professional" or "down home" according to how she chooses to present herself to others.[2]

Amidst her sermon, "How I Got Over," we hear of a God who assists a divorced black woman struggling to complete theological education while working a full-time job and raising her children. Evans intones:

I know that God got me through seminary. I was about to lose my mind. Somebody gave me the power to read in the midnight hour. I can say like David, I got over because "of *thee*," not because of *me*. That's why I don't let nobody play with my title. *God* gave me the strength "to run against the troops and leap over walls." God gives power to overcome any obstacle and for Isaiah-Matthews to work as a team. I had enough sense to put my intellect up and lean not on my own understanding. I've learned to lean on the Lord.

Acknowledging her femininity in the pulpit, Dr. Evans is adorned in a soft and colorful gown. Her selection of clergy apparel seems to say, "In my pulpit, I don't choose to dress in a standard clergy robe designed for a male but sized for a female." As she came to the celebration climaxing her sermon, Dr. Evans removed her large earrings, kicked off her high heel shoes and finished her message (and the rest of the service) in her bare stocking feet. Apparently, she wanted to get out of her heels to do the foot stomping, dancing, and walking that is a part of how Dr. Evans "celebrates in the preacherage."

Furthermore, Dr. Carol Evans, empowered from her traditional role of housewife and healed from the wounds of an abusive marriage, has accepted the burdens of confronting the unofficial tradition of a "males only ministry." Working with other church leaders, she is transforming a merged mission church into a place of healing, while confronting prevailing patriarchal attitudes in the church and society. That she is determined that "nobody play with her title" also suggests the critical link between theological education and liberation for aspiring black women preachers.

Many burdens are shouldered by black women in the black church. In particular, the burdens of gender and race have historically resulted in a "weight of weariness she had to share" and a "load of loneliness she had to bear."[3] The burdens of being a black woman in the church are indeed heavy. These burdens include the burden of women's history, the burden of the Bible, and the burden of the church.[4] The burden of women's history is the historical creation of patriarchy, a system of male domination on the basis of gender alone. The effects of patriarchal systems and attitudes are experienced by women across the world from antiquity to the present. The burden of the Bible is that it is a male-dominated book that has been used in the past as well as in the present as an instrument to legitimate the subordination of and mistreatment of women. The burden of the church includes the fact that patriarchy has been accepted as the divine intention in the policies and polity in the white hierarchical patriarchal church as well as in the attitudes and practices of the black church. Moreover, denominational insiders assert that the practices of this "ecclesial patriarchy" in the CME Church include the exploitation of women for fund-raising and as objects of sexual favors.[5]

Despite the fact that women have had "full clergy rights" since 1966 in the CME Church, CME Church scholars illumine further burdens of women in ministry in the CME Church. These include some bishops' reluctance to take a chance on assigning females to the larger churches, lay male officers not wanting a "woman preacher" as their pastor, negative reactions of many CME women with respect to female preachers and pastors, and slights by male colleagues in ministry because of their gender.[6] In fact, it is not uncommon to hear female members say, "If they send a woman to pastor my church, I am leaving!"[7] Thus, a paradox of the CME Church and other black churches is that it is an institution in which the majority of its members are women; yet, its leaders are predominantly men.[8]

Through the healing catharsis of joyfully singing "Glory, glory . . . since I laid, I laid, I laid my burdens down" I see Dr. Evans attempting to lay down her own concrete personal and pastoral burdens by faith in God. Dr. Evans's specific pastoral burdens include her working without salary at the church while working another full-time job, dealing with the pressure of paying the mortgage and other bills, proving that a woman can do a "man's job" without being a crybaby, and nurturing "baby Christians" while trusting them as key leaders. Despite these and other burdens, Dr. Evans, a spiritually gifted and theologically educated clergywoman, has been shaped by the experience of her struggle to overcome male oppression at home and institutional oppression in the church. While leading her congregation's valiant effort to empower women and men in Isaiah-Matthews gentrifying community, she is one pastor among a growing wave of women, challenging the unofficial tradition of male-dominated leadership in black Methodist churches.[9] These women have been shaped to lead in a different way from male colleagues like Rev. Harrison. Yet, they are determined to achieve the same, if not superior results. My representation of Rev. Dr. Carol Evan's experience in ministry should be seen within this social and ecclesial context.

Black Women's Experiences as Sources for Pastoral Leadership

The experiences of black women struggling against the oppressive forces of racism, sexism, and classism in church and society are beginning to find legitimation as sources for a more inclusive theological understanding of leadership in the black church.[10] Rather than simply imitating white male strategies of leadership, women have questioned whether these strategies were adequate for males or females and have begun to develop their own leadership strategies based upon their experiences as women.[11]

Furthermore, because of black women's struggle with the tripartite oppression of race, gender, and class, they can glean only so much from the leadership strategies of white women. As Vashti McKenzie, the first woman elected as bishop in the African Methodist Episcopal Church, writes:

> African American women are products of their struggle with racism, sexism, and classism. Their style of leadership is a legacy from the Mothers of Struggle, who raised other peoples' babies while their own were sold away; who dreamed great dreams while doing menial labor;

who learned how to collect the pieces that life gave them and quilt them as a covering for the whole family; who marched, sat in, picketed, protested, and were jailed.[12]

Since answering her call to preach in 1968, Carol Evans has continued to be shaped by the crucible of her life experiences, educational training, and experiences as a lay and clergy church leader. In her short time in the CME Church, she has become an exemplary female pastor in the CME Church context. Forced into the workplace in 1978 from her primary roles as a housewife and church leader, she struggled with the harsh realities of trying to support her home and two children as a black woman battered and neglected by her husband. She says that she heard the Lord's still small voice saying, "I am your provider" after her valiant struggle to hold together her twenty-year marriage ended with divorce in 1987.

Growing in faith as well as in her ability to manage her finances, she says that she heard the Lord say, "get yourself over there in school." Twenty years after she began preaching, she entered a program designed for adults with significant life experience. Putting together a portfolio of her community and professional work, she completed a bachelor's degree. At the same time, she applied to seminary as a special student. After maintaining the required grade point average, she was accepted into the regular degree program. During this period of managing work, school, and family, Evans says that those four years were "nothing but work, school, and preaching."

In contrast to Rev. Harrison's experience of being a "student of the system," a system in which he benefited from many mentors, we might say that Evans had to "search for the right system." In the CME Church, she found an ecclesial system where she could feel at home. Concerning how she left her Pentecostal church home in this search Evans explained:

Primarily, as I continued to grow in the Pentecostal church, I ventured outside the church to join an ecumenical choral group and in that choral group, I found a new place in God. I was able to fellowship with sisters and brothers of all denominations which broadened my horizon. . . . We used to travel the length and breadth of this country singing God's praises and I saw through that group how it was important to expand my walk from just being salvation conscious to becoming socially conscious. In so doing, I began to seek out other denominations who offered me what I was growing into.

Her expanded environment of relationships resulted in broadened social horizons and discontent with what she later recognized as self-righteousness in herself. She says she had to lose her "Junior Jesus-ness." In this process, a crucial lesson was learning to "love people where they are" whether or not they were where she might want them to be morally and spiritually. She began the ordination process in the United Methodist Church (UMC), one of the progressive mainline denominations with respect to its stance on women in ministry.

Not surprisingly, Evans has found few male or female mentors along the way. However, after she joined a black United Methodist congregation, the pastor, an African American male, began to tutor Evans. She says that in this congregational environment, the teaching and example of this social activist pastor helped her learn "to embrace all people of all walks of life." She regards him as her first instructor, trainer, and mentor in ministry. There, she says, she began to think seriously about getting an education. She also credits him with first teaching her how to "exegete a text" from the Bible.

However, when she began the process toward ordination, denominational officials assigned her to another church. Eventually, it became clear that she would not be ordained in this system. Evans says it is because they did not "embrace the gifts and graces" that she had "learned to be at home with." When pressed to explain what "gifts and graces" may have caused her to be rejected in her journey of ordination Evans said:

> I am an African American sister and I am an African American preacher. I embrace the tradition of black preaching everywhere I go and our tradition is to celebrate in the preacherage, if you will. I believe in sermon preparation [and] that one should enjoy the sermon as much as the congregation. I am somewhat a jubilant kind of preacher. I'm not staid or stuck. Sometimes, that rubs persons the wrong way and that was the reputation that I had in the United Methodist Church.

Furthermore, Evans says she did not fit into a United Methodist ethos because of her willingness to operate in her spiritual gifts including the supernatural spiritual gifts of a "word of knowledge."[13] Continuing with her response to my question concerning her perception of gifts and graces that were not embraced as she sought ordination in the United Methodist system, Evans responds:

> I'm a radical preacher. I am extremely radical in terms of my demonstrations in the sermon. I get excited and sometimes that does not

work for some people. I can sing a little bit and sometimes if the Lord leads me I will sing before a sermon, and if not, sometimes, I sing after sermons. Then there are times that God uses me in the gift of discernment. It's something that I don't apologize for. It is a gift, the word of knowledge that God gives me and I use it as I feel led of God. Some persons will say, "How does that happen and where does that come from?" It comes from God and when God gives me a word for people I tell them what God has given me to tell them. I used to draw back and hold those gifts and let those gifts lie dormant because I did not want to be looked at as a queer person or somebody who was trying to be deep, if you will, for lack of a better term, but I've learned to embrace the gifts that God has given me.

When she did not find that her manner of expressing her gifts and graces was accepted in the United Methodist Church, she gave up her efforts to be accepted in the UMC.

It is a common pastoral observation that local churches have "personalities." Extending this reasoning to denominational systems, we can also observe that denominations have unique identities, self-understandings and ways of engaging the world.[14] Furthermore, it is common wisdom that a pastor's personality may not match the personality of a church. A pastor may succeed in one parish that matches her or his personality and fail in the next as the personality of the pastor and church fail to mesh. Evans's beliefs and behaviors ran up against previously unknown sanctions in the UMC. Indeed, beliefs and behaviors related to the Holy Spirit have divided Christian churches in the past and present. Like a ship nearly wrecked because of a collision with an underground iceberg, Evans decided to change her course.

An out of town preaching engagement to a CME Church was Evans's first encounter with the CME Church. That she was the church's first Women's day speaker suggests to me that the congregational leadership was just beginning to address the issue of the pulpit being off limits to women. In my observation of another female colleague who was warmly embraced as a Women's day speaker and later rejected by male and female members as the next pastor of that same congregation, I can say that congregations have different attitudes toward women as preachers than they do toward women as pastoral leaders. Nonetheless, Evans's warm acceptance by a particular CME congregation planted the seed in her mind that the CME Church might be the place to pursue her calling to be a pastor. Introduced to Rev. Harrison's ministry by seeing his television broadcast, she later joined Christopher Temple and served as a part of his ministerial staff.

Of her feeling of being a part of the CME Church and her analysis of its politics with respect to women preachers, Evans says:

> I have found the CME Church to be a warm church, a church that will embrace sisters. A church that has its own level of politics, but it's not so thick that you cannot get through and you cannot find a home. I have found a home in the Christian Methodist Episcopal Church where people are loving and people are caring. That is not to say there are not flaws because there are; however, the love and friendliness that I found seem to outweigh everything else that I encompassed. I was a new kid on the block and I was treated from day one as if I belonged. That is what won my heart to come over into the Christian Methodist Episcopal denomination.

In her first interview with Rev. Harrison, before joining Christopher Temple, she told him of her desire to become a pastor. No doubt, Rev. Harrison's support of her desire to pastor was instrumental in Bishop Douglas's willingness later to take a chance with this "new kid on the block." In 1994, the bishop appointed Rev. Evans to the newly merged congregations of Isaiah CME and Matthews CME Churches.

Her preparation for this appointment was much more than the sum of her seminary education and denominational course of studies. Indeed, her particular experiences as a black woman would not be included on a traditional profile outlining her preparation for her first pastoral assignment. Her struggle toward healing the wounds from her divorce, her experiences of nurturing and caring for family as single head of her household, her growth and development in the workplace, her prior experiences as a laywoman raising funds in the church, and lessons learned from her search for the right ecclesial system to exercise her gifts in ministry are experiences that would be discounted from a traditional male developmental perspective. However, with the advantage of hindsight, we can see that they enhanced Rev. Evans's preparation for transformative pastoral leadership in her first pastorate.

Transforming a Merged Mission Church

In her first pastorate, Dr. Evans was given the difficult assignment of merging two small churches and finding a suitable home for the congregation. Convincing the small congregation, her bishop, and a bank to loan the church $260,000, she led the Isaiah-Matthews Church in renovating a burned out church edifice. Departing from the more typical circumstance in which ordained women are tolerated but offered little assistance,[15] Bishop Douglas supported the building project with a significant influx of funds from his various conferences. Building the faith community has proved to be an even more difficult process than her working with bishop, banker, architect, and contractors. With her seminary degree in hand, Evans admits that, at the outset, she had hoped for a better church, "a more established church." She accepted the challenge nonetheless. Her life experience helped her to take on such a task. Evans says, "I'm used to taking nothing and making something out of it."

A new location was needed because one of the church's buildings had been sold for taxes and owed several thousand dollars for past due utilities. The gas and water supply had been disconnected. The other church's building had burned down in a recent electrical fire. Moreover, there were internal problems in each of the little churches. The previous pastor on one side of the merger was the mother, sister, daughter, and aunt of several of the members. Family members resented the bishop moving the pastor, who was their family member. On the other side, a congregation of about six remaining members, Evans faced opposition because they had never had a woman pastor.

Transforming the Pastor First

Transformation of the church began with transformed perspectives of the newly appointed pastor. Displeased with this assignment, she called several friends to pray that she would have the right spirit about this difficult assignment. From this period of prayer, Dr. Evans gained a new perspective and approach for dealing with this situation. Evans says:

> The Lord began to work on me and to teach me that all people were His. I was to get in there and to help bring about reconciliation between the two congregations. . . . I began to look at ways that I could empower the people to feel good about the merger. . . . I had to come in very prayerful because people were very vulnerable and they were hurt. I did my best to take on the Spirit of Jesus, to come in with a very caring spirit, to be very nurturing. . . . I knew that some of the hurt and the pain was their own fault because they just took things for granted in the church. They did not take the Lord's work seriously enough to keep the gas on, to make sure that the roof was not leaking, to make sure that the building was tuck pointed. Then on the Matthews side there was a fire that had burned out that church because of neglect.

It would not be an exaggeration to describe this situation as a mess. Ackoff writes:

> Managers are not confronted with problems that are independent of each other, but with dynamic situations that consist of complex systems of changing problems that interact with each other. I call such situations *messes*. Problems are abstractions extracted from messes by analysis. Managers do not solve problems; they manage messes.[16]

The challenge before her was to learn how to manage the mess and to devise a fitting leadership strategy growing out of her experience and strengths as a female leader. Having overcome her earlier fear of going to school, Rev. Evans entered doctor of ministry program to learn how to revitalize this urban church. Dr. Evans's thesis gives insight into the analysis and approach that resulted from her study and prayer.

Seeing the vulnerable and hurting people who had failed in their responsibilities to manage their lives and their church, she formulated a solution path. After renovating the chosen facility, she would attempt to lead a nurturing and caring ministry to transform the attitudes and behavior of her inner core of leaders so that they would learn to accept responsibility as partners in stewardship. In her mind, she envisioned that these church officers and leaders must be transformed to accept responsibility for the total shared life of the congregation, for the care of the property, and for the development of ministries to serve the needs of the congregation and community.

Dr. Evans's transformed perspective included her learning to see the interconnected nature of the mess. The mess included the physical condition of the two buildings that she inherited, properties that she described as, "one run down and the other burned down." The situation was exacerbated because of the limited financial and human resources of the merged church of thirty-one members, many of whom were retired or out of work. The low levels of trust in pastors and church officers because of the abuses of past church officials would make it difficult to lead. Then, there was the inner condition of vulnerable and hurting black people, burdened by poor self-image. On top of this was the need for developing caring ministries to serve in a poor and gentrifying community. Despite all of the dimensions of this mess, Dr. Evans saw the *opportunity* of developing a new congregation in a developing community.

With a transformed perspective of the challenges ahead and belief in her role in helping the fledging congregation to fulfill its purpose,

Evans moved forward in developing her team approach to ministry. As a team leader, she experienced the struggle of balancing the members' needs for patient nurturing as well as for firm challenging. At core, she exemplified two important keys for effective leadership. More important, perhaps, than any special leadership qualities that she possessed or extensive training that she had for this position, she proceeded with a strong belief in the congregation's purpose and in the people with whom she had been sent to work. This enabled her to strike a balance between action and patience working toward fulfillment of purposes and goals that were meaningful to the membership as well as to herself.[17] From the struggle to help the vulnerable and hurting members of the congregation emerged the idea of the theme now written on every church bulletin:

> "A Sharing and Caring Church Where Everyone Reaches One, Everyone Teaches One, and Everyone is Someone."

While other persons assigned to a merged mission congregation might have been overwhelmed by the mess, Rev. Evans sensed a new purpose and new possibilities working with the people of the church and community. Transformation of the merged mission began with transformation of the pastor.

Overcoming Resistance to Female Pastors

Male and female pastors will encounter resistance to their leadership at various times during their tenure from various people in their congregations. The common maxim is true: "you can please some people some of the time, but you can never please all the people all the time." Some resistance to leadership is expected because people tend to resist change and leaders are at the center of change movements. Others resist strong leaders "on g.p. (on general principle)." Believing their role is to be a check and balance to strong pastoral leadership, some follow the practice of the ill-informed Baptist deacon who often stated to my father (a deceased Baptist deacon) that "my role is to oppose whatever the pastor proposes and to propose whatever he opposes!" At other times, poor leadership or abusive leadership (illegitimate uses of authority) should be resisted. Because Methodist pastors are appointed by bishops and not selected by congregations, it is not uncommon for new pastors to face resistance when parishioners are not ready for pastoral transitions.

Notwithstanding the sources of resistance that all leaders face, the question posed to members of Isaiah-Matthews was "do you think that women face unique struggles as pastors?" Michael Evans, a trustee from the early days of the merger and the son of Dr. Evans, recalls resistance from some of the female members in the beginning of Dr. Evans's pastoral tenure:

> Well, I can remember one lady saying that, "I don't have to obey her. I'm a woman just like she is." I heard that several times, "I don't have to do this" or "she can't tell me this because I'm a woman just like she is." Instead of looking at it as she is a leader and the pastor, women just had a hard time with it. They would rather listen to a man and be in the presence of a male pastor.

Confronted by resistance of this type from female congregants, the new pastor initially used the power of her position. She lovingly but firmly declared, "If you can't follow my leadership, you'll need to make other decisions." The result of this bold, but risky, stance is that at least two of these women left the church; others decided to stay. Yet, there were women who stayed that tried to sabotage the new female pastor. By "shutting down the finances," "back stabbing the pastor," and "running away new members" church leaders impacted key resources: money, membership, and trust.

A critical part of Pastor Evans's neutralizing those who opposed her on the grounds of her gender was her evangelistic work that brought in new people. These people were not only dedicated to Evans's ministry, but they provided new membership strength by their commitment to "pay tithes." Dr. Evans regularly teaches that the tithe is sacred and belongs to God. Based on biblical passages, she consistently preaches and teaches that to give less than 10 percent of one's income is "robbing God."[18] Failing to "pay tithes" brings curses rather than blessing from God to the individual, the church, and the community, which ought to benefit from the ministries of the church. Furthermore, one cannot properly "give an offering" until one pays the tithe, which is holy to God. Hence, while those resisting the new pastor's ministry were talking, new members were coming in tithing.

I interviewed a husband and wife, Penny Aikens, a steward, and Bob Aikens, a trustee, probing the gender antagonism resulting from the appointment of a female pastor. Bob, a lifelong member of CME churches and grandson of a respected female CME minister, recalls witnessing females opposing the new pastor. He says,

> There was some of that still going on, but you had people that would come into the church and, no matter what, they became very dedicated to her. It just eliminated automatically, there was nothing they could say to change our perspective of the pastor. So . . . [Penny interjects, "It died away."] It died away because we came in . . . paying our tithes and the tithes were paying some of the bills. No matter what they say, if they weren't tithing, it overcome anything that they were talking about. Now, the bills were being paid, alleviating some of the stress off of the pastor. Now, she can concentrate on the things that she was doing.

Bob speculates that these types of parish struggles impact CME bishops' willingness to appoint female pastors to pulpits in positions other than entry level or other token appointments. If it is observed that one female pastor cannot overcome resistance encountered in one situation, Bob thinks that bishops, whom he refers to as "the men in the old regime" remain more comfortable with the unofficial "males only tradition." Continuing his analysis of the struggle of female pastors Bob says,

> When you were talking about the women relationship to a woman pastor, it's the basic thing I was talking about: man's relationship to themselves. Then it gets to the point if she's had a relationship problem with . . . the women [in the] congregation and you got the men in the old regime, right, the struggle has begun. Can she move up? Because like you said, they are cutting off the revenue, they are doing these different things and the male [the all male college of bishops that holds the power of clergy appointment and promotion] is saying, "You know, if a male was there, they wouldn't do that. Yet, at the same time, she can't seem to get this thing off the ground. Here we go again."

Acknowledging that these parish dynamics indeed impact the CME system, Bishop Douglas says that he has exercised care in his appointment of female pastors. He has not forced female ministers into situations where they would be roundly rejected. In response to my questions as to whether there is a "stained glass ceiling for woman preachers" and how the church might help women to succeed in larger appointments, Bishop Douglas asserts that bishops can attempt to determine the congregations that would be most receptive to a woman pastor and prepare these congregations to receive them. In addition to appointing women as pastors, Bishop Douglas has made the still rare appointment of a woman to the "middle-management" position of a presiding elder. This female presiding elder, like her male counterparts, assists the bishop in supervising a district of churches. Of the struggle of women ministers receiving and handling larger church appointments, Bishop Douglas says,

> The women [preachers], their largest problems come from women. . . . That's the problem women are having. It's not with us, but, it's with women who lead them to believe, oh, they would like to have a woman pastor . . . I have to be careful to know the real temperaments of the congregation. I use women as far as [I] can . . . I know in congregations this can help you to know where a woman might be effective. This is not FEPC [Fair Employment Practice Commission], so you can't shove a woman down someone's throat. . . . It's not where you can discriminate between the sexes. It's a kind of thing where you try to prepare a congregation. When I first sent Cathy Denny [fictitious name for female sent to pastor a larger congregation], I went to some of the key people in the congregation and said, "Look, I'm thinking about sending you a woman. I want you all to be good to her." I didn't *ask them could I send*. I said, "*I'm going to send* you a woman and I want you all to receive her. OK?" And the people said, "Well, OK." The bishop has a lot of power but if he's aware of situations, he can help work people into these situations. All congregations are not ready for women, but more of them are than you would imagine. A lot of women are not ready either for pastoring.

In order for women preachers to overcome resistance to their leadership on the basis of their gender, they must be ready to face the real challenges of pastoral leadership as Dr. Evans was. Her strategies included being willing to risk losing people in order that an atmosphere might be created where new people brought in by intentional evangelistic ministry might be incorporated into church life. She also formed healthy alliances with women and men in the congregation who were open to the idea of a woman in the role of pastor. However, bishops and presiding elders must also use their best skills not only to prepare women for leadership, but to also prepare congregations to receive women as their pastors.

Though the CME Church and other black-controlled Methodist denominations do not utilize a formal system of consultation between the local church leaders and the bishop's cabinet,[19] Bishop Douglas's experience, nonetheless, suggests principles for increasing the number of female pastors appointed and promoted within the ranks of

CME clergy. These principles include bishops and presiding elders understanding how to gain and exercise legitimate authority in mutual ways that show care for clergy and for congregations. This may include utilizing formal or informal systems of consultation with wise and trusted laity in congregations.

In addition, ministers at all levels of the Methodist hierarchy—bishop, presiding elders, and pastors—must be proactive in seeking to transform attitudes resistant to change. A mentor of Dr. Evans, Bishop James Norman of the AME Zion Church, says that he has made it plain as to where he stands relative to gender and ministry by "a proactive teaching, a proactive philosophy, a proactive principle, a proactive biblical understanding that is articulated in any number of times in any number of settings." Intentional efforts to address gender prejudice at all levels of the church are necessary to overcome resistance to women clergy.

Proving Herself, Earning Respect

Women and minorities in American society are accustomed to the contemporary reality of having to "prove themselves" in a world that privileges white males. Overcoming hurdles *to enter* nontraditional fields is one thing; gaining respect *to be promoted* in those fields is another thing. In the CME Church, pastors may be appointed on the basis of their gifts and graces while satisfying the minimum requirement of two years of college.[20] However, I think that most observers would agree that women almost always require a college and/or seminary degree to even be considered for a decent appointment in a black Methodist church. Furthermore, they must prove their skills in the practice of congregational ministry. If an individual female pastor "fails" it simply confirms critics who say, "Women don't belong in the pastorate." This pressure drives women such as Dr. Evans to succeed despite the odds.

Penny Aikens, a registered nurse, thinks that Rev. Evans and other female pastors have to do more to prove themselves than men. A steward of Isaiah-Matthews, Penny said:

> I don't know if necessarily she would have to do that all the way [earn a doctorate in ministry] to prove her knowledge . . . if [she was] a man coming out at the same time. . . . She came out very well educated and very well prepared and on top of being able to teach the Word and to teach people how to follow the Word and how to live their life through the Word, she has been able to be a great administrator.

Penny's husband, Bob, says that "as a strong black man" he has no problem respecting and following a woman "who is a strong woman who has her stuff together," "lifts up black men," and is balanced in speaking to both men and women without putting down either sex. He finds that Dr. Evans's teaching ministry contributes to more positive relationships between black men and women. Bob says:

> For example, and I am always relating this to a lot of people, she says the number one killer of a black man is that we don't communicate. We hold in things. In holding in things, we build up pressure, stress, and die of heart attacks. That gives you something to think about. When you got a black man that is dealing with a lot of stress and he's not communicating, it takes only an inch to push him over the limit when his woman comes in and challenges him, comes in and degrades him.

Dr. Evans draws upon her strengths and experiences as a woman to pastor her flock. In an interesting segment of our interview, Bob sees Dr. Evans as "the mother hen of us all" finding ways to challenge and nurture church members. Dr. Evans teaches grown men how to be accountable, a lesson in male responsibility that he says is crucial to the black race. He says:

> She's also the mother hen of us. She spanks us but she holds us close to her bosom. And at the same time, we forget about the spanking and we realize she still loves us. She will get on you, if you're an officer and you do not do your duties. She doesn't hem and haw and pretend it doesn't happen. She'll say, "And you!" She'll call your name right in front of the congregation. "You said you was going to do this and you did not do it." I can respect a woman like that because I'm a very direct person. . . . She doesn't do it to embarrass you, but to hold you accountable. Through our lives, being black, and what I've seen, in my opinion again, is that we as blacks do not hold each other accountable.

In contrast to his "mother hen" image of leadership, Bob, a former police officer, also uses the image of a commander personally leading the troops to battle in the following description of Dr. Evans:

> She's a leader that you wish to follow. She's the one that says, "Come on. Follow me. We're going to fight this battle." Yet, at the same time, she's in the middle, she's not there [saying] (he hollers) "All right! Let's go fight this battle. Everybody just go ahead on!" No, she's not [in the back]. She's there [in front, saying by her example] "Come on, follow me.

Follow me." She makes the path and we just stroll through the path like a support group. And in order for our church to be successful, we need a strong leader.

Manford Billings will readily tell you that he and Dr. Evans do not always "see eye to eye." The son of a Methodist pastor, Mr. Billings says he was "born into the Methodist church" eighty years ago. Mr. Billings is quite knowledgeable of the church, having served in the past as a superintendent of Sunday School, a trustee, steward, and class leader. Asked what he appreciated about Dr. Evans as a pastor, Mr. Billings responded:

> Well, I would say, first of all, she is a [good] speaker and she is a beautiful person. Sometimes, you know, we don't see eye to eye sometimes, she and I, but we always get back together. She'll tell you that. Something that I dislike, I'll tell her. Something she dislike, she'll tell me.

In addition to Mr. Billings's appreciation for Dr. Evans's skills as a speaker and her direct manner for resolving conflicts, he respects her ability to reach out and bring people into the church. Early in her pastoral administration, Pastor Evans teamed up with Mr. Billings picking up people from local housing projects in the church van. Perhaps most significant is his unsolicited tribute of Dr. Evans as "a spiritual leader." Asked what he means by his use of the term, "spiritual leader" Mr. Billings responds:

> Well, a spiritual leader, the way I can see, I can't look within her. Seemingly, she practices what she preaches. In other words, if there be anything different in there, I can't see that. That is between her and her God. That's the reason I say a spiritual leader, you've got to practice what you preach. If you don't practice what you preach, then there's a falsehood somewhere.

The praxis of transformative pastoral leadership requires considerable knowledge, Christian virtue, and skill. Encountering initial resistance to her position as pastor on the basis of her gender, Dr. Evans has worked to prove herself and to earn respect. Sources of this respect include her being an educated minister, preacher, teacher, administrator, "mother hen to her members," commander of the troops, conflict manager, evangelist, and spiritual leader.

Spiritual Healing for Inner City Ills

Having joined her friends, Bob and Penny Aikens, at Isaiah-Matthews seven months ago, Mona Daniels has struggled with Dr. Evans's expectations of her as a new church leader as well as what she perceives as shortcomings in Dr. Evans's leadership. The previous ten years, Mona practiced Buddhism. Dealing with the demands of her new church, which struggles to pay its bills, Mona is trying to get her own spiritual needs met. At the same time, she has quite a juggling act in developing her own business as a legal nurse consultant. Her view of Dr. Evans's leadership is through eyes that have been trained by years of practice as a nursing supervisor in hospital emergency rooms. When asked what qualities she most appreciates about Dr. Evans's pastoral leadership, Mona says she most appreciates "her psycho-social skills." Asked what she means by her use of the term, "psycho-social skills" with respect to the subject of pastoral leadership Mona said:

> When I'm working with families with functional dynamics that's psycho-social skills, so when you're working with the congregation you're dealing with people who may have ineffective coping skills, they may have dysfunctional families. Those are the two. There might be issues in relationship to health needs, so to be an effective leader, that's what I mean by I appreciate her psycho-social skills.

As this nursing supervisor warms up to the subject and realizes that her nursing perspective is a valuable lens for interpreting the work of this pastor, she grows in her level of respect for the magnitude of the urban pastor's job in poor communities. A commuter from an integrated middle-class neighborhood, Mona, recently appointed as a steward, judges the socioeconomic background from at least two pieces of evidence: the meager giving of individuals and the many prayer requests for better jobs during the period of sharing joys and concerns. Ministry in this context (and other social contexts) requires not only conversion by faith in Jesus Christ, but also transformation of lifelong beliefs and habits. Comparing the work of the pastor to the work of the nursing supervisor Mona says:

> It's just like myself. I'll use myself as an example. I went to my boss. I saw many problems with the nurses I supervise. Many of them come from lower socio-economic situations and many of them have habits that are very, very bad habits. When I went to my boss, I went to her

with a solution. She looked at me and said, "Mona, you have a good idea. How are you going to apply that? What is your goal? What do you want to achieve in this situation?" I couldn't really verbalize it, but she helped me out. She said, "You want to achieve a change in people's thinking." If I was going to analyze Dr. Evans's role and goal, I would think that is what she is trying to achieve.

On Easter Sunday, Mona saw Dr. Evans's manner of dealing with a number of problems that she sensed in the congregation. Dispensing with the prepared Easter message, Dr. Evans called people up for prayer and exercised her "gift of knowledge" to speak prophetically into the lives of the congregants. To those who might wonder about her departing from the order of worship Dr. Evans simply says, "I make no excuse for the Holy Ghost!"

As people stand in line before her at the altar, Dr. Evans says to one, "We declare healing into this young lady's life, in her mind and body." To another she says, "I see a brand new job and more money than you've ever made. God says He must be first in your life!" Mindful of the local gas utility publicizing the possibility of gas supplies being cut off in homes across the city as gas prices soared, Pastor Evans prays for God's favor in making suitable payment arrangements. Summoning worried members forward she says:

> All who have a high gas bill and aren't ashamed to come forward for prayer, we're going to pray for God's favor that your gas will not be cut off. Pray for favor to work out a plan to pay the bill.

Fifteen persons, about one-third of the adults present, came forward in response to this specific call. Anointing people with oil, laying hands on persons, praying for the sick, Rev. Evans clarifies her belief on the relationship of divine healing and healing through medical science:

> I'm not telling anybody not to go to the doctor or to throw away their medicine; I'm praying that you will trust God for your healing as you go to the doctor and take your medicine.

After briefly sharing her story of how God had blessed her life, Dr. Evans concluded, "The Lord has preached today. We're going to be an untraditional CME Church. I'll preach next Sunday."

I would think that a nursing professional coming out of ten years of Buddhism might be turned off by prayers for divine healing and other "signs and wonders." However, Mona says that she has personally experienced convincing results from Rev. Evans's prayers. What Rev. Evans calls her "gift of knowledge," Mona calls "her intuitive spirit." Speaking with me the day after Easter Sunday about this Mona says:

> Yesterday was a perfect example of her intuitive spirit to deviate from her written plan, sermon, and address issues that I hadn't spoken to her about, but had truly been something I had been dealing with all last week. That was to get off of the medication that I was on, the antidepressant medication. Do you remember when she asked people to come up if you weren't embarrassed? That was a [answer to a] prayer. All last week, I kept saying to Jack, "I've got to get off this medicine. I don't want to take it anymore. I just got to get off it." For her to say that yesterday was like, "Where did she get that?"

Deviating from the written plan, the textbook, is one characteristic of Dr. Evans's ministry. Describing what she saw in this Easter event through her nursing lens, Mona sees Dr. Evans adapting her ministry to deal with challenges that "the textbook" would not address anyway:

> What she did yesterday is the equivalent of my doing ten patients with large gaping wounds. . . . As a patient, what would you rather have happen? . . . You have an 18 centimeter by 20 centimeter wound in your abdomen. I don't have anything large enough to cover it. The textbook says it's not doable. Or would you rather see another nurse walk in who throws away the textbook and finds a way to heal the wound? That's how I saw yesterday.

Perhaps the image of a nurse in an urban hospital's trauma center is a fitting image for Dr. Evans's work in this context. The work of the pastoral leader may be akin to nurses' and physicians' work of assessing a situation, determining the best possible intervention, and implementing a plan of addressing the wounds of hurting people.

In this context, the key phrase for leadership is "best possible." Many problems are not "routine problems" with known solutions. Many of the pastoral challenges might be termed "adaptive problems," problems that demand innovation and learning. Dr. Evans is not a savior but a shepherd helping people to face their problems while changing their attitudes, behaviors, and values.[21] Previously rejected for ordination in a system that did not want to embrace her manner and gifts, Dr. Evans is developing "an untraditional CME Church," a congregation in which her gifts can be received and utilized.

Keeping It Real

Invited to visit the church by a family member soon after Rev. Evans became pastor, Wendy Sanders was initially impressed by this "little lady who would preach and take her shoes off." Later, she was attracted to Pastor Evans because she was "a real person." Asked what qualities that she appreciated about her pastor, Wendy responds:

> She's a real person. I've always put a minister above no reproach. They are on a certain level. Rev' explained to me that reverends are people too. They make mistakes. They do things wrong as well as anybody else. She said, "Don't put a minister on a pedestal because they're human beings as well as anybody." . . . But, I found out they are just like everyday people. I can always reach out and touch her.

Wendy does not perceive Dr. Evans in a role, "putting on a mask" or "putting on a show." In her sermons, members comment, "she just tell it like it is" and "she don't sugar coat nothing." Being "real" as a pastor made it easier for Wendy to hear and respond to what the minister was trying to teach through her sermons. Asked what role the church has played in her life, Wendy responds:

> For me, it filled a void in my life. . . . I know I need a church in my life, but I guess I wasn't ready to accept it at the time. When I started, it filled that void for me because Rev' was so real about things and that touched me so much. She was a real person to me. I learned the Word more than I ever learned it before and I was interested, I was hungry for the Word, so therefore it wasn't hard for me to adjust to certain things and put myself aside on a lot of issues.

In this age, a time when television ministers and mega churches are oft-revered as the ideal models of contemporary ministry, the value of pastoral ministry in small membership churches is often devalued. There, the fellowship of face-to-face relationships between pastor and people as well as among the members is important to sustained Christian faith. Wendy's husband, Israel, is appreciative of his pastor's availability and encouragement. Asked what qualities he appreciated about the pastor Israel responds:

> Pastor's beautiful, she really is. She takes me in her office and we sit and talk and something on your mind and she talks to you about it and tells you, "Don't worry about it. Everything is going to be alright. You know

you got God on your side." Just keep your head up in the air and just fight the good fight of faith is what she was saying. . . . If she wants to talk to you, she'll come to your house and sit and talk, pray at the house. She's a beautiful reverend. She's all right with me!

Israel also shares his observation that the church often provides food or concrete assistance to people just walking off the street. In that capacity, Dr. Evans's years of working with people in her career in social services pays off in her capacity of discernment. The way that Israel puts it is, "She look at you and can tell if you jokin' or jiving!" Wendy simply reiterates, "Like I said before, she *knows* people."

"Keeping it real" is a model of ministry that Dr. Evans says is rooted in the pattern of Jesus' life and ministry. This is a way in which Dr. Evans shares her life with people, being socially conscious as well as salvation conscious, being concerned with her self-care as well as caring for others, and moving persons toward greater health, happiness, and wholeness. This model allows this pastor to resist being put on a pedestal and to enter the arena where people live and die as one ministering from the scars of their own life. "Keeping it real" sees risk and opportunity, human problems, and human potential.

Struggling without the benefit of a supportive spouse, as many clergywomen do, for the first seven years of her pastorate, Dr. Evans talks frankly about how being "real" acknowledges her own desire for a supportive spouse. Of this model Evans says:

Jesus was always with people where they are and that is the model that I pray that I am demonstrating as I continue to be real. To be real simply means that I am just as vulnerable as other persons. I don't have two faces in terms of pastoring. Who you see is who I am. As you know, Richard and I began to date and I decided I would not act as if the church were not a part of my family. When we began to date, I went before the church and I told them we were seeing each other. I have shared my life with the congregation and I feel a good pastor is who, moving towards healthiness, happiness, and wholeness can do so. . . . In so doing, it brings about a spirit of being transparent. I don't have anything to hide. This is also part of what I learned from Rev. Sanders [her African American male mentor pastor in the U.M.C]—just to be real. If people are going to embrace you, they will and if they don't, you just let them be who they are.

Seeing herself in a process of moving toward health, happiness, and wholeness, Dr. Evans says that she chooses to be real and transparent even in the personal matter of her dating a member of the congregation to whom she is now married. Every pastor would not openly share this. McKenzie counsels single clergywomen, "Don't play where you pray!"[22] Others might see this as a violation of clergy sexual ethics, dating within one's congregation. Yet, by "keeping it real" she staved off unhealthy speculation that could damage her reputation and ministry. As Evans has been open about her struggles in her first marriage, she is open about her joy in her new marriage. Indeed in this second marriage, coming after years of being alone, she is jubilant about serving a "God of a second chance."

Confessions of Fallibility

In her opening remarks prior to preaching at a special conference celebrating the gifts of women in ministry, Dr. Evans was unusually frank confessing her ongoing struggles in her ministry at Isaiah-Matthews. Speaking to a congregation that included many women preachers who were not pastors Dr. Evans said:

> I told my people this year that if you don't follow my leadership, I'm outta here! I don't want to be one of those who is said to draw a good bucket of milk and then turn around and kick it over with the other foot! . . . I made up my mind that if I didn't see a difference in the life, in the faithfulness, in the finances, in the growth of the church, I've got to go! . . . I'm not going to stay in the ministry and kill it. . . . I think that we've got to be big enough to walk away gracefully if you've put your all into the ministry and I am praising the Lord, Reverend [looking towards me, a participant observer in the congregation] that we're moving to another level! I can truly see that we're moving to a different place of growth and development. I am just happy in the Lord that I don't have to leave! (She laughs and the congregation joins in laughter and clapping). So, I thank the Lord.

Despite "putting her all in the ministry" there are just some days when pastors, male and female, feel like quitting or feel it best to move on, hoping that somebody else can move the congregation to another level of growth and development. The idea of transformation includes the notion of growth and development in a particular direction. However, the direction of congregational transformation is not strictly linear; in the ebb and flow of viewing such measures as the faithfulness, finances, and growth of the people of God, transformation may be difficult to discern.

People of many vocations who exemplify lives of commitment must find places for confession of their struggle with fallibility. This is one of the conclusions of an ethnographic study of more than a hundred citizens who were committed to the common good, demonstrated perseverance and resilience, showed an ethical congruence between life and work, and engaged with diversity and complexity. [23] In this vein, Dr. Evans joins others who have learned to "give voice to the inner conversation," that is to say, "the capacity to see and reflect upon one's own inner world."[24] Indeed, the ability to chair such a range of voices, acknowledging her strength and her fallibility as well as her faith and her doubt is a healthy possibility if she is not paralyzed by it. Of this ability for committed people to "acknowledge, reflect upon, and give voice to all parts of one's inner conversation"[25] Daloz, Keen, Keen, and Parks write:

> Indeed, it is our perception that when the ability to entertain internal counterpoint is poorly developed or wanes for whatever reason, when some voices are suppressed and others amplified, burnout or destructive behavior is most likely to occur. When all are heard, none can fall away.[26]

Counseling her sisters in ministry, Dr. Evans knows that women have fought in the past and in the present for the right to exercise their gifts of leadership in the black church. From her own experience, she knows that these women may face opposition in the home, in the church, and in the community. On one hand, the struggles of pastoral leadership go with the territory. Like a soldier, you cannot just work when you feel like it. In this sense, she advises her sisters to be "tough like the brothers" and not to wear their emotions on their sleeves. She warns the woman that if you're looking for favors, then you have the wrong idea. It's tough for the brothers and it's even tougher for the sisters. A part of this toughness is recognizing that you can't depend upon all brothers in ministry to come to your rescue. They have their struggles too. "Keeping it real" for the sake of sisters Dr. Evans says that a certain amount of toughness is necessary amidst one's femininity:

> I'm not going to be one of those crybaby sisters. I'm going to learn to be faithful in season and out of season. I'm going to do it like the brothers. The brothers go rain, shine, sleet, or snow. Don't want to go, but they go anyhow and that's the mode that we sisters in ministry, that we've

got to take on. How many sisters in ministry? Raise your hand. This is a women's ministry conference. Gotta be tough! Ain't nobody giving away nothing. . . . No sugartits in this thang! You got to roll up your sleeves and work it. . . . Ain't no specialties for us in ministry. We fought to get in here, now let's roll up our sleeves and go to work!

No pacifiers (sugartits) will be handed out for crybaby sisters in ministry. To succeed as a pastoral leader, women and men must have the toughness of a soldier, the discipline of an athlete, and the patience of a farmer.[27] Ministry is a calling that must be embraced with a full awareness of the cost of full commitment. Of the costs experienced by committed persons that they interviewed, Daloz, Keen, Keen, and Parks include the loss of income that they might have received given their intelligence and credentials, potential costs of relationships with children and spouses, increased health concerns,[28] constant busyness, and limited recognition by society for their choices and sacrifices.[29]

God of a Second Chance

"Keeping it real" acknowledges the journey that Dr. Evans describes as "moving toward health, happiness, and wholeness." Along the way, we have all suffered pain, been wounded, and messed up along the way. A relevant question is, "can these experiences be transformed so that they become inner resources for healing ourselves and others?" Of the possibilities for dealing with our pain, Daloz, Keen, Keen, and Parks write:

> Since none of us can escape at least some pain in our lives, the question is not whether one is hurt, but what one does with the pain. Some people absorb it, understand it partially, and spend their lives at a safe distance from others' suffering. Others bury it so deeply that they scarcely know it is there. So armored that they are unable to love well or make good friends, they drift through life without focus, severed from any deep sense of love and purpose. . . . The people we interviewed . . . had avoided falling into these traps. Somehow, they allowed the pain to touch them, but did not become lost in it. Rather, they healed in such a way that they became neither immobilized or self-absorbed on the one hand nor anesthetized on the other. They were able to choose healing work rather than be merely driven to it, and thus served both others and themselves simultaneously.[30]

One of the keys for understanding Dr. Evans's ministry is her coming to grips with human fallibility. Because all humans are fallible, we must learn to be compassionate and learn how to forgive ourselves as well as others. This conviction has been gained on Dr. Evans's faith journey. A product of her Pentecostal church upbringing, she says that she had to deal with her own self-righteousness to learn to embrace people and to love them where they are. As one who openly shares from whence she has come—a battered and lonely woman—to where she is today—a confident and successful minister—she has chosen the healing possibilities of pastoral work.

In the following excerpts from the sermon delivered at the women's conference, "The God of a Second Chance," we can see how the experiences of the preacher form the backdrop for the message and ministry of this pastor. In her introduction to her sermon Dr. Evans declares the following:

> I think we all know that God, because many times you and I have messed up . . . and we need to know that we serve a forgiving God. Come with me, if you will, to the book of John. I want to tell y'all about a lesson here that we don't like to talk about too much in the church. Some of us in Christendom have not worked it out. And I'm going to try to look at the woman in the 8th chapter, the adulterous woman, a sister if you will, who could be either you or me. Since we want to be inclusive, brothers, it could be you or me. The God of a second chance. I'm so glad that I know Jesus that he is a God of a second chance, because for years, many of us have been beating ourselves up because we have not been willing to forgive ourselves of stuff that happened in '62, '73, '85 and so on.

In this introduction, Dr. Evans signals that she wants the congregation to take seriously the experiences of a woman in the Bible as an interpretive lens for understanding our human fallibility and vulnerability.

In a private interview, Dr. Evans insists she is not a feminist. Her aim is the liberation of black women and men. Hinting at her womanist[31] leanings she says:

> I'm not trying to be over my brother. I'm trying to be with him. I want black men to be free as me.

Dr. Evans, like many black women striving for freedom from patriarchal systems of domination, do not readily identify with the feminist movement. Some have found the term, womanist, first coined by Alice Walker to be a more useful description. A womanist may be described as a black feminist who sees the necessity of confronting the evil of gender oppression as well as racial and class oppression. For many womanists, empowering black women does not imply putting down black men. Dr. Evans's goal of "trying to be with him" and not "over my brother" alludes to the inherent tensions in this theological project.

Declaring her interpretive freedom as a biblical expositor, Dr. Evans says, "I want to nuance this text to bring this woman out." Painting a visual image of a vulnerable, insecure woman in pain and embarrassment, Rev. Evans makes the point that, except for the grace of God, this could be you or I:

> Look at her, if you will, in your mind's eye. Here's a woman that had been rushed into the temple, clothes half on, makeup messed up, hair all over her head, slip maybe hanging out from under her skirt 'cause she had to move in a hurry. Just discombobulated, nothing in place, feeling insecure and embarrassed. Look at that girl if you will, for because of the grace of God, go you or I. I hope I can get through this because my heart is filled for this woman in the text. I'm not bringing her out to make her look bad, but I feel her pain in this text.

As she develops her sermon, Dr. Evans challenges the church's reticence to "keeping it real." Beyond the moralistic "thou shall not" propositions, the traditional black church avoids open talk about our sexuality. Confronting this taboo, Evans says, "Y'all want to watch this on Oprah, but you 'sposed to get it in the church!" In her eyes, the woman caught in adultery in John 8 was a vulnerable woman enticed by a man, because she was lonely, insecure, and sexually unfulfilled by her impotent husband. This becomes a warning to sisters today:

> Now, sisters, let me tell you something (women shout, "Come on now!"). Brothers can detect a hungry spirit anywhere we are! If you are a hungry, insecure woman, with your antennas up, "here I am, married or single, I need somebody," they can detect it a mile away! Oh, I know I'm right about it. They can sense your spirit, if you will give it up or not! . . . That's all that happened to the girl in this text. She was lonely. She was longing and was needy of something to fulfill her and evidently brother boy [her husband] didn't have it going on! Just maybe he needed a little Viagra! (congregation, "ooh, my, my") Oh, y'all don't want to go there with me 'cause y'all want stuff sugar coated.

Like many other African American female leaders, Dr. Evans draws support for her ministry from seeing how Jesus exemplifies a model for human relationships, especially in his social interaction with women.

Breaking the social taboos, Jesus spoke with women in public, paid attention to their predicaments, and listened to them. Throughout the gospels, Jesus promoted egalitarian relations between women and men.[32] Just as significant to our understanding of Dr. Evans's portrait of Jesus is how she uses her own experience of oppression as a resource for understanding the Bible.

Despite the research of feminist and liberation scholars showing that specific texts "are unalterably hostile to the dignity and welfare of women"[33] and that the Bible has been "an instrument of the dominant culture that was used to subjugate African American people"[34] African American females such as Dr. Evans have not given up the Bible as a resource for liberating women and men. Weems argues that marginalized female and male readers "have to be able as much as possible to read and hear the text for themselves, with their own eyes and with their own ears."[35]

Thus, Dr. Evans imaginatively contrasts the compassion of Jesus with the condemnation of the church folk who claim to be his followers. In this way, Dr. Evans fosters internal self-critique of the church and its shortcomings:

> I just want us to look at this woman left there alone in the midst with Jesus. Alone with Jesus, what better place could she be? Alone with the one who could do something about our situation. All of the people that could harm her were out of the way. That's why it's important for us to know that we serve a God of a second chance! See, in the church world, we condemn everybody. We send everybody to hell! . . . And we keep the mess going on, like the Duracell bunny rabbit, instead of having mercy and somebody bringing the sister in right relationship. We keep the mess going on and condemn her.

Dr. Evans teaches, through her portrait of Jesus, that God is one who forgives us and gives us a second chance. With this precious second chance, there is the possibility of new life. Furthermore, she teaches that "open confession is good for the soul." Dealing with human fallibility, our personal sins, Dr. Evans preaches that individuals must realize that we've messed up, confess that we've messed up, get up out of the mess, don't allow others to stop us because they remind us of our past, and work toward reconciliation of relationships as difficult as this may be. In her sermon, the joy of reconciliation is pictured as the ecstasy of the rekindled romance between the husband and the forgiven wife who confessed her affair with another man.

Dr. Evans has been impacted by a statement that she attributes to Howard Thurman: "We wish only to bring our better parts to God." Her application of this insight is that we must all deal with our weaknesses and wounds. Her gospel is of the radical possibilities of the transforming grace of God. When this grace is experienced, she says, we can go home rejoicing telling somebody else about this God of a second chance.

Through faith in this God of a second chance, this female pastor in the CME Church continues the blessed burdens of pastoral leadership seeking to transform a black church in a changing urban community. In a sense, this story simply confirms many of the struggles faced by other black women who deal with the ecclesial patriarchy described by Lakey and Stephens. However, what I have tried to capture in this tale of transformative pastoral leadership is the development of the relationship between the pastor and people as they respond to their set of challenges in this changing context. Through my eyes, the call and response of "Glory, Glory, Hallelujah Since I Laid My Burdens Down" is a fitting image of their interactive style of congregational leadership. Dr. Evans strong initiative and sacrificial example, "the call," is eliciting a joyful "response" from her expanding core of supporters. In addition to this image of call and response, I have tried to capture a sense of the spiritual gifts, qualities of leadership, skills, competencies, and commitment that Dr. Evans displays, particularly through the eyes of her followers.

I have also suggested that the crucible of Dr. Evans's life experiences as a black woman shaped her differently from a male pastor and enhanced her capabilities for leading the household of faith beyond what one might expect from one fresh out of seminary. Frankly speaking, the years of being a wife, mother, and active laywoman were not wasted. I believe that this God of a second chance redeemed these experiences as useable in the leadership formation process. In the tradition of Sojourner Truth, Jarena Lee, Julia Foote, and many other strong black women, she has developed survival strategies in spite of racial and gender oppression to save her family and her people.[36]

4

Emerging Strategies of Transformative Pastoral Leadership in the Black Church

We need leaders—neither saints nor sparkling television personalities—who can situate themselves within a larger historical narrative of this country and world, who can grasp the complex dynamics of our peoplehood and imagine a future grounded in the best of our past, yet who are attuned to the frightening obstacles that now perplex us.

—*Cornel West*, Race Matters

The premise of this work is that a new vision of pastoral leadership in the black church is needed at the outset of the twenty-first century. My vision is that "transformative pastoral leadership" is needed to transform individuals, churches, and society. This new vision is needed because many denominational black churches do not have the capacity to carry out the black church's dual mission of salvation and liberation.

In the present post-Christian context, the mission of "salvation" or making disciples of all cultures cannot be assumed. The cultural supports for the age of Christendom, going back to the intervention of Constantine, have collapsed. The church cannot assume that Christian values will be taught and reinforced in the institutions of family, school, or government. Hence, the ministry of evangelism must be intentional if Christian agents of transformation are to be recruited, formed, and sustained in black churches that nurture a moral vision of communal responsibility.

At the same time, the mission of "liberation" cannot be neglected in the present post–civil rights era context. The black church is yet called to be a symbol and instrument of freedom in a society that continues to oppress persons on the basis of race, gender, and class. The black church itself must be transformed as it struggles with the issues of its own sexism and grapples with class divisions in the segregated black communities in which many of them are situated.

The New Context of Black Urban Religion

Discovering the particular strategies of transformation emerges from the work of taking seriously both the internal structure of black churches and their response to societal conditions. When a pastor, his or her church members, and community leaders choose to transform the church in response to changes in the world around it, they will fashion a range of adaptive strategies. Of the work of inventing new strategies of action in these unsettled times Ammerman writes, "Often ideological entrepreneurs are active in such times, promulgating new strategies and the rationales for them, answering the question not only of what to do, but also of why it should be done."[1] Using the cultural tools available to them, these strategies will result in a range of public actions that may include cultural production, social service, community organizing, and community and economic development.[2] Before looking at the strategies developed by the leaders of Christopher Temple and Isaiah-Matthews, we examine the common urban context in which they work.

In this chapter, I explain some of the strategies of action emerging from the interaction of Christopher Temple and Isaiah-Matthews in a new black urban context that may be characterized as post–civil rights, post-Christian, and postindustrial city. That is to say that this study attempts to see the pastoral vocation in relationship to three social processes shaping urban religion as we enter the twenty-first century: the social transformation of the 1960s and 1970s; religious restructuring; and urban restructuring.[3] According to Livezey, those who studied urban religion in the late twentieth century should have done so in light of these social processes.[4]

Urban restructuring is the first of these social processes that forms the context for studying urban religion. Prior to World War II, cities were designed with the growth of the "industrial city" in mind. Since that time, many cities lost manufacturing industries on which their economies were based and on which their physical layout was organized. As employment shifted drastically from the central industrial cities to industrial suburbs, a fundamental change occurred in the place and means by which residents of the metropolitan area made their living. Major challenges of the postindustrial city include the economic polarization of people and the spatial dislocations of people. In our present postindustrial cities, we see economic polarization of upper-class, middle-class, working-class, and working poor people from a growing "ghetto underclass," a population of people whose skills were adequate for the requirements of manufacturing jobs of a previous era but do not qualify in the present postindustrial economy.

At the same time, the concept of the spatial dislocations of people characterize the urban experience of people being constantly on the move going to places other than where they live to work, shop, go to school, and to worship. This results in eroding neighborhood ties and the social cohesiveness of communities.[5] This postindustrial city urban restructuring significantly complicates the ministry of black urban churches and others committed to ministries of social service and social justice in their communities.

A second significant social process to be appreciated in the urban context is a restructuring of American religion. Mainline denominational and ecumenical organizations reached the peak of their strength in the 1950s. Since that time, there has been a significant fragmentation and realignment of religious organizations that once were able to mobilize significant segments of religious communities to speak and act as one body. Another significant development is rapid immigration from South and East Asia, the Middle East, Africa, and Latin America since the 1960s. As a result, large numbers of people from countries where Christianity is not the dominant religion are present in the metropolitan area forming a new context of religious pluralism in many communities.[6]

A third social process for understanding the context of urban religion is the present impact of the social transformation of the 1960s and 1970s. According to scholars of American culture, the primary direction of these changes is from traditional sources of collective authorities (e.g., neighborhoods, Catholic parishes, unions, and churches) toward personal autonomy and individual choice. However, the civil rights movement and feminist movement of this period not only advanced the rights of individuals but enhanced the consciousness of blacks and women who continue to press their moral claims for equality and justice in American society.[7]

As a result of a two-year study of black congregational life, Robert Franklin focuses on this last social process in his study of significant changes in post–civil rights black churches. According to Franklin, post–civil rights urban black churches must reckon with the declining significance of denominationalism, church and community conflict, the Afro-centric aesthetic, exposed gender tensions, a decline of black folk preaching, the rise of Word nondenominational churches, and new innovations in black congregational culture.[8]

In a separate analysis of the culture of black congregations, Franklin asserts that clergy must learn to nurture and then mobilize these alternative prophetic religious communities for Christ's mission in the world. Different styles of leadership will be exercised by different black ministers operating in a variety of situations. These styles of leadership include a consensus building style of leadership, a crusading style of leadership, a commanding style of leadership, and a campaigning style of leadership.[9]

Two Tales of Transformation

Rev. Harrison and Dr. Evans accepted different challenges in pursuing their aim of leading a transforming church. Rev. Harrison, appointed to a church focused on its own internal mission, was instrumental in helping Christopher Temple to gain a new identity through development of a set of ministries that established their growing niche within the large number of congregations in its metropolitan region. Isaiah-Matthews faced the complex challenge of merging two congregations and developing its internal and external mission in a new facility.[10] As we examine more closely these two tales of transformation, it is clear that there is a wide difference between the available resources, internal structures of authority impacting their ways of making decisions, and the internal congregational cultures[11] available to these pastors as they entered their respective pastoral appointments. Hence, our understanding of the range of transformative possibilities and transformative activities is expanded.

In 1986, the context of Rev. Harrison's work at Christopher Temple was its being an established large church with substantial resources: 1,200 members on roll, a financial surplus, and no indebtedness on the church property and parsonage. As a result of a legacy of successive high-quality pastoral appointments to Christopher Temple, there were competent male and female lay leaders in place with church leadership training. As a result of being a middle-class church, there were leaders with skills honed from their occupational work. Despite the fact that his first church paid about $25 per week,

Rev. Harrison started his seventh pastorate, Christopher Temple, as a "full-time pastor." As one of the estimated 10–20 percent of black clergy with professional ministerial training from an accredited seminary,[12] his compensation was above most of his black urban clergy peers—about $25,000 per year.[13] A few years later, the income of the church was nearly one-half million dollars and the value of church property was over $1.5 million dollars.

By contrast, the context of Rev. Evans's efforts to transform the newly merged mission of Isaiah-Matthews CME Church was a situation of meager resources and significant resistance to her leadership as a female pastor. Many of the thirty-one initial members were senior citizens or young people with no jobs. Despite the fact that there was an $80,000 insurance settlement from the fire at the old Matthews Church site, the two properties—"one run down and the other burned down"—were a net liability. None of the existing leaders had the professional skills that would mesh with Dr. Evans's vision of a professional ministry. As a result, she would later choose to integrate new "baby Christians" with professional skills into her leadership team along side of existing lay leaders who demonstrated their commitment to the mission and vision of the church.

Despite the fact that the CME Church reportedly has a 92 percent "approval" of women as pastors by other clergy,[14] Dr. Evans joined a cadre of black female religious professionals, 98 percent of whom feel they are heavily exploited and treated with indifference or suspicion by their male colleagues.[15] Starting her pastorate as a single woman, this seminary graduate had to work another full-time job while renovating her church building and developing her congregation. In her first year of pastoral leadership, the total church income was $17,623, of which $3,450 was used for the pastor's "salary and expenses."[16]

These different congregational contexts in the CME Church system provide settings for understanding particular conditions within which essential activities of leadership can be related to the central phenomenon of interest: transformative pastoral leadership in the black church. These congregational contexts are analyzed within broader structural contexts that facilitate or constrain the praxis of pastoral leadership. It would be a gross exaggeration to conclude that pastoral leadership is the single cause of transformative ministry. Likewise, transformation is not always the consequence of pastoral leadership. Nevertheless, I argue that, in both of these congregational contexts, pastoral leadership is a decisive factor in intentional congregational leadership efforts to transform persons, churches, and society.[17]

Transformation of persons, churches, and society are not discrete phenomena. I find that they are in fact interrelated phenomena as would be expected in this study of an organization (the CME Church), groups (two congregations), and persons (the experiences of two pastors as they interact with others) in society. Transformative pastoral leadership in the black church is necessary because of causal conditions—past, present, and future events in society—that impact the course of life in the black community and the black church. These two tales of transformation provide data which expands our emerging theories of transformation, effective ministry, and spiritual leadership.

Strategies of Transformation

Shift from Traditional Worship to Culturally Affirming Celebrative Worship

One of the changes under Rev. Harrison's pastoral leadership was the strategic shift from the traditional Methodist worship service to a culturally affirming celebrative worship experience. In the past, if someone got up to praise the Lord and "shouted," they would get disapproving looks from the members who said, "That's not Methodist!" Meanwhile, wise observers of black religion noted that black Holiness and Pentecostal bodies, such as the 3.5 million member Church of God in Christ,[18] were growing in the black community whereas the historic black denominations were losing their young people to these churches.

In response to my question regarding forces hindering the growth of CME churches, Presiding Elder Crider said:

> I think it's a lack of understanding what growth is all about. I think it's too much holding on to tradition. By tradition, I mean, "We've always done it this way." We've always had, "Holy, Holy" for the procession or something. We've always had, [hymns like] "Jesus Keep Me Near the Cross" and "Pass Me Not Oh Gentle Savior." We didn't allow any praise service or testimonial before the worship service started. If I clapped in the church and raised my hand [people would say] "that's not Methodist." That really has stunted the growth of our church. We're losing our young folks because they cannot let go. They're going to these congregations where they can rock, where they can holy dance, where they can clap. They can speak in tongues. They can go there and do all of these things. I really think what happened is, as Methodists, we got carried away with people bragging about us: "y'all those educated folks." It went to our head and they [the Holiness and Pentecostal

churches] were steady out there preaching and praying about the love of Jesus and we were teaching them about all of these theologians. Professional people want to hear the Word of God. They want to hear the Word of God. What I'm saying, pastor, is we've got to reach out to these young folks. We have to help the young people understand that they are just as far from understanding where the old senior citizens are as the senior citizens are from understanding where the young people are. So my philosophy is this: that we must have a common ground when you bring them all together.[19]

In his over forty years in the ministry of the CME Church, Presiding Elder Crider has noticed a certain transformation in the thinking of some of the persons that his church is trying to reach and teach for Jesus. He sees a new generation less concerned about "holding on to tradition" and remaining loyal to the denomination of their parents. He sees that many of the younger generation look for worship that is "for real."[20] That is to say they shop for an experience of worship that helps them to feel the presence of the Holy Spirit while celebrating their indigenous culture's music, dance, and spontaneity.

Contemporary observers of the black Methodist church notice that behaviors such as clapping, lifting up hands, affirming spiritual gifts, and dancing, previously rejected by class-conscious black Methodists in northern urban settings, are now more widely embraced by younger blacks. These "newer behaviors," influenced by the rise of Pentecostalism across the world, are defended by worship leaders as biblically supported acts of praise and worship across lines of race and class. New congregational cultures are being fashioned celebrating the gifts of the Spirit and reclaiming biblical patterns that led to the growth of the early Christian church. As Presiding Elder Crider notes, these biblical patterns include meaningful prayer, demonstrative praise, relevant preaching and teaching of the Word of God, and demonstrating the love of Jesus by concrete acts of service within and beyond the household of faith.[21]

As a result of these forces, some educated black Methodist clergy, like Rev. Harrison are "ideological entrepreneurs" who perceive a need to reinterpret the black worship traditions of Methodism in ways that reflect and creatively respond to these changes in their environment. As theologically educated preachers—many of whom are students of African American religious history, contemporary black culture, academic forms of theology, and black "folk theology"—they are transforming worship from "traditional worship" to culturally affirming "contemporary worship."

The rationales they articulate may include reclaiming their Wesleyan heritage as "shouting Methodists"; invoking biblical authority for ways of praising God found in the Hebrew scriptures; rejecting the old black middle-class ways of worshipping as dignified as white middle-class Protestants by embracing the "emotional and demonstrative";[22] defending the cultural integrity of black folk culture—its music, preaching, worship style, and theology;[23] and promoting Afro-centric cultural elements (rituals such as black male role celebrations and celebration of black women as queens, symbols such as kente cloth and liberation colors, and theologies that promote African centered worldviews).[24]

Thus, this strategy of transformation, changing the congregational worship from a traditional "old middle-class" Methodist service to a culturally affirming "new middle-class" worship experience is an innovation seen under Rev. Harrison's pastoral leadership. This culturally affirming worship service not only lifts up the name of Jesus and spiritually builds up the worshipper; it also affirms the personhood and identity of black believers. It should be noted that Rev. Harrison made these changes with the support of the patriarchs and matriarchs of the church. After gaining their trust, he invited them to be his allies in building a church that their children and grandchildren would not mind attending.[25]

Shift to Intentional Strategies of Evangelism, Discipleship, and Church Growth

Despite the positive aspects of his pastoral appointment to Christopher Temple, Rev. Harrison faced a number of challenges. One challenge was the task of evangelism, discipleship, and church growth.[26] Rev. Harrison had a theological commitment to church growth in the CME Church wherever he served as a pastor. By a theological commitment to church growth, I mean one who is not primarily driven by pragmatic motives of institutional preservation or denominational growth, but by theological motives of sharing faith and love with a concern for making disciples of Jesus Christ. Church growth, for Rev. Harrison, involved both the quality of ministries and the quantity of persons recruited into the ministry.

We can surmise that he saw the need for evangelism, discipleship, and church growth in particular at Christopher Temple. *Although* there were 1,200 members on roll when Rev. Harrison was appointed as a pastor in 1986, only 400 were active in worship in an edifice that seats over 1,000 persons. Meanwhile, the religious environment in which his church was imbedded was a competitive one. Potential members, shopping for new churches, would bypass traditional Methodist churches and join other religious movements, such as the fast growing Pentecostal and Holiness churches, nondenominational mega churches, and even non-Christian movements like the Nation of Islam. Not withstanding his theological commitment to the salvation of souls, in this environment, Rev. Harrison was also pragmatic and recognized the need for many changes if his church was to grow in this competitive environment.[27] He immediately embarked on a "soul winning campaign." You could say that he never stopped his efforts to "win souls" and disciple them within the local church.

For the first five years of his ministry, he curtailed his community activism and denominational duties to prioritize his work of equipping and discipling leaders for present and future salvation within his local church base. As we shall see, Rev. Harrison's vision of ministry embraced both congregation and community from the start. However, by disciplining himself to first lay a foundation of church growth and leadership development, the number of workers with spiritual vision and training for ministry to church and society were multiplied; the growth of the church helped Christopher Temple to later emerge as a stronger community stakeholder in the political, economic, educational, and social life of the community; and Rev. Harrison was later able to give more time to community activism and denominational duties confident that good ministry would continue in his absence. Beginning his work with the end in mind, he envisioned a legacy of strong ministerial and lay leadership ready to carry on ministry whenever the time would come for him to pass the pastoral leadership baton to his successor.

At his fifteenth anniversary as the pastor of Christopher Temple, it was noted that 3,958 new members had been added in those fifteen years. It must be acknowledged that this total, developed by the membership registration chairman, is not a net figure that accounts for members lost by death, transfer, moving away, or those "lost otherwise." Nevertheless, the resulting spiritual growth, net numerical growth, and financial growth of Christopher is evidence of one strategy of transformation, the growth and development of the congregation through intentional ministries of evangelism, discipleship, and church growth.

This strategy of transformation that I am examining certainly is not the result of the pastor's efforts alone. Often, Rev. Harrison credits his leaders for the success of the ministry. For example, in one of the pastoral statistical reports we read his concluding comments:

> Our 60 ministry leaders of clubs, organizations, and needs meeting ministries is the strength of our church. . . . The stewardship program of tithes and offerings of our time, talent, and treasure along with celebrative worship, 17 paid staff, children and youth ministry help us to grow spiritually and numerically each year. Our TV ministry each Sunday from 10:00 a.m. to 11:00 a.m. reaches over 100,000 households weekly.

These comments highlight the importance of a shared leadership approach. It also gives a glimpse of Christopher Temple's multiple strategies of church growth:

- developing ministries that meet needs,
- developing a stewardship program that develops faith as well as funds to operate the church,
- developing a celebrative worship experience,
- augmenting volunteer leadership with skilled paid staff,
- investing in children and youth ministries, and
- using technological media to reach more people than can be reached through face-to-face ministries.

Christopher Temple's other strategies for evangelism, discipleship, and church growth include regular training of ministers and laypersons in principles of evangelism and regular "love journeys" into the surrounding community sharing faith with their neighbors. In sum, in this strategy of transformation, Christopher Temple has created a systemic approach to congregational evangelism.[28]

Shift from Pastor Centered Leadership to Shared Transforming Leadership

A third strategy of transformation at Christopher Temple has been the shift from the tradition of pastor centered leadership to shared transforming leadership that transforms the pastor and followers. The following excerpt from Mrs. Cora Nolan, who has been a member of the CME Church all of her eighty-one years of life, reveals different assumptions about nature of pastoral authority:

> So many people do not know that you do not organize no club or name another club unless you go to your pastor. When I tell someone that,

"You can't do that unless you talk to pastor," [they say], "Why?" [I tell them] "Pastor's our leader. So we have to ask the pastor can we do this." And when they tell me, "We're going to do something," [I say] "Have you talked to the pastor?" Some people don't know that. [They ask] "What he got to do with it?" [I answer] "He's our leader. So we have to ask him. Don't care nothing about how old you are. You still have got to ask the pastor. You've got to come by him." And I do it gladly because I know that's what we're supposed to do. I was taught that down through the years. "Don't do nothing in the church without you talking to your pastor concerning the church!"

Reflecting the traditional assumptions in the black church that the pastor is expected to play a preeminent leadership role, Mrs. Nolan has been taught that "pastor" is "leader" and that you must get approval from the pastoral leader to do anything in the church. We might say that she regards the "pastor" as not simply a spiritual "priest," but as a political "king" as well. In her view, the pastor "rules the church"—not just the pulpit, but its programs and policies as well. As she notes, this traditional view is challenged by "many people" who question her view of the pastoral authority.

This tension regarding the rule of the black preacher and the rights of the membership is not new. Taylor Branch describes these tensions in his analysis of Dexter Avenue Baptist Church, once served by Dr. Martin Luther King, Jr. Branch writes:

From the beginning, Dexter Avenue operated as a "deacons' church," meaning that the lay officers took advantage of the full sovereignty claimed by each Baptist congregation. They were free to hire any preacher they wanted—trained or untrained, fit or unfit—without regard to bishops or other church hierarchy. . . . Not surprisingly, these powerful characters [the black preachers] sorely tested the ability of congregations to exercise authority guaranteed them in Baptist doctrine. As a rule, the preachers had no use for church democracy. They considered themselves called by God to the role of Moses, a combination of ruler and prophet, and they believed that the congregation behaved best when its members, like the children of Israel obeyed as children. The board of deacons at Dexter Avenue Baptist Church was one of the few to defend itself effectively against preachers who regularly tried to subdue the membership.[29]

Even if this description is in the context of Baptist congregational polity, there are relevant insights that are useful for the black Methodist context as well. It has been my observation that many of my colleagues in pastoral ministry adopt what I think is a selective reading of the role of Moses as a basis of presuming their preeminent authority over against the laity. They may not say this; but, by their actions, they regard members of the congregation as spiritual "children," who are expected to simply "pay, pray, and obey."

Apparently, King began his ministry with such a view of himself as ruler and prophet. On his first Sunday as resident pastor of Dexter Avenue on September 5, 1954, he surprised his congregation with a document for their prayerful consideration: "Recommendations to the Dexter Avenue Baptist Church for the Fiscal Year 1954–1955."[30] In it, King reportedly made it clear that this "deacons' church" was not going to run him or the church:

> "When a minister is called to the pastorate of a church," King declared, "the main presupposition is that he is vested with a degree of authority." . . . "The source of this authority is twofold. First of all, his authority originates with God. Inherent in the call itself is the presupposition that God directed that such a call be made. This fact makes it crystal clear that the pastor's authority is not merely humanly conferred, but divinely sanctioned. Secondly, the pastor's authority stems from the people themselves. Implied in the call is the unconditional willingness of the people to accept the pastor's leadership. This means that the leadership never ascends from the pew to the pulpit, but it invariably descends from the pulpit to the pew."[31]

While I agree with the first source of authority mentioned—that the pastor must have a divine call, I would argue that King's views of how the people confer authority is a flawed paradigm. As there is transformation in the thinking of the people, their expectations of legitimate pastoral authority changes as well.[32] Although blacks tend to be some of the most forgiving people and thus are forgiving of their leaders' flaws, I think it is an exaggeration to say that their acceptance of leadership is unconditional. In fact, pastors need to exemplify personal qualities by which they earn the informal authority granted by the people. We see this in Mrs. Nolan's response to my question, "what qualities to you look for in a pastor." Mrs. Nolan said:

> First thing is being yourself, because, a pretender, it finally comes out. . . . And don't ask Pastor Harrison to pray for you, don't care where it is or what he's doing, he's going to pray right then and there. The pastor is somebody that you want to always look up to and that is where I stand with our pastor, somebody you can always look up to,

that you have faith in. We know they're not God, but they know that they are leading us toward God. Now we can go astray anytime we get ready, but, most of the time, you follow your pastor you'll be on the right road. I feel good about all of my pastors. They've been good teachers, good lecturers, good advisors, spiritual leaders, somebody we can go look up to—not somebody that we can go and say, "Oh well, I would ask the pastor, but, you know, he ain't right his self." [She laughs.]

Despite Mrs. Nolan's view of the pastor as leader, it's clear from her response that her willingness to follow the pastor's leadership is not unconditional. There are certain qualities that she looks for—being themselves, a real person; evidence of a spiritual vitality that enables the leader to pray for and with their flock; moral and ethical character that is exemplary of a spiritual calling; and competency in the work of a religious leader. She's optimistic that in most instances, the leadership of her pastors is trustworthy. However, she allows that there are those men (and presumably women) that "ain't right his self." These persons are not trustworthy persons that she would turn to for spiritual guidance.

A second reason why King's paradigm of legitimate pastoral authority is flawed is because it views the pastor as an expert in all matters pertaining to the church. This assumption neglects, in particular, one of the features that will shape the black church of the twenty-first century: the dramatic increase in black participation in higher education following the civil rights movement. This not only produced a more credentialed clergy; it also produced a more professionalized laity that not only demands an educated ministry and quality services but are capable of volunteering professional skills that may well exceed the pastor's competence in their area of training.[33]

Rev. Harrison, in fact, is keenly aware of the possibilities and challenges of utilizing the expertise of his laity. Of his vision to implement a spiritual leadership development process in light of the professional volunteers available to him, Rev. Harrison says:

I think we wait much too late to involve our 25–35 [year old] age group. If they're out running industry, running the world, why can't they be a part of the steward board or stewardess board or other meaningful ministries in the church giving leadership to it? If they are accountants, why can't they help set up the books and do all the things that are necessary to keep the accountability of the church financially in the best possible shape so that you have accountability to your membership, to

IRS, and any other responsible agencies? Why can't they also help create programs that create separate corporate not-for-profit CDC's and not-for-profit organizations that can provide other meaningful services for children, seniors, HIV/AIDS, other homeless shelters that might be needed in the community. Many times, I see too many human and social services being provided by white agencies in the African American community. Why can't our best minds be paid executive dollars to provide human and social services in our community? Why can't that happen? That's part of the paradigm shift I think we have to bring to the table.

A selective reading of passages about Moses extracts a model of the pastor as a ruler and prophet who demands obedience of members who remain as children. A better reading of passages such as Exodus 17: 9–14 yields a snapshot of Moses and Joshua in a mentoring relationship that transforms them both.[34] Burns would call this "transforming leadership." Burns writes:

> Such leadership occurs when one or more persons *engage* with others in such a way that leaders and followers raise one another to higher levels of motivation and morality. Their purposes, which might have started out as separate, but related, as in the case of transactional leadership, become fused. Power bases are linked not as counterweights, but as mutual support for a common purpose.[35]

When the pastor and other church leaders are secure persons, they can engage one another in mutual relationships of trust and respect for each other's gifts. Then, it is possible, I believe, for "leadership to ascend from the pew to the pulpit."

Although the pastor has a special responsibility for envisioning the whole ministry on behalf of the congregation, guarding against threats to this shared vision, and articulating this vision repeatedly, it is possible that different specific visions, initiated by those in the pews, may complement and not compete with an already articulated vision that is more broadly owned.[36] I think that this is particularly the case in developing social ministries that utilize member's capacities for vision, spiritual leadership, skilled planning, and management. Thus, the practice of insecure pastors treating the members "as children" is an unacceptable practice that must be transformed in the black church. As Rev. Harrison says above, meaningful ministries, such as services to children, seniors, and those afflicted with HIV/AIDS, are often best initiated and sustained by those "in the pews." Transformative pastoral leaders foster the emergence of other leaders who are empowered by the Holy Spirit and committed to serve with compassion, humility, and excellence.

Shift from "Members Only" Orientation to Communal Orientation

A final challenge that I examine here in my analysis of the ministry situation of Christopher Temple was the unmet plight of the community and the resulting competition of the Muslim faith and black religious sects for the souls of black folk. Since the 1960s when the Nation of Islam began baiting black Christians out of their "blood sucking churches" and criticizing "chicken-eating nigger preachers,"[37] various forms of Islam in the black community have grown in their ability to compete for the "souls of black folk." Members of African American Islam religions, both orthodox Sunni Islam and the Nation of Islam, have grown from perhaps 2,000–3,000 in the 1960s to over one million today.[38] Malcolm X, Louis Farrakhan, and other Muslim ministers have convincingly argued that many black churches have done little to alleviate the black condition.[39] Factors for the growth of the Nation of Islam have included their attention to the economic plight of black people and their reclamation of young black men from the criminal justice system. Furthermore, Islamic groups have a much stronger ministry in prisons and impact on poor black men and women.[40]

In this light, one strategy of transformation at Christopher Temple included their shift from a church with a primarily "privatistic orientation" to a more "communal" orientation. By the term, "privatistic orientation" is meant the tendency of the church to withdraw from the concerns of the larger community and to focus strictly on the religious needs of the members. By the term, "communal orientation" is meant the historic tradition of the black church to be involved in the political, economic, educational, and social concerns of the community.[41]

Mrs. Janice Parker, who has been a member of Christopher Temple all of her sixty-one years, has witnessed this transformation. In response to my question of what Christopher Temple has been transformed from and been transformed to, one of her responses was as follows:

> The other transformation that I think has happened is that we are doing more things in the community outside of the church. We're doing more

things to nurture and to meet the needs of the larger community than just what happens inside of this building. We're feeding the homeless, we're clothing and having the mentoring and tutoring in the schools outside of the church and having things here at the church that bring the community in. That's the transformation that I have seen.

Christopher Temple had been at its present location for just over twenty years at the outset of Rev. Harrison's ministry there. The clubs and organizations that were in place were those that were needed to promote basic Christian worship and discipleship, to maintain Christian fellowship and the CME Church administrative structure, and to increase the finances of the church. It might be argued that these ministries, to invite persons to Christian discipleship, fellowship, and service, were and are a faithful response to the universal mission of the church. Indeed, despite Rev. Harrison's apparent "black consciousness" he constantly uplifts the "Great Commission" to make disciples of all nations as the *central* mission of the church.[42] Yet, community outreach has been stressed so that Christopher Temple is making an impact on the political life of the community by serving in capacities such as the "Get out the Vote rally"; on the educational life of the community by sharing in the education of youth through tutorial programs, their One Church One School outreach to local elementary and high schools and summer Freedom School Programs; on the economic life of the community by its development of housing and commercial businesses; and on the social life by being a "safety net" for both members and nonmembers by contributing to "legitimate needs" through their benevolence offerings[43] as well as by their outreach to the homeless through their "More Like Christ" ministry.

Building a Community for Survival, Healing, and Wholeness

As we examine the strategies of transformative pastoral leadership at Isaiah-Matthews we begin with Dr. Evans's acceptance of the appointment to Isaiah-Matthews, a challenge that resonated with her life experience in which she says she was used to "taking nothing and making something out of it." Indeed, it is through the merging of two dying congregations that transforming possibilities of new life were generated. Whereas the "miracle" at Christopher Temple includes "fast growth," the "miracle" at Isaiah-Matthews is one of steady growth and the development of a community of people who are themselves on the difficult journey of survival working toward healing and wholeness.

Indeed, the transformation of Isaiah-Matthews should be celebrated by the CME Church as much as the transformation of Christopher Temple. From the time of Bishop Douglas's decision to merge the two dying congregations in 1994, Isaiah-Matthews started with thirty-one members and the *liabilities* of two church buildings—"one run down and the other burned out." It had grown to a 2001 total membership of 249. The average worship attendance was then about 60 persons. The church facility renovated in 1997 was valued at nearly $370,000.[44]

These measures of "success"—numerical growth of the membership, increase in worship attendance, and increased property value—is noticed by the denomination. In my interview with the presiding elder of both Dr. Evans and Rev. Harrison, Presiding Elder Crider indicated that both Isaiah-Matthews and Christopher Temple were recognized as "really growing." In fact, he says that they are two of the only three churches that are "really growing" on his presiding elder district, the other one being a new church start. Christopher Temple, he says, is in an elite category of three or four "fast growing" churches in the entire denomination. The remainder of the twenty-two churches on his presiding elder district he describes as "declining" or "holding their own." By "holding their own" he means that there is no net growth in membership. Congregations that simply attempt to "hold their own" are those that simply do what they have always done and thus experience a slowly declining membership. Because they fail to discern the changes they should make due to the internal and external forces in their environment, many congregations that simply "hold their own" will eventually close their doors or merge into another congregation.[45]

However, beneath these numbers, which denominational officials collect in quarterly conference reports, district conference reports, and pastors' annual statistical reports, is a story of a people, some of whom have had to struggle for their very survival, self-image, and personhood. For those who have not had similar experiences, these themes may not appear to signal "success." Yet, these themes are common to those who identify in some way with "the least of these" in our society. And thus, the lessons of the praxis of pastoral leadership in the context of this small membership black church led by a black female pastor should resonate in communities where there is any type of suffering and oppression.

The womanist theologian, Jacquelyn Grant, argues that the condition of "the least of these"—descriptive of different human experiences of suffering and oppression—connects with the experience of black women. Grant writes:

> It is in the context of Black women's experience where the particular connects up with the universal. By this, I mean that in each of the three dynamics of oppression, Black women share in the reality of the broader community. They share race suffering with Black men; with White women and other Third World women, they are victims of sexism; and with poor Blacks and Whites, and other Third world peoples, especially women, they are disproportionately poor. To speak of women's tri-dimensional reality, therefore, is not to speak of Black women exclusively, for there is an implied universality which connects them with others. Likewise, with Jesus Christ, there was an implied universality which made him identify with others—the poor, the woman, the stranger.[46]

Dr. Evans's experience as a "poor Mississippi (black) woman" has allowed her to become well acquainted with this tri-dimensional reality. In this congregational setting, she brings a high level of compassion, courage, and competence to the ministry of reaching the "least of these." Transformed from her "Junior Jesus-ness," she says the church must "love people where they are" and refrain from judging people. Of her faith that people's lives can be transformed by the power of God Dr. Evans says:

> It is important to me that people reach their fullest potential regardless of their educational background. I believe that if a pastor would work with people, we can do what Jesus did. Jesus would go into communities and pick out people as He did with the bent over woman in the synagogue. He looked over everybody in there and looked to her and healed her as He did [the woman] in Samaria at the well, as He did with the woman with the issue of blood, as He continues to do with me every day.

The Gospels' accounts of Jesus' attitudes and actions toward people that are "bent over" by all manner of debilitating life conditions is received by Dr. Evans as substance for her hope that people of all backgrounds can be transformed through the church's ministry. She believes that a vital church must say what Jesus said and do what Jesus continues to do in the lives of those who trust Him. While her members speak of the personal impact of her ministry she understands that she cannot do this alone. She envisions that, as she continues her ministry of nurturing the congregation, people will emerge with gifts to lead small ministry support groups for persons with HIV/AIDS, cancer, and various forms of addiction.

Operating as a part of a larger community network of institutions, Dr. Evans understands the importance of collaboration within her ecological environment. Because of her position as Director of Social Services, she has ready access to community agencies and services to which she refers individuals of her congregation. She taps these resources also to bring health fairs and medical screenings as a way of caring not only for the members of the church, but also for the persons in the surrounding community. She also connects her missionaries to serve residents in the senior citizen development where she works on occasion. In this way, this bi-vocational pastor bridges her secular employment with her ministry vocation.

Although there is not yet a structured ministry for community outreach, Dr. Evans reaches out to bring "the least of these" into the faith community in which she believes they can become stronger by the power of God. When asked how these are reached, her son, Michael, responds:

> That goes back to her people skills. It doesn't matter what kind of lifestyle you have lived in order for you to want to accept God into your life. I mean, God did it. God reached down to the homeless, to the nasty, to the stanky, like she always says, reached down and helped those people who were the lowest, and I believe she has taken on that challenge as God did. There are several people on her job who she's been in contact with who have problems and [she] invited them to church, gave them hope, showed them that, this is the way according to the scripture. . . . Through teaching and preaching and leadership, some of these brothers have turned around and decided to say, "Hey, I don't want to do this anymore. Let me see what this lady is talking about. You can believe this Lord, trust this Lord that she's talking about."

Once people are brought into the life of the congregation and exposed to the basic tenets of the CME Church in the new members' class, they are embraced in the faith community and taught how to be faithful followers of Jesus Christ.

Influenced by the men's ministry model of Rev. Harrison and Christopher Temple, Dr. Evans has also instituted a Male Emphasis Sunday celebration. This puts within the context of worship their efforts to reclaim the black male for the family, church, and community. Driven by the historically formed perception that white male dominance is threatened by strong black males and that through systemic sin black men are castigated in the media, in the educational system, and in the criminal justice system, Male Emphasis Sunday seeks to uplift the role and presence of men and boys in the church. Dr. Evans uses this time to encourage brothers, challenge them, and teach them the truth about their role in the family, church, and society. At the end of this period, specific prayers are offered for them. In this, she is moved by the conviction that both male and females are made in the image of God and are to be partners in the stewardship of all creation as well as in the struggle for human dignity and equality.

It may seem paradoxical that a black female pastor would systematically uplift the role of black men in the church. But, Dr. Evans insists, "I'm not trying to be over my brother. I'm trying to be with him. I want black men to be as free as me. *I am not a feminist.*"

Similarly, it was surprising to me that this congregation led by a female pastor has a higher proportion of men than most black congregations that I have observed. After all, black women have been marginalized from the standpoint of power and leadership in the black church. At the same time, they have been exploited by male clergy for their ability to raise money. In so doing, it could be argued that women have helped to create, in many black churches, a fund-raising culture of teas and fashion shows that repels men. As a result, churches that would reach black men must be intentional about providing "hooks" to catch them and provide hospitable spaces where they can enjoy the fellowship of the church.

Mrs. Billings, a sixty-nine-year-old stewardess, has been amazed by this growth in the number of young men, particularly by the fact that many were converts. By her account, on one baptism Sunday, forty young men were baptized. The passage also alludes to the challenge of holding the young men in the church after they join. Mrs. Billings says:

> Pastor Evans brought in 40 young men to join that church and I didn't know they hadn't never been in no church. I saw the baptizing because I was holding the [baptismal] bowl. I asked her later if those people had ever been in the church and she said, "Never." I said, "You mean to tell me that all of those half grown boys, I called them young men, they were around about 25, 30, 35 [years old] maybe and they all joined the church and I said they ain't never been in church?" And she said, "Never." I said, well some how or another they just like the way she preaches, *something* brought them there. They stayed there so long, so long and then they started falling off and their people still coming there and I asked them, "Where's them boys, cause I'd always like to hear

and guides me along right pathways for his **Name's** sake.

Though I walk through the valley of the shadow of death,
I shall fear no evil; *
    for you are with me;
    your rod and your staff, they comfort me.

You spread a table before me in the presence of those
               who trouble me; *
    you have anointed my head with oil,
    and my cup is running over.

Surely your goodness and mercy shall follow me all the days
            of my life, *
    and I will dwell in the house of the LORD for ever.

them sing. Where's those boys? " He's say, "They're at home." Well, you tell those boys I said, "Come on to church." Well they start back to coming, because they still got their membership there. When they come, they pay. I think they send money when they don't come. Young men, 40 boys, that was amazing to me.

The Male Emphasis Sunday is one of those hospitable spaces that is appreciated not only by the men, but also by the women who are thankful that they will not have to be, in the absence of responsible men, "the mules of the world."[47] At the same time that gender-specific ministries are offered for the men, including male seminars and retreats, they are also offered to teach and uplift the role of women in the family, church, and society.

That two dying congregations have been merged so that the pastor, individuals, and the congregation might grow on their journey of survival working toward healing and wholeness is evidence that a difference is being made. There is no claim that healing has been instantaneous or that healing and wholeness has been finally achieved. Furthermore, pastor and members alike agree that the level of community outreach has been hindered by their own internal struggle to pay their bills as a congregation. The vision of Isaiah-Matthews as a "center for nurturing in the community" through One Church One School partnerships, becoming God's woman classes, AIDS awareness workshops, youth delinquency Christian prevention, feeding program for the homeless, after-school tutorial, and day care for seniors has not been fully realized to date.

This should not be surprising because congregational studies of the public ministry role of religious institutions in their communities reveal that congregational resources is a significant factor in the number of outreach ministries that can be effectively carried out. As these researchers note: "The more money a congregation has in its budget, the more connections it is likely to form, and the more high-income parishioners it has—over and above the size of the budget—the more connections it can sustain. It is money, in fact, not sheer size, that makes a difference."[48]

Besides money being a constraining factor in the outreach of this congregation, an intentional leadership development process must be successfully implemented to create a team of leaders working to envision and carry out these programs. This will take time. As self-image is raised, spiritual growth takes place, and the wounded are made whole, this will occur. But, the most significant transformation to appreciate is the growth and healing that is taking place, making possible a community in which all persons might find resources for their survival, healing, and wholeness.

Transforming Attitudes and Behaviors

The claim was made in chapter 3 that Dr. Evans learned not only to "manage the mess" of interconnected problems that she encountered in her context, but that she also devised a fitting leadership strategy growing out of her experience and strengths as a female leader. Nurturing and caring is a natural part of her makeup as a person. Fund-raising was a strength that she gained from church leadership as a layperson.

In the beginning of her ministry, she utilized various strategies to add new members to the church. However, she noticed that something was missing. Newly formed Sunday School classes would meet but she observed that people did not seem to interact with one another after class. The content of mid-week Bible classes seemed to be well received; however, people seemed to distance themselves from one another. Church leaders would announce in church conference that they were planning ministry activities; however, in the first one and a half years, they did not follow through on any of their plans. She perceived that not only was the congregation in need of nurture and caring, but they also needed to learn how to nurture and care for one another. The members of the congregation had a poor self-image and were in need of healing.

After an extensive reading of her congregational context through her participant observation and interviews, she decided on a strategy of leading a nurturing and caring ministry to transform the attitudes and behaviors of her ministry leaders so that they would learn to share responsibility as "partners in stewardship." This project resulted in a series of stewardship classes for the executive board and for the congregation. Despite the fact that new ground was broken, this "schooling approach" was not transformative. There were some temporary changes; however, it later became clear that the changes in thinking and behavior were not accomplished.

However, the seminal idea of transforming attitudes and behaviors through a nurturing and caring ministry has persisted throughout her ministry. Change in attitudes and behavior has come about very slowly. Some people have "caught the vision"; others continue to lag behind. This is a source of Dr. Evans's open "confessions of fallibility."

Having brought the church this far, can she continue making a positive difference? Change processes can be progressive or regressive. As she says, "I don't want to be one that draws a good bucket of milk and then kicks it over!" As she watches, works, and waits, Evans defines specific criteria by which to discern the shape, direction, form, and character of transformation: she looks to "see a difference in the life, in the faithfulness, in the finances, in the growth of the church." As she looks for these differences, will she see growth, development, and movement? Or, at the other extreme, will she see the failure of growth, a sliding backward, even stagnation?[49] One of the valuable pieces of practical wisdom that Dr. Evans learned from a seminary professor is the insight, "*If you give the Holy Spirit time to act, your work will be so much easier.*"

Slowly, results are being seen by the pastor and the people. This is as a result of her struggling to be patient with a developmental process. Privately, she speaks of having to "spoon-feed" members and teaching "pre-primer stuff." Most of her membership were previously unchurched, were out of church since childhood, or in congregations in which they were never nurtured and discipled to know who they are in Christ. Of this leadership challenge Dr. Evans says:

> I believe that one must lead by example especially to help persons who are in the early developmental stages of church growth. The majority of our congregation is made up of persons who have been un-churched or have had little experience in church work. They are learning as we move forward. They are learning as we grow in the Lord.

In this context, Dr. Evans is challenging her members to get hold of existing dysfunctional processes and transform them to embody Christian faithfulness. This has occurred as she has broadened the notion of fashioning a people from the limited educational approach of holding stewardship classes to an approach that embraces the whole course of the church's life as the "curriculum."[50] Basic lessons that she is trying to teach are faithfulness, consistency, and accountability.

Indeed, three prominent signs on the sanctuary walls stress the one theme of faithfulness. On the south wall, there is a neatly painted sign reading:

Be faithful in attending church *each* Sunday (Hebrews 10:35)

On the west wall, there is another neatly painted scripture stressing faithfulness in service as an expression of stewardship:

Their Lord said to him/her, well done good and faithful servants! Thou hast been faithful over a few things. I will make thee ruler of many. Enter into the joy of your Lord! (Matthew 25:23)

On the north wall is the message:

Be faithful in your giving of tithes and offerings (Malachi 3:8)

Faithfulness in worship attendance, faithfulness in service, and faithfulness in giving of tithes and offerings are three elements of members' developmental journeys. These elements must be stressed in the infancy stage of this congregation. This understanding of developmental stages and process is crucial for transformative ministry. Individuals are in various stages of growth and development and the congregation itself is in a stage of growth and development. Indeed, "process" may be the strongest educational element in a church for we may "act our way into thinking more than we think our way into acting." The lens of process thinking is helpful in analyzing the dynamics of congregational life. Careful attention to process exposes the interaction of behavior with beliefs and values with actions. Process is always present; but, it is elusive to the observer because both formal and informal processes must be examined. And, we must see that there are often tensions between the formal processes and the "taken for granted" informal processes.[51]

In the following account, we glimpse some of the tensions between the formal processes and the informal processes. The congregation has agreed to the idea of holding a formal Pre–New Year's banquet to raise money for denominational assessments and past due church bills. In an earlier executive board meeting, Dr. Evans has stressed to her officers the necessity of their leading by example. The results were disappointing. Despite the formal decision made in the church conference, only 50 percent of the people voting for the event felt obligated to support it with their presence or their fund-raising. In a church meeting following the event, Dr. Evans says:

We didn't get but *50% cooperation*. . . . I've learned in terms of communication, it's best to hear things from the pastor's mouth and that's the spirit that I'm sharing this. . . . We need to catch the vision that a church needs a budget. What is a budget? You determine needs, allocations, and you raise what is needed. . . . If you make a commitment and don't follow through it *hurts* the church. . . . I'm weary of people who say they're going to do something to look good. Don't lie, just say, "I can't do it this time." I have the list (she holds it up as she continues to convene the meeting standing in the pulpit) of those who helped. I won't read it now. But, I *will* say thank you to those who did help in the bulletin. If your name is not listed, it means that you didn't do anything. If you have questions, call me. Ask me. I am approachable. I will share with you. I will address your questions.

In this account, we see several tensions in church process. We see the pastor's belief that people need to be held accountable for their commitments. For some reason, there are those who "say they're going to do something" and do not seem to understand the process in which plans are made on the basis of their stated commitment. Many of the members, formerly unchurched members or CME members who have not had a pastor with administrative skills, do not understand the formal process of a church budget and knowing that members will be expected to do their part to raise it. Lacking the personal financial resources to pay for the $75 tickets or a network of associates with financial resources to pay for this, some have not learned the simple lesson that in the church, a voluntary association, one can simply say, "I can't do this, but I can do that!"

That money is a problem for several of the members is evident in the following account of Mrs. Billings. I had asked her about the struggle of raising money in the Pre–New Year's banquet. As a church leader, she had to teach some people that they did not need stay away from church when they did not have an offering to bring. Mrs. Billings says:

I'm going to tell you what some of them asked me. They said, "When we don't have no money, we going to stay home." And I said, "No, don't stay home, come on to church." I say, "When I'm tired and I don't have no money to pay in the church, I come on to church." And I told Pastor Evans, "I ain't got it today." And she say, "You ain't got no money today?" I say, "I ain't paid no money in church today." I just kind of talk to her and tell her, "I ain't got no money today. Won't have no money." . . . And she say, "Well don't stay home when you ain't got no money." And I have told a lot of folks "Don't stay home cause they ain't got no money. Come on to church. You're going to get some one day." So she started coming. And Pastor Evans got up and told her, "If you ain't got no money, just come around and hit the [offering] basket."

As many of the members of Isaiah-Matthews are in their "infancy" stage of spiritual growth, so the congregation is in its infancy. As such, theorists in congregational life cycles predict some of the struggles at this stage will include undeveloped programs, disillusionment, and possible erosion of membership and potential. The challenge at this stage is to generate a sense of community and mission, developing specific ministries.[52]

Sometimes, a single successful project can signal a turning point increasing the confidence of members and encouraging them to go to the next level.[53] Such a turning point was realized in a recent stewardess program. When asked her assessment of how her process of development is working, Dr. Evans gave the following account:

> I am encouraging as you heard when you came in, encouraging the different groups in the church to have different activities that are assisting in the struggle of the financial situation in the church. I am encouraging them to put on programs, to invite persons to do healthy projects that will bring more funds into the church. They are catching on fire. The stewardesses just had a lovely day yesterday that grossed an additional $725.00. For them, that is a biggy and they still have funds that are coming in. The stewardess department has never, in the seven years of our pastoring, brought forth that kind of money into the life of the church. I must add that the stewardess group of the church, until here recently, has been persons who are in their late sixties. But, we have empowered another group of younger women, stewardess board No. 2, and it brought about a lot of energy and a lot of activities. They now have uniforms alike, shoes alike, their head dress alike. There is inspiration from the younger ones to the older ones and now the stewardess board No. 1 wants the same uniform and the same shoes so there is some life, some growth that has taken place, where people are beginning to feel good about themselves and in their feeling good about themselves and what they're doing in the church is bringing in more finances in the church.

Surprising to me was the perceived relationship between the growth in their self-image—people feeling good about themselves—and in their level of productivity. Indeed, because self-confidence has not been nurtured in other areas of life, these stewardesses seemed to "catch on fire" as they were empowered by a shared vision (assisting the financial situation in the church), experienced a synergy in the fellowship of shared work (the inspiration and energy exchanged between the older and younger stewardesses), tasted the "success" of achieving their objective (net funds raised), and felt good about their visible status and role on the church (wearing new uniforms, shoes, and headdresses). With all stewardess board members wearing new uniforms, class and status differences were erased. Whether they had money when they came to church did not matter. That they could or could not afford certain dresses did not matter. For a few moments, at least, a sign of their unity in the kingdom of God was glimpsed.

This was, in fact, an example of Dr. Evans's Doctor of Ministry thesis in action—that people had to learn how to nurture and care for one another and for themselves before they would feel good about caring for their church and giving to it. In response to my question about the relationship of her nurturing efforts and the attitudes and behavior of members of the congregation, Dr. Evans responded, "It's coming. It's coming [We laugh together]. *Slow, but it's coming.*"

Educating the People of God for Continuity and Change

Though Rev. Harrison and Dr. Evans employed different strategies of transformation, one common characteristic of their transformative pastoral leadership is their intentional educational ministry. In the spirit of Ephesians 4:11–12, they are pastors *and* teachers equipping the saints for the work of the ministry in the world. They teach extensively from their pulpits. They teach in workshops and classes. They are involved in shaping the educational programs of their congregations. They are mentors to individuals who have become educational leaders in their congregations. They are aware that they teach by their personal example. They teach through a variety of processes. Inspired by the Apostle Paul's statement, "be transformed by the renewing of your minds (Rom. 12:3)," their ministry of transformational pastoral leadership is one that is significantly enhanced by their commitment to educating the people of God.

Rev. Harrison is a pastor and teacher who engages congregational leaders on a journey that provides continuity with the heritage and traditions of the CME Church, but moves beyond them to create new paradigms so that the faith community survives and thrives in new circumstances.[54] These new circumstances include social transformation of black communities following the civil rights movement and the influence of black power and black theology movements, and womanist movements upon educated preachers; religious restructuring in the black community including the rise of black Pentecostalism and the Nation of Islam, and the decline of denominational loyalties; and urban restructuring in a postindustrial city era, including the economic polarization of the community into poor, working-class, and middle-class populations.

Change must not be made simply for change's sake. There is no need to "throw out the baby with the bath water." As a transformative pastoral leader, Harrison fosters processes that educate the people of God for continuity and change. Mentored in the living tradition of the black preacher, his preaching, teaching, and leadership draw on the accumulated wisdom of the race.[55] Critiquing the tradition of the black preacher, one of ecclesial privilege for males and patriarchal domination for females, his ministry is oriented not only toward reclaiming the black male for family, church, and society, but also toward fighting "sexual apartheid."

It is one thing to explicitly preach and teach against "sexual apartheid." It is another thing to utilize the implicit curriculum of church processes to teach against the ingrained sexism of the church. That is to say, we teach not only by what we say, but also by what we do. Black pastors have tremendous influence on whether or not women are accepted as leaders in the church. Rev. Harrison made sure that laywomen and women clergy were appointed to ministry leadership. Powerful church leadership positions such as chairman of the board of trustees, church treasurer, and chairman of the board of stewards have been held by women under his pastoral tenure. Two of the six women clergy on his staff are employed as full-time paid staff. Other women clergy formerly on staff, such as Dr. Evans, have been supported by Christopher Temple as they are launched into pastoral ministry. Exemplary women working for change in the community are honored on Dr. Martin Luther King's birthday as "dream keepers."

The resources for this journey of continuity and change, which opens people up to the possibility of transformation, are historical, contemporary, and visionary. Dealing with contemporary issues in the black community offering future visions for it in light of God's relationship to it prevents the church from being stuck in continuity without change—repeating traditions that have outlived their usefulness. Accessing the historical tradition of the black church prevents the church from making changes without continuity with its rich past.[56] In this way, new practical wisdom is added to the old.

In contrast to the well-developed situation of Christopher Temple, Isaiah-Matthews is still in the infancy stage of its development. Consequently, Dr. Evans is playing the role of a "founding mother." Leading the merged congregation in completely renovating and furnishing the facility was quite an accomplishment as was her dealing with initial resistance with her leadership as a female pastor. However, other issues loom. At the beginning of this group's life, Dr. Evans is a charismatic authority, a strong presence needed to direct, orient, resolve conflicts, and establish norms at Isaiah-Matthews. Yet, she is trying to find a way to do this in such a way that the people do not remain dependent on her.[57]

How shall Dr. Evans transform the attitudes and behaviors of such people whose creativity has been stifled and their dreams deferred? How will Dr. Evans keep her own creativity alive in the face of such a daunting task? This is a challenge that black women have faced in the past and face in the present. Alice Walker writes:

> How was the creativity of the Black woman kept alive, year after year and century after century, when for most of the years Black people have been in America, it was a punishable crime for a Black person to read or write? And the freedom to paint, to sculpt, to expand the mind with action, did not exist. Consider, if you bear to imagine it, what might have been the result if singing too had been forbidden by law. Listen to the voices of Bessie Smith, Billie Holiday, Nina Simone, Roberta Flack, and Aretha Franklin, among others, and imagine those voices muzzled for life. Then you may begin to comprehend the lives of our "crazy," "Sainted" mothers and grandmothers. The agony of the lives of women who might have been Poets, Novelists, Essayists, and Short Story Writers (over a period of centuries), who died with their real gifts stifled within them.[58]

Dr. Evans believes that despite peoples' apparent issues and needs, they come with gifts and potential that can be developed.[59] With visions of Isaiah-Matthews being a nurturing center in the community, she educates the people of God by nurturing and challenging the membership. She educates the people of God believing that leaders will emerge who have the creativity, compassion, and skills for effective ministry. This faith in people's potential is not utopian naïveté; a patient, developmental, educational course is being followed. Transformation of adult learners takes place in a larger environmental context. The church, an educational institution, is one of the arenas that has the capacity to help people adopt new attitudes and behaviors or to simply reinforce old ones. As a transformative pastoral leader, she is attentive to these educational processes. Although preaching, teaching, praying, laying hands on the sick, evangelizing, fund raising, mentoring, making sure that bills are paid, and participating in CME Church conferences are essential leadership activities of this pastor, she challenges the belief that the pastor must do all the ministry. The only way that she can share ministry with others is to equip her members through her educational ministry.

It is Dr. Evans's belief that even "the least of these" needs nurturing, and not coddling. If people do not learn to be accountable and consistent in church, they may not learn to do this in everyday life. Church training for some of the members of Isaiah-Matthews is the training that they never got in life. Hence, growing in self-image and learning the lessons of accountability and consistency are needed to be elevated in society. In particular, she is working to elevate the role and presence of black men so that they can stand along side of the women in the human struggle of survival, healing, and wholeness on earth while accepting future salvation in heaven.

The Praxis of Congregational Adaptation

In this chapter, I have examined the new context of black urban religion and selected strategies of transformation adapted by these congregations to deal with their changing environments. I have also suggested that a common characteristic of these transformative pastoral leaders is their commitment to educating the people of God for continuity and change. Both Christopher Temple and Isaiah-Matthews are exemplary in their ongoing efforts of transforming their churches seeking to fulfill the black church's dual mission of salvation and liberation. In many ways, the adapted strategies of transformation discovered in these black church settings are quite similar to strategies of transformational churches in mainline churches.[60] What is unique is that, in every situation, congregations must invent transformative strategies using the cultural ideas and practices available to them.[61] The range of strategies and their effectiveness is impacted by the resources, structures of leadership, and internal cultures of each congregation.

While the decisions to merge two congregations or to develop a new niche in the metropolitan region were not theologically driven decisions, these pastoral leaders are to be commended for their creative theological and ideological work. As Ammerman says:

> Having said that congregational adaptation is not well explained by
> theological and ideological factors, it is also important to note that
> ideas do matter. Each of these adapting congregations had to do some
> ideological work. They had to discover elements in their own heritage
> that could be turned to the task of explaining and encouraging
> change.[62]

Clearly, transformative pastoral leaders must lead their congregations
in interpreting the gospel in varying cultures amidst the shifting
changes of history. These CME pastors have retrieved elements from
varied sources including the following: their Wesleyan evangelical
heritage, their African roots of engaging the sacred and secular
dimensions of communal life, their black church tradition of being an
instrument for the survival, elevation, and liberation of their people,
the Holiness traditions related to Methodism, and their CME Church
tradition of participation in educational ventures through the "Three
Rs for the CME Church" (reading, race, and religion).

They do critical hermeneutical work not only in their interpretation
of the texts of Scripture in their sermons; they also do critical hermeneutical work in their interpretation of mission in ever-changing circumstances. Of this critical hermeneutical approach, Bosch writes:

> The approach called for requires an interaction between the self
> definition of early Christian authors and actors and the self-definition
> of today's believers who wish to be inspired and guided by those early
> witnesses. How did the early Christians as well as subsequent generations
> understand themselves? How do we, today's Christians, understand
> ourselves? And what effect do these "self understandings" have on their
> and our interpretation of mission?[63]

As a scripture text may be interpreted and preached in a myriad of
creative ways, a context of ministry may also be interpreted and innovative adaptive strategies devised in innumerable ways. The strategies
of transformation described in this chapter are by no means exhaus-
tive or definitive of the ways that transformative pastoral leadership
can be carried out. Yet, the emerging strategies described and explained
is suggestive of the active, reflective, and creative work that is necessary
and possible.

5

Independent Black Methodist Systems as Contexts of Transformative Pastoral Leadership

"African" and "Christian" in the names of our denominations denote that we are always concerned for the well-being of economically and politically exploited persons, for gaining or regaining a sense of our own worth, and for determining our future.... Our churches work for the change of all processes which prevent our members who are victims of racism from participating fully in civic and governmental structures.

—John H. Satterwhite, "The Black Methodist Churches"

At the outset of this work the thesis was stated: transformative pastoral leaders are needed to cooperate with God's work of transforming the Church, the people of God, in light of the perspectives of the past and the challenges of the present and the future. This is essential if the black church is to effectively fulfill its mission in the world—an age of crisis and rapid change. By transformative pastoral leadership, I mean spiritual leaders who are intentionally engaged in transforming persons, churches, and communities. Spiritual leaders are women and men called of God to lead in the pastoral vocation of priestly and prophetic ministry. The purpose of my research is to strengthen the praxis of pastoral leadership in the black church so that it can be a renewing agent in American society.

My quest for discovering praxis of ministry theories for transformative pastoral leadership in the black church has yielded two ethnographic tales of transformation of one male pastor and one female pastor in the CME Church (chapters 2 and 3 respectively) and strategies of how pastoral leadership has been a decisive influence in, but not the singular cause of, particular modes of transformation (chapter 4). Because this research was conducted within the particular religious tradition of the CME Church as well as my commitment to the praxis of ministry as clergy in the AME Zion Church, I offer a brief assessment of the independent black Methodist denominational systems as a setting for transformative pastoral leadership.[1]

Comparing the Experiences of One Male and One Female Pastor

My comparative analysis of the ministries of Rev. Harrison and Rev. Evans highlighted what I perceive as the striking differences in the experiences of this male and female pastor in the CME denominational system. Rev. Harrison, an astute "student of the system," rose through the ranks of the CME traveling ministry. Relishing this ecclesiastical gamesmanship like an athlete who aspires to move up from the minor leagues to the professional leagues, he loyally supported the Episcopal system of ministry, which he sees as a political system that also rewards one's spiritual gifts and graces for ministry. He made appropriate choices for his path of ministry in this ecclesial system in which the bishops have the sole power to make pastoral appointments.

I argue that his navigating through the system is not an incidental part of the story for it brought him to an urban context and a mature congregation with significant resources for the support of ministry. Thus, there was a suitable match of his calling and the context. His gifts and calling as an evangelistic and community-oriented pastoral leader found a home at Christopher Temple, where, over the course of a relatively long pastoral tenure, fruitful ministry was possible.

Along the way, Rev. Harrison was alert to the rich possibilities of mentoring in the church and in the communities where he served as pastor. A lifelong learner, he actively learned from the positive and negative examples of others. While his bishop acknowledged that he has brought Rev. Harrison with him as a part of his team, Rev. Harrison says that his mentors have been many. Not only bishops, but also Sunday School teachers, pastors within the CME Church and beyond the CME Church, civil rights activists, black seminary professors, and laypersons are specifically acknowledged as mentors who have aided his personal development as a minister. As he has been transformed (and we hope is continually being transformed) from the forces in his mentoring environment, he has been a mentor to clergy and lay leaders and fosters a teaching and learning environment with the intention of developing leaders for church and society.

With these leaders, he makes "the dream work through team work." My data suggests that Rev. Harrison's formative period in ministry was in the context of the northern civil rights movement and black power movements of the late 1960s and early 1970s. I argue that in light of Rev. Harrison being a student of black history and of the black church, Rev. Harrison envisioned the transformation of this traditional middle-class denominational church at the outset of his pastoral tenure. He prioritized the development of spiritual leaders who were trained to keep "the big picture (of the mission of the church) in mind" while dealing with the operational realities of ministry.

I claim that the strategies of transformation examined in chapter 4 were primarily theological responses to his perception of the changes in the black community and the call to be change agents in the world. There are many changes that are judged as meaningful by the pastor and the people. At the same time, there is continuity with the black church historical tradition of meaningful worship and involvement in the political, economic, social, and educational life of the community. The strategies of transformation include systemic approaches to congregational evangelism, discipleship, and church growth; the shift from traditional Methodist worship to worship as culturally affirming celebration; the shift from a "members only orientation" to a more communal orientation; and the shift from pastor centered leadership to shared transforming leadership. I believe these to be intentional adaptive strategies in a post–civil rights, post-Christian, and postindustrial city environment.

These changes can be understood as part of a larger social pattern that Gilkes identifies as the ongoing tradition of adaptation of exemplary black churches that manage to carry out their traditional religious mission while dealing with the mighty causes of the race.[2] Also, the strategies of urban ministry adopted by this congregation are part of a post–civil rights movement pattern in which black churches are focusing on internal strategies to serve their communities rather than external strategies of protest against racial injustice.[3] Unlike many other black churches that are constrained by their small size and limited budgets, Christopher Temple is an example of a stable and resourceful congregation with strong leadership to which the community can turn to in times of social crisis.[4]

In general, denominations are hindrances, irrelevant, or, at best, supporting players to the transformative efforts of congregations led by strong clergy in creative partnership with lay leaders and members.[5] The CME denominational context does not appear to be a limiting factor for Rev. Harrison and Christopher Temple members in this study. In particular, Rev. Harrison was able to work in tandem with those "above him" (bishop and presiding elder) and those "below him" (members over whom he exercised pastoral oversight) to carry out a shared vision of ministry. As Rev. Harrison is "on board" with the vision of his denominational leaders, his bishop and/or presiding elder appear(s) to be "supportive players" of Rev. Harrison's local ministry at several key moments. For example, Presiding Elder Crider is present as the bishop's representative for the "Gospel Get out the Vote Rally." On another occasion, he uses Rev. Harrison's "Let's Go Fishing" annual theme when he serves as guest Sunday morning preacher. I argue that Rev. Harrison makes the case for being "proud to be a CME" in an era of declining denominational loyalties by reminding his flock that God has produced fruitful CME institutions in the past (such as the denominational schools that support an educated ministry) and that God is still producing fruitful local congregations like Christopher Temple, "the Miracle on Middleton Street."

In contrast to this, Dr. Evans's progress as a female minister was initially hindered as she "searched for the right system." After her journey from her black Pentecostal origins through the United Methodist Church, where it became clear that she would not be ordained, she finally "found a home" in the CME Church. Switching denominations is common for women and men during and after seminary. This may reflect, to some degree, the climate of declining denominational loyalty that impacts clergy as well as lay members. However, Carpenter's research of black seminary graduates suggests that, of the women who switched denominations, more than a third of them switched for ordination-related reasons or to enhance their chances of obtaining paid employment in ministry.[6]

Dr. Evans describes the CME Church as "a church that will embrace sisters . . . a church that has its own level of politics, but it's not so thick that you cannot get through and you cannot find a home." In contrast to Rev. Harrison, who has been transferred to different conferences of the CME connection, as a part of his pastoral sojourn, she has made her mark through a localized ministry.

A bi-vocational, or "tent-making"[7] pastor, she does not receive the material support of salary, housing, and benefits. Because her church is in an "infant stage" of development and has responsibility for the mortgage payments on their complete renovation and refurnishing, there are few resources for ministerial support or for community ministries. In the first few years of the newly merged congregation, she received financial support from the denomination through the leadership of Bishop Douglas. According to Presiding Elder Crider, after the conference provides initial support, mission churches are expected to be self-supporting.

In the CME system, it is not unusual for pastors to begin at "starter churches" like Isaiah-Matthews. Bishop Douglas began his ministry at a mission church. Rev. Harrison began his ministry at a small church with meager resources. Presiding Elder Crider is developing other mission appointments with male and female clergy. Mission pastors are being urged to develop their charges with the vision that one day it may become a leading church.

However, there are different patterns of pastoral ministry after the initial "starter church." Some pastors are promoted to larger more-established appointments in the denomination. Others receive fairly lateral moves to other churches of the conference. Another pattern is that of pastors choosing to "make their promotion where they are at" by steadily building their churches. These pastors are wary of the immense challenges of the historically prestigious "flagship" churches that have declined in resources (membership, finances, property value, and reputation). Meanwhile, expenses have increased due to increased maintenance and operating expenses on aging buildings as well as large, mandatory denominational assessments. Some very capable and enterprising pastors are convincing bishops that they would be better off staying at their churches and building them over a longer tenure.

Because my research at Isaiah-Matthews concluded at the end of her seventh year of her first pastorate, I leave open the question of what is next for this female pastor whose effectiveness in this context is acknowledged by her bishop, presiding elder, and church members. Even in the black Methodist denominations, which have the most progressive attitudes regarding female pastors of the black church leaders surveyed,[8] few women have advanced beyond entry-level missions or small urban churches like Isaiah-Matthews. Their second and third appointments tend to be lateral appointments rather than true promotions to more established churches.[9]

In my analysis, I drew upon the research of CME scholars, Lakey and Stephens, who elaborate on what they call the "ecclesial patriarchy" of the CME Church. This patriarchal system of domination includes the burden of women history, the burden of the Bible, and the burden of the Church.[10] From a local perspective, Dr. Evans's specific pastoral burdens include her working without salary at the church while working another full-time job, dealing with the pressure of paying the mortgage and other bills, proving that a woman can do a "man's job" without being a crybaby, and nurturing "baby Christians" while trusting them as key leaders. However, she is actively supported by some male clergy and enlightened laity who are trying to free themselves and the Church from its ingrained sexism.

As a minority, working in a male-dominated system, she has few clergy sisters to turn to for mentoring and support in the professional practice of ministry. This does not preclude the possibility that male mentors—presiding elders, senior pastors, and bishops—cannot also make themselves available to mentor Dr. Evans and other women. But, I have found little evidence that this often happens for women clergy over a sustained period of time.

As a result, Dr. Evans says that CME's clergy sisters just "hold all of our stuff" as they work in relative isolation. However, female pastors "steal away" to encourage one another and to share wisdom about their respective situations at annual conference and Episcopal district gatherings. Of the CME clergy-sister clandestine experience of networking and mentoring Dr. Evans says:

> When we get together, the sisterhood, we get together maybe three times: winter council, spring convocation, and the annual conference. We all know, those of us who are pastors, that we are going to have some time where we steal away in somebody's room at night when everybody is still and quiet and we just share. The room is packed. We are all in our pajamas. We are all in our gowns with our cups and stuff and we come and we empty up and we share. It's very rewarding. [Laughs] . . . We get together and seemingly we hold all of our stuff until we get there. We just go around, we have to monitor the time so everybody will get a chance to share what is happening in their world and then at the end we share what we think would be helpful for the other.

Perhaps not named as "mentors" by Dr. Evans are women and men who are "faith mentors."[11] Although these people may not have directly assisted Dr. Evans in her professional ministerial development, there are some influential supporters who may be characterized as a faith mentors. Faith mentor being defined as "a co-creator with God, who, as a living representative of God's grace, participates in the relational, vocational, and spiritual growth of others."[12] Matthaei argues that limiting the definitions of mentoring to people who hold professional, executive, or administrative positions usually excludes the relational mentoring that women and people of color excel in doing.[13]

It is clear that, along her ministerial journey, and particularly at turning points, there have been persons who have helped to sustain her in faith as well as in her growth and healing.[14] We glimpse unnamed "faith mentors" who Dr. Evans calls upon soon after her appointment to Isaiah-Matthews. Dr. Evans acknowledges this need to be in relationship with those who could join her in prayer. Dr. Evans says:

> At first, I was not pleased with the assignment, but I knew that God had called me to pastor so I called up a couple of friends after leaving the annual conference, after getting the appointment, and asked them to pray that I would have the right spirit concerning the assignment, to pray with me that I would have the right spirit.

Strengthened in her faith, she nevertheless, encountered resistance to her leadership on the basis of her gender. She, like other minorities, worked to "prove herself," not only in the classroom, but in the church by her effectiveness as pastor. Despite the fact that she had been a pastor in the CME Church for only seven years at the time of my study, her purposeful and process-oriented praxis of ministry has enriched our understanding of the trials and triumphs of pastors determined to make a positive difference in the lives of their congregants as well as in their communities.

In the highs and lows of ministry, Dr. Evans shows her vulnerability to her congregation in her "confessions of fallibility." She openly muses that she would rather leave gracefully if she cannot see a difference "in the life, in the faithfulness, in the finances, in the growth of the church." In the itinerant ministry, she recognizes that sometimes it may be time to move on and that this is what is best for the person and the situation. In particular, the inordinate physical, emotional, and financial sacrifices that she has made in the building process of Isaiah-Matthews have not been mutually shared by the congregation and its leaders. Hence, there are moments when the relationship of the church to the pastor feels like, in her words, "an abusive relationship." I argue that these "confessions of fallibility" are healthy as it allows committed persons, like Dr. Evans to maintain a more balanced perspective. These feelings must be acknowledged and addressed if she is not to join other women and men who are victims of clergy burnout.

Nevertheless, I argue that Dr. Evans, as "founding mother," successfully establishes this merged mission not only from the perspective of the physical renovation, but also from the perspective of what I describe as her "building a community for survival, healing, and wholeness." In so doing, this is a transforming experience for herself and others. Also, she is working to transform attitudes and behaviors that not only equip the members to be faithful on their journey toward heaven, but also to be consistent and accountable in everyday living on earth.

Like Rev. Harrison, I analyze her ministry in a post–civil rights movement historical context. As such, Dr. Evans is part of a "growing wave" of black preaching women seeking legitimacy through full ordination and theological credentialing in the wake of the black consciousness movement and feminist movement of the 1960s and early 1970s that sought parity for women in church and society beyond the traditional designated roles.[15] As Dr. Evans says in one of the messages cited in chapter 3, "I don't let nobody play with my title."

I cannot say, of course, that the different experiences of this particular male and female pastor are representative of other males and females in the CME Church. However, these different experiences illuminate some of the complex spiritual, personal, and political realities of "the system" of the black Methodist denominations. These dynamics must be better understood by male and female pastors as a context for the praxis of transformative pastoral leadership in the congregation and community.

Clearly, there are strengths and weaknesses inherent in the practices described above and there is no one way to navigate "the system." Some persons, like Rev. Harrison, will learn to thrive in this system of the traveling ministry. Their pastoral ministry will be enriched from a rich symbiotic relationship with the denomination. Others, like Dr. Evans, will survive the system and learn how to carry out their pastorates despite the challenges of paying financial assessments to the denomination while attempting to develop resources for ministry in their local communities.

Still others will find the spiritual, political, and economic realities so daunting that visionary ministry is impossible for them in this context. Discussion of the issues that are motivating pastors to leave the black Methodist denominations is beyond the scope of this study as I have chosen pastors committed to ministry in the CME Church. However, I note in passing this silent and not so silent group of pastors who are choosing to leave the black Methodist denominations.

If the leadership of the Church, particularly the Episcopal leadership of the black Methodist denominations, does not develop greater empathetic understanding of the motives of these persons it is possible that others will join gifted male and female ministers who have left their denominations and established ministries elsewhere.

The Itinerancy and Pastoral Tenure

The pattern of a pastoral tenure of eight years or more is being embraced by the CME Church as a strategy for creating more healthy ministries. When asked the average tenure of pastors in the CME Church, Presiding Elder Crider responded. "It used to be 3–5 years. Now, I know in this Episcopal district, as long as you've done a good job, the bishop would prefer you staying there."

The CME Book of Discipline now states, "No preacher is to remain at the same charge or enlarged charge more than eight years successively, except where the Presiding Bishop thinks a longer term will promote the welfare of the charge."[16] Thus, the welfare or health of the charge, rather than the historic Methodist tradition of frequent moving of preachers, is becoming a principle for the yearly appointment of preachers, many of whom need to work at other vocations.[17]

I believe that transformative pastoral ministry cannot occur without the development of healthy trusting relationships that usually takes several years. It is unlikely that pastor or members will invest significant time, talent, and treasure in transformative ministries when there is a belief that the pastor will be moved in a year or two. Asked about the AME Zion tradition of moving pastors every four years,[18] Bishop Norman explains why he thinks that pastors need more time than this if anything transformative is to occur in the relationships among God, self, and others. Bishop Norman comments:

I believe the changing of lives are the results of a couple of things: either there's a divine intruder where God steps in and there's the dramatic change that He brings about through His Holy Spirit, or there is the slower process of change that comes out of relationships. It takes time for an individual to understand the self. It takes time for an individual to understand other individuals. It takes time for an individual to understand the human social dynamics in a given setting. It takes time to help others to see that which perhaps the leader has perceived. Once they see, it then it takes time to motivate them to want to do something about it, to want to change. Then it takes time to process change. Then it takes time to see the evidence of that change in terms of the ultimate mission of the church.

The deployment of preachers in the itinerancy is a practice that must be transformed. Preachers should be appointed to carry out ministries of personal and social transformation. The trend toward appointing ministers for a time sufficient to see transformative results is a practice that should be affirmed for the sake of the mission of the church.

Vision and the Itinerancy

Transformative pastors in the itinerancy must risk being visionary leaders. Visions given by God to pastors and leaders who dare to ask for it have the power to charge, challenge, and change congregations and communities. However, a pastor or church may resist efforts to develop a vision and strategic plan because of the fear of a leadership change. Inherent in the Methodist itinerant system are transient expectations of the pastor's tenure. This was, in fact the case at my Chicago pastorate.

I entered the church with no grand plans. Soon afterwards, I learned that we needed a new roof. Previous roof problems in the ninety-year old building had caused the previous pastoral administration to gain approval from the membership to divert funds raised for a new air-conditioning system to address persistent water leakage problems. Soon after my arrival, a break-in occurred, causing the officers to consider new proposals to secure the building in our "new poverty area" urban neighborhood. Within six months of my arrival, it became clear to me that a major financial investment was needed to address the several renovations and repair needs.

At the same time, right outside of the imposing wrought iron gates installed on the front door of the church, I witnessed people driving into the community to buy drugs sold on the corner of our church property. Over the last twenty years, the previous pastors and church officers had dealt with prostitutes, the homeless, the drug dealings, and the car thefts on this corner.

Reflection on a counseling session with a young couple whose children I was preparing to baptize helped me to see the impact of poverty and joblessness on my own ministry. A faithful leader of our church requested that I baptize her two grandchildren. I requested that the parents accompany her for counseling with me as well. I learned that this unmarried couple had seven children together. Neither of these parents, who were in their late twenties, had a high-school diploma or GED. Most of their children had been adopted by family members so that they would not become wards of the state. The father, who had been recently incarcerated, was marginally employed. The mother indicated that she was a "certified housekeeper."

When I asked the man, "Why, after seven children, haven't you married the mother of your children?" He responded, "I've got to get myself together first . . . get myself stable." He seemed to want to provide for his family. He at least had enough respect for his girlfriend's mother to come to my office for counseling with respect to baptizing his children. Yet, knowing that he did not have the tools to provide for his family he would not marry. When I asked him about his plans for education, he was very vague and noncommittal. At that point, the grandmother chimed in with a sociohistorical perspective. She said:

> When we moved from Alabama there were plenty of jobs. You didn't even have to fill out a job application. There was somebody at the desk that would ask you questions and fill out the application for you. Today, if you can't fill out an application you can't get a job.

Clearly, this grandmother of limited formal education was reflecting to me what social scientists have written about in their impressive structural analyses. In a previous generation, this young man being counseled in my office would have had the sufficient skills to be employed in the plentiful manufacturing jobs available in the central cities. But now, following the massive loss of jobs from the central cities to the industrial suburbs, this young man had been sucked into the "ghetto underclass" of people whose skills do not qualify for employment in this postindustrial economy.

This experience provided a microcosm for my reflection on how poverty and joblessness impacted my ministry. Learning from this example, I had to accept the fact that the fate of the church and community were linked. No longer could I allow the church to simply be a "refuge" "for members only" while, to the community, the church looked like it was "closed" and "out of business." This was in fact, the impression conveyed to me by a barber just down the street from my church. When I told him I was the pastor of the church, he said, "Man, I thought that that church had closed down for a minute!"

Later in the midst of studying my community from an ecological perspective, I was struck by the impact of urban restructuring on my church's neighborhood. I began to ponder the question, "What is the impact of neighborhood poverty and the loss of jobs on neighborhood institutions—families, social service agencies, formal neighborhood groups, schools, businesses, and churches?" As I walked the neighborhood, Wilson's analysis of the decline of neighborhoods vulnerable to societal economic restructuring came to life. His portrait of a severely depressed neighborhood looked liked an amazingly accurate portrayal of the neighborhood around my church as he wrote the following:

> As the population drops and the proportion of nonworking adult rises, basic neighborhood institutions are more difficult to maintain: stores, banks, credit institutions, restaurants, dry cleaners, gas stations, medical doctors, and so on lose regular and potential patrons. *Churches experience dwindling numbers of parishioners and shrinking resources* [emphasis added]; recreational facilities, block clubs, community groups, and other informal organizations will also suffer. As these organizations decline, the means of formal and informal social control in the neighborhood become weaker. Levels of crime and street violence increase as a result, leading to further deteriorations in the neighborhood.[19]

In my spirit, I was pressed with the burden of how I could ethically lead the congregation in investing nearly $100,000 for renovation and repairs to a nearly one-hundred-year-old building without seeking a vision to revitalize the church and community.

When I first proposed to my church officers the idea of creating a "dream team" to develop a three-to-five-year strategic plan for the church, one of the most influential leaders of the church looked me in the eye and asked, "Rev. Tribble, I don't think you'll be here in five years. I've been a member of the AME Zion Church all my life. Once the bishop sees that you're doing a good job, he's going to move you. If you're not going to be here five years from now, then I don't want to waste time working on a five year plan!"

In that moment, I think the Spirit prompted me to say, "I don't know if I will be here five years from now or not. I can't promise you that I will be here. But, I believe that this church needs a vision for its work in this community. If a written vision is in place that has been developed by the pastor and people, then, at least, the new pastor can prayerfully evaluate that written set of directions, goals, and objectives in consultation with the officers and members. I would expect that a new pastor would do some things differently because they have different gifts, talents, and experiences. However, at that point, with a written set of mission, vision, and action plans, the new pastor can work with the leaders and decide what aspects of that vision to continue, to modify, or to discard."

Apparently, my answer was sufficient to persuade this influential leader to be a member of our "dream team." His influence and commitment was a key factor in convincing other church members to invest time over the next several months in developing our mission statement, vision statement, and action plans in several phases of ministry. Our vision was impacted by interviews with community leaders in the political, educational, economic, and social-service arenas.

As a result, our church opened its doors to the neighborhood association for its meetings. The local elementary school expressed interest in renting space for its after-school programs. We became involved in the alderman's efforts to revitalize the commercial corridors, improve the housing stock, and to encourage faith-based community ministries. We initiated a partnership with a local homeless shelter to bless homeless families in need of supplies as well as ministry. Thankfully, we did not simply make a set of plans to sit on a shelf. Many of the action plans were implemented before the final strategic plan was in place.

The leader who initially resisted beginning the visioning process was right, in a way. I was not at the church for five years. It was not because the bishop moved me. Three years after my arrival, I accepted a full-time faculty seminary position with the blessings of my bishop. One of my last pastoral acts was to work with my vision team to complete our strategic plans as well as a set of policies and procedures. These documents were left to my female successor as a part of my legacy of leadership. Some of the plans were already in motion and continued. Other plans were discarded. But, the words of my successor have been, "you left a good foundation."

Carlyle Fielding Stewart III, a black United Methodist pastor, also advocates for churches developing and implementing a vision plan in the Methodist itinerant system. Stewart writes:

> If every pastor and congregation developed and adopted a vision plan for the church's future, that vision would already be in place when the next pastor arrives. The vision's success need not be predicated on whether a certain pastor serves a church. The vision or strategic plan can continue regardless of a change in pastoral appointment.[20]

Yes, the vision can continue regardless of a change in pastoral appointment if the articulated vision is not simply what the pastor wants or what the laity want. In a transforming church, clergy and laity must share the pastoral vocation of vision seeking, rooted in their covenantal relationship with God. They must talk with the Lord and expect to catch sight of what God would have for them to do. They must "write the vision and make it plain . . . that he/she may run that reads it."[21]

Yet, at the same time, denominational officials need to be supportive of creative visionary partnerships of transformative pastors and transformative lay leaders. Bishops and presiding elders must ask, "What will be the impact of pastoral appointments on the health of churches and of communities?" In the best of situations, denominations can help create a climate for transformative pastors to have time to discover God's vision for their church's mission in their changing communities. As in the cases of Christopher Temple and Isaiah-Matthews, they can find ways of encouraging change, provide resources for assistance, and make sure that pastoral appointments meet the needs of congregations and communities. This may mean that a different set of questions must be asked when appointments are confirmed at annual conferences. Instead of asking simply how a particular pastoral appointment serves the interest of the connection, or even the interests of a particular pastor, the critical question must be, "How does a particular pastoral appointment serve the interests of transforming individuals, church, and community?" Perhaps, looking at the complex interplay of the interests of the denomination, local churches, pastoral families, and communities will transform thinking about the use of the itinerancy.

When asked the question, "Is there a way to reconceptualize the appointment system so that the itinerancy better serves the congregation and the community?" Bishop Norman of the AME Zion Church responded:

> I think there certainly is a way that can be done. We need to revisit the original intent of the itinerancy. We need to understand that it was designed to serve a purpose and we need to evaluate whether or not that purpose is being served. . . . That's a slow process. That's a process of calling into question some sacred cows. That's a process of making people deal with things at a level that often is painful and uncomfortable and just tedious. And we would rather not function at that level. We have so much pain in other areas, so we are not looking for more pain. We're not looking for more things to perplex us and to stretch us. We don't want to be stretched. We want to be comfortable and you know we live in a day and time where the culture says you ought to be served and we want to serve you and we want to give you choices so you can select that which is comfortable for you. . . . I'm talking about the

greater society, the greater culture that carries over into church. That same mindset is in the church that we find in the greater culture. It's a culture of self-service, self-serving, and being served. To deal with anything that requires systemic change is painful, it's stressful, and the people are just seeking to avoid things that are painful and stressful. Yet, if we are going to honor the tradition, if we are going to honor itinerancy and at the same time seek to do those things ultimately which itinerancy was intended to do, we've got to go back and look at it, we've got to wrestle with it, we must ask ourselves what does itinerancy mean in this day and time and how ought it be interpreted and how ought it be applied in this day and time.

Yes, the hierarchical structure of leadership in the Black Methodist systems means that visionary transformative pastors are hindered or supported by their bishops' use of the itinerant system. Bishop Norman admits that transformation of the itinerancy is a difficult process that is, in fact, hindered by the American culture of individualism. Impacted by this culture, the institutional church is a reflection of its leadership. The larger question becomes, will the black church simply be a self-serving institution or will it wrestle with needed transformation of its practices to fulfill its mission? Are leaders at all levels of the church willing to do the difficult critical hermeneutical work of examining the structures put in place to support the mission and changing them if needed? Is there vision and determination to do this transformative ministry? If not, we can predict the "State of the Black Church." Playing on Tavis Smiley's conference, referred to in chapter 1, we can be sure that the black church will be, in the absence of such vision and determination, irrelevant, repressive, and in a continued state of decline.

The Upward Mobility of Women Clergy

Other studies of black women and the black church have noted the issue of the upward mobility of black women clergy. On this issue Lincoln and Mamiya write:

> Even in those black denominations (mainly Methodist) where women have been officially accepted as pastors and preachers, their upward mobility to larger black churches, historically famous preaching posts, and positions like bishop remains troubled with varying degrees of hindrances and resistances. . . . As a result of the opposition they have encountered in the historic black denominations, a growing

number of theologically trained black women have opted for posts in white denominations that have shown more progressive attitudes on the issue of sexuality. Whether and when this trend will change depends upon the changes in attitude and practice among the historic black churches towards greater tolerance and equal treatment of women clergy.[22]

Whether more equal treatment of women clergy is imminent in the CME Church and other black Methodist denominations is an open question. When asked the question of how the CME Church is being transformed by the presence of gifted female clergy, Presiding Elder Crider responds:

> I think that many of the congregations are accepting them quite well. One of the things that we have not had [is] a major pastoral appointment of a woman pastor, but it's coming and I think that if the person can deliver, they would accept them. . . . We have more women coming into the ministry than we have men. One of the reasons that I have been able to expand [the number of churches on his presiding elder district] is because of the women that are coming in. I would say that within the next couple of years half of my appointments will be women.

It is clear that Presiding Elder Crider has a vision of increasing the number of CME churches on his district and that he is relying on the increasing supply of women preachers to accomplish this.

When I asked Bishop Douglas how the CME Church is being impacted by the growing numbers of female clergy in seminary, he responded:

> If we don't use them we're going to be out of business. What I'm saying is that, personally, I have no problem with it. . . . I have three or four other women preachers who I have assigned to good churches. . . . First, I don't have any problem with women preachers. The CME church, for the most part, has adopted that stance. The fact that the AMEs elected a woman [Bishop Vashti McKenzie as first woman bishop] should help things even more. If we don't use women, you won't have enough preachers. Like I said, I'm already using retired preachers. Down South . . . it's even worse . . . I visit the seminary once a year, ITC [Interdenominational Theological Center], for Founder's Day. We have a large class of women preachers. Most of them will be pastors, some in Christian Education, but most will be pastors. . . . Without women preachers I would not have been able to fill my pulpits.

These perspectives of influential male leaders regarding the crucial role of female clergy in the building of the CME Church suggests that women will be appointed to pastor "starter churches" despite continuing lay resistance to this. However, if the pattern of not promoting women and/or giving them lateral moves continues, I think that the prospect of gifted female pastors being exploited as "the mules of our race" is great.

Social change is needed within the black church. One of the needed social changes is gender equality. Carpenter identifies four building blocks for the social change of gender equality in the black church:

1. A Spirit-led religious liberation movement addressing not only the need for liberation from racism, but also from the sexism of the ecclesial patriarchy of the black church;
2. The acceptance of the historical-critical method of interpreting the authoritative biblical texts as a tool of freeing women and men of the black church from the bondage of restrictive texts against women;
3. The formulation of womanist theology within the structures of liberation theology transforming how people think about the God ordained system of the church;
4. The socio-psychological freedom of black women and men removing gender as the defining characteristic of institutional leadership.[23]

To these four building blocks, I would add the necessity of identifying and mentoring promising women clergy for positions of greater responsibility in the church. Implementation of these building blocks into a Spirit-led movement would amount to a spiritual "affirmative action program" in the life of the black church.

I agree with Bishop Douglas who noted that, in some instances, the bishop can prepare the congregation for the appointment of a female pastor. Also, Bishop Norman notes that proactive teaching is needed in this area. Substantial dialogue is needed at all levels of the church to transform attitudes that hinder women's progress in the black Methodist denominations. As Lincoln and Mamiya note, these theologically educated women cannot be taken for granted in the black Methodist denominations. Some will choose paths of lesser resistance such as in progressive white denominations. Certainly, they will face issues of race and gender there also; but, may choose to at least have minimum salary and benefits[24] amidst the struggle.

The ministry of Dr. Carol Evans provides a provocative example of a pastor who has "paid her dues" in an entry-level pastorate. Furthermore, she has been fruitful in transformative pastoral ministry. When I asked one of the members of Isaiah-Matthews, Mary Duncan, if Dr. Evans deserves a promotion she gave this response:

> (Sighs) Now as a member of her church, no. (She laughs and I join her in laughter.) I love my pastor I'll be clear about that, no . . . NO!! But, because of her, lovingly and just to what is right, yes. Other than my personal prejudice, yes. I could see her leading even a district, if you will. I could see her doing that. She would be fair and she would be excellent in that. She has excellent people skills. She can put you at ease and at the same time you know that you are talking to a formidable person. She doesn't put on airs. She's as plain spoken as she knows how to be and I can see her in a role like that. She would be excellent at that. I would personally hate to lose her as a pastor at any point in terms of being a CME church person. I would not be upset if she was promoted. I think [she would be] well deserving of it and indeed well trained for it.

This is a remarkable endorsement of a laywoman in the pews who feels she and her family has much to lose if Dr. Evans was promoted.

Finally, I asked Bishop Douglas, her supervising bishop, his candid assessment of the qualities and skills of leadership that Dr. Evans exemplifies in her work. Excerpts of his response are as follows:

> I think she's a very good leader. First of all, she's very articulate. She has a background of social work which helps her understand people to that degree. She's spent a lot of time as a singer. She's a stomp down good preacher. . . . She has what we like to experience, but it's structured and it's not noise. It's information in a loud format. She's a good woman. She's a determined woman. She brings class to it. She has a very good job. She has the kind of appearance that I believe causes people to enjoy her presence.

The point of my publicly sharing these private perspectives is simply to raise consciousness of the question of the upward mobility of deserving clergywomen in the CME Church and the other black Methodist churches who are capable of moving from bi-vocational to full-time ministry because they have gifts and graces to offer transformative pastoral leadership in the church and community.

Fostering a Movement Mentality in Black Church Structures

I believe that there is a hunger to see ongoing transformation of the black church so that it can be a renewing agent in society through its priestly and prophetic ministries. There are committed individuals here and there who love their church too much to let it descend to the depths of mediocrity, irrelevance, and impotence. Too often, however, these progressive-minded lay leaders, pastors, presiding elders, and bishops, may be compared to the CME women pastors who "hold their stuff" and work in relative isolation. Only here and there are opportunities to "steal away" and share with one another in helpful ways.

Perhaps the Spirit is fostering the wind of a social movement to encourage the development of transformative pastoral leaders. In August of 2003, I was approached by my pastor with his vision of a Transforming Church Conference. The objective of the conference was to provide pastors and church leaders with progressive and culturally relevant strategies in transitioning traditional churches into transformational ministries. After several discussions, I agreed to serve as a co-convener of the conference along with Pastor Lester A. McCorn. African American pastors who had proven strategies of transforming traditional ministries were invited along with seminary professors who served as facilitators of panel discussions and workshops.[25] The bulk of the preachers and presenters were from the AME, AME Zion, CME, and United Methodist Churches, while some served in autonomous Baptist structures of leadership.

Among the ideas that surfaced at this conference was that of developing a transforming church network that would be a vehicle for ongoing encouragement, support, and sharing of ideas throughout the year. Pastors, in particular, expressed their weariness from working in isolation to transform churches that are resistant to change. One pastor, also serving as a presiding elder, was nearly in tears as he expressed his gratitude for such a gathering. Too often, leaders inspired by the practical possibilities of new ideas are tempted to fall into despair amidst the institutional impediments to even minor reforms. The conservative forces of organizations and the conditions of society often seem to overwhelm the transforming forces of change.

In the previous section, I shared Delores Carpenter's model for working toward the social reform of gender equality in the black church. In this section, I would like to explore the implications of a model of social reform that was developed by Parker Palmer out of his work in educational reform. His model is inspired by his study of the civil rights movement, the women's movements, the movement for gay and lesbian rights, as well as movements for freedom in Eastern Europe, South African, and Latin America. Paradoxical thinking is needed to embrace the creative roles of organizations and movements in the work of social change. Of the "both-and" thinking needed to think together the tensions of organizational thinking and a movement mentality, Palmer writes:

> Organizations and movements both play creative roles, but to quite different ends. Organizations represent the principle of order and conservation: they are the vessels in which a society holds hard-won treasures of the past. Movements represent the principle of flux and change: they are the processes through which a society channels its energies for renewal and transformation. A healthy society will encourage interplay between the two. *Reform-minded organizational leaders will often welcome movement energies, despite the chaos they can bring, and leaders of movements must understand that they need organizational structure to sustain whatever reforms they achieve* [emphasis added].[26]

Four stages of development of this movement are proposed by Palmer. In stage one of the movement, there are isolated individuals who make their own inward decisions to live "divided no more." Suffering from a situation that is chronic and severe, they finally come to a point when they are tired not only of systemic wrongs, but of their silent complicity with the system. The price of loyalty to the system, whether right or wrong, can make a claim on the self to the detriment of one's living with personal integrity. Although remaining invested and committed to the institution, these individuals are discovering a new center for their lives outside the institutions. From this center, they find the courage to honor their deepest convictions risking the sanctions of the system. Parker compares this stage of the movement to the decision of Rosa Parks, who decided one day that the punishment that she might face for refusing to go to the back of the bus was not as great as her conspiring in the diminishment of her personhood.[27]

In the black church, I imagine that there are many such individuals with visions of change. They try to convince the authorities—the General Conferences, the Board of Bishops, their administrative committees, their pastors, the trustee or steward board members, the members—of a needed change in the church. These desired changes, on all levels of the church's life, may grow out of a myriad of concerns including: a desire for diverse styles of worship; despair with the church's inability to reach and minister to many of the youth of the church and community; a "traditionalism" that stifles the life of the Spirit; the need to restructure antiquated systems for determining the financial assessments for overburdened local churches; wrestling with uses of the itinerancy that honor the intentions of the founders; a suitable response to a perceived epidemic of young adults and innovative younger pastors leaving denominational churches for nondenominational ministries; gender tensions around the need for upward mobility of women clergy and the need to elevate the presence of black men; community crises demanding sustained collaborative responses to systemic problems; styles of leadership that signal attitudes of clergy being unapproachable; members' fear of change, so on and so forth. Reform-minded pastoral leaders, whether class leaders, pastors, presiding elders, or bishops, will simply be consumed in a sea of despondency if they work in relative isolation.

Palmer's second stage of the development of the movement occurs as individuals discover one another and form "communities of congruence" in which they can offer mutual support and opportunities to develop a shared vision.[28] As these "communities of congruence" coalesce, they fill at least three characteristic roles. First, they serve as a gathering place for those who need to know that they are not alone in the struggle of social reform. Second, they serve as conceptual space, developing the vision, language, and symbols that the movement will need to survive in the public arena. Third, the "community of congruence" provides a training ground to develop the knowledge, skills, and habits needed to take the values of the movement into the broader community.[29]

I believe that these "communities of congruence" concerned with the kind of leadership needed in our communities may emerge in many places. Some will be formed within convocations and workshops of denominations. Others may be formed by conferences developing out of the ministries that are self-consciously "teaching churches." Still other "communities of congruence" may form across lines of church and academy as well as across denominational lines.

Some models of transformative ministries may come from theological seminaries working closely with graduates skilled in the praxis of ministry. These reflective practitioners see strengths and weaknesses in theological education. They may be interested in shaping models of theological education that build on the classical tradition, yet critique it from the perspective of the black experience. With a critical understanding of the critical issues facing the African American community, they will gladly mentor their parishioners toward theological education if they are assured that the seminary is committed to equipping women and men with the knowledge, skills, and virtues for transformative ministry in the church and community.

A third stage of the development of the movement emerges when the movement goes public. At this point, the movement is exposed to public critique, a critique that it must take seriously. There is much risk in the give and take of the public arena. Potential allies will have different visions and values. Yet, when the movement grows, it can attract unlikely allies as well as attract the criticism of unexpected enemies. Yet, this is all a part of the painful process of growth.[30]

Transformative pastoral leaders in the black church will work on internal strategies of transformation within the black church and black community. However, they will also see the relationship of various movements addressing social injustice and discover ways to work beyond their "tribes" toward the common good. This is demanding work, this work of working within one's own community as well as beyond it. Being a bridge between communities and seeing one's ministry within the globalizing forces of our time is an immense challenge. "Going public" is necessary for those who minister in response to the love of a God who loves the whole world, not just their localized corner of it.

In stage four of this model of the movement, an alternative system of rewards emerges to sustain the movement's vision and to alter the system by putting pressure on its standard system of institutional rewards.[31] In a transforming church, transformative pastoral leaders in the black church draw strength from their commitment to living out of the integrity of their inner convictions, from the mutual support that they discover by working with like-minded people, and from the reward of working in a more public sphere within and beyond their own institutions.[32] Somehow, those who work for change must be freed from their fear of punishment of the system, their worship of its rewards, and the rejection that they might experience from colleagues who cling to the old ways of being, believing, and behaving.

Unfortunately, Frazier's analysis of a dark side of the ministerial tradition in the black church, in some instances, still rings true. Reflecting on a period of time between Reconstruction and the modern civil rights movement, Frazier sees the church as the main arena where the struggle for power of men who are starved for status could be satisfied. Frazier's scathing criticism of the ministers of the denominations most dominant in that era illumines a dark side of the tradition of ministerial leadership in the black church. Frazier writes:

> As the result of the elimination of Negroes from the political life of the American community, the Negro church became the arena of their

political activities. . . . In the Baptist churches, with their local autonomy, individual Negro preachers ruled their followers in an arbitrary manner, while the leaders in the hierarchy of the various Methodist denominations were czars, rewarding and punishing their subordinates on the basis of personal loyalties. Moreover, the monetary rewards which went with power were not small when one considers the contributions of millions of Negroes and the various business activities of the churches.[33]

Thankfully, this portrait would not fit many ministers. Yet, there is a dark side of religious leadership. The temptations of ambition, power, and greed, are very real. Furthermore, socialization in this tradition fosters attitudes of authoritarianism and arrogance. Unfortunately, some powerful clergy have not made the shift from their self-perception of "magisterial" to "ministerial."[34] The fundamental shift needed is from a perspective of leadership that reaps power and rewards on the leader to a view of leadership that benefits those that are led.

This model of a Spirit-led movement of spiritual leaders with the vocation of transformative pastoral leadership is offered to help persons find their place in the movement and to inspire vision to help the movement along. The work of transformative pastoral leadership is hardwork. It is a continual process. Sometimes, changes will be incremental. Often, the process will be messy and involve managing conflict. As one theologian puts it: "Grass roots studies of transformative praxis often recognize discernment of small steps . . . [it] is often a convoluted process, working through a mess."[35]

Conclusion

In this book, I have attempted to recognize, understand, and define the emergent concept of transformative pastoral leadership in the black church. I did this by comparing similarities and differences in the experiences and transformative praxis of one male pastor and one female pastor in the Christian Methodist Episcopal Church. "Theories in process" have been developed in the form of thick descriptions and explanations of strategies of transformative pastoral leadership in their contexts of congregation, community, and denomination.

Systemic forces hindering and helping transformative pastoral leadership in the black Methodist itinerant system were explored primarily by raising questions of church leaders at the local congregational level (pastors and other church leaders), district level (presiding elder), and annual conference level (bishop). In this system, some pastoral leaders thrive, others survive, and still others leave. I selected a male pastor who I would characterize as one who has "thrived" in this system and a female pastor who I would characterize as one who has "survived" in this system. Beyond the scope of this study is the category of persons who leave for a variety of reasons, one of which may be because they find it impossible to do visionary transformative ministry in this context. It may be worthwhile to do a study of pastors who have left the system as a way of understanding how to keep the church a healthy place for as many people as possible. I have only scratched the surface of the question of the possibilities for transformative pastoral leadership in the larger systemic contexts of black Methodism.

Of course, the local congregation is the primary system for understanding transformative pastoral leadership. Rather than trying to fix denominational systems, our best hope is in fostering healthy congregational ministries. My approach was to select two healthy congregations that had managed the inevitable conflict of working through the transitions of transformation.

My study is constrained by the discipline of generating insights from my grounded theory approach to research. In this approach, "theories" are generated from the data of my two cases, although ideas from other sources can also be correlated with data from my cases. Hence, the strategies of transformation that I examine are only suggestive of the possibilities, problems, principles, processes, and practices of transformative pastoral leadership in the black church. As the gospel is interpreted in a variety of circumstances in the preaching moment, so the mission of the church must be interpreted in a variety of circumstances and strategies of adaptation must be devised.

Although I have attempted to place the practical wisdom, insights, principles, and strategies in larger contexts, there are many other situations of transformation in the black church that this study does not address. Hopefully, the breadth that I lack is compensated for, to some degree, by a depth of insight from my analysis of my two contrasting cases. Transformative pastoral leaders must tend to the souls of their congregations while enlarging their capacities for transformative communal ministry. We need the gifts of all of God's people for the ministry of transforming people, churches, and society.

Appendix A: Research Method

My research, although drawing extensively on sociological methods of field research, was conducted in the tradition of late twentieth-century religious researchers who have related theological reflection and the social sciences with the goal of understanding and transforming the practices of congregations. Utilizing the diverse methods developed by scholars in the area of congregational studies,[1] I have attempted to bridge theories of practices of ministry, biblical and theological reflection, and the century-old tradition of the sociological study of the black church.[2]

Critical and constructive reflection on the diverse experiences, understandings, and activities of two pastors in their congregational, communal, and denominational contexts has been done with the aim of sharing practical wisdom. In this study, the practices of pastors and congregants as well as the perspectives that lay and clergy leaders have of pastoral leadership and of congregational ministry were the focus of one moment of critical reflection. I have also reflected on the social and cultural contexts of pastoral leadership in my two research sites. This moment of reflection engaged the history of the black church in America, classical and contemporary sociological studies of the black church, urban history of the communities in which the congregations are situated, and social theories related to the transformation of the black church since the social movements of the 1960s and early 1970s. My reflection on the biblical and theological roots of the practices of these pastoral leaders and their congregations engaged biblical images of pastoral ministry, the theological traditions of Methodists, and black and womanist liberation theologies. Finally, I suggest new transformative practices for the black church. This takes the speculative, coherent, and critical insights of the other interrelated moments of reflection and puts them back on the ground of concrete experience and practice.[3]

The Ethnographer as Minister

I must acknowledge that I have a special connection to this research because I am a practicing minister of the AME Zion Church. Although I was not serving as a pastor during the field research, I am aware of the politics of this research for myself and for others. Hence, my professional experience as a pastor in a similar ministry context is both a resource for this research as well as a hindrance to my being as fully critical as one detached from the life and ministry of the black church. Yet, this "insider research" is done in hope that any criticism that I offer of the church and its leadership is out of love and respect for the black church. Redemption may grow out of my courage to model a prophetic internal criticism, a stance that not only affirms the black church, but critiques it.[4] Through my field research, reflection, and writing, I am attempting to create a dialogue between scholars and the words and actions of those who are not usually privileged in scholarly discourse: black female and male lay church leaders as well as black female and male clergy.

Philosophically, my field research is shaped by the phenomenological approach, a social-scientific approach for studying human experience that seeks to interpret the underlying perspectives, motives, rules, and practices that determine human behavior. Using this approach, I strived for what Max Weber called *verstehen*, accurate empathetic understanding of the motives and beliefs behind people's actions. I wanted to understand what lies behind particular beliefs and practices of pastors and their congregations. Using ethnography as a tool for studying social reality, I disciplined myself to use multiple methods of data collection (participant observation, interviews, and document analysis) and to treat each of the congregational cultures as "anthropologically strange." I followed the methods of grounded theory[5] and used existing theories in my reading of a variety of streams of literature to enhance my theoretical sensitivity in preparation for my field research. As a result, new "theories in process" were generated inductively through the method known as theoretical sampling.

My selection of congregations in the CME Church grew out of my desire to do field research on pastoral leadership in a black Methodist context that I reasoned would have similar issues and concerns as my own AME Zion Church. But, because of my awareness of the politics of my own relationships within my denomination as well as the ethnographer's methodological concern for "marginality," I decided to study congregations outside of my own denomination.

Because of my theological interest in studying how black Methodist churches might embody the evangelical and liberation dimensions of their heritage in their mission practices, I looked for growing ministries exemplary of a useful concept of pastoral leadership in the black church called "prophetic ministry." Stewart defines prophetic ministry as a concern for wholeness of individual and community.[6] Furthermore, in conceiving an inclusive study of pastoral leadership in the black Methodist church, I decided to include the experiences and perspectives of a theologically educated female pastor as well as a theologically educated male pastor. Conversations with the presiding elder as well as a minister of the district led to meetings with Rev. Harrison and Dr. Evans who were receptive to my study aims and methods.

The resulting comparative analysis has helped me to reflect on how I benefit from a patriarchal church system as a theologically educated black male clergy. My journey of healing from my own sexism includes my advocacy for the acceptance of qualified female clergy at all levels of the church through my research and writing as well as by my teaching and mentoring of female and male clergy.

The field research began in the summer of 2000 with my visit to the Tri-State Annual Conference of the CME Church. This visit was explicitly approved by Bishop Douglas with the encouragement of Presiding Elder Crider. The ethics of this research with human subjects required me to ponder the potential risks to congregations, individual members, and pastors. One of the potential risks that I identified was that my intent to interview pastors about their experiences with powerful bishops could put their pastoral appointment at risk. In my own denomination, "pastor's rights" have been a real concern. Some have charged that pastors, appointed annually by their bishops in these Episcopal systems of governance, have sometimes been left without pastoral appointments, moved to distant pastoral appointments, or demoted to lesser paying appointments because of supposed disloyalty or disagreements with their bishops.[7] In addition to this, I was aware of the need to create safe spaces for laity to engage in frank discussions regarding their own pastoral leadership.

As a result of these and other risks, a research protocol was established to conduct this research with a full awareness of the need for collecting, protecting, and presenting information in a sensitive and ethical manner that would maintain trust and integrity between people. As a graduate student of Northwestern University, the research for this work was conducted under the auspices of Northwestern University's Institutional Review Board (IRB).

After gaining written congregational consent from both congregations as well as formal approval by the IRB, my field research continued with participant observation research in both Christopher Temple and Isaiah-Matthews from November 2000 to April 2001. Thus, for a period of approximately six months, I was a participant observation at the two congregations conducting participant observation of congregational activities, including regular worship services, special events, administrative meetings, and educational events. In both congregational settings, I had many informal conversations with members over fellowship meals at the church as well as before and after services and meetings.

The six-month period of rudimentary participation observation and writing of field notes accomplished several aims. It enabled me to gain firsthand knowledge of the settings by my participant observation in multiple ministry settings at multiple times, to build rapport with persons, to develop my own "theories in process," to formulate strategies for selecting and/or recruiting knowledgeable persons that I wished to interview, and to determine specific questions that I wished to pose in subsequent semi-structured interviews.

Adopting a range of "nonacademic" membership roles in the field,[8] I would describe my roles as ranging from "active participant in the pulpit" (being actively involved in the worship services sitting in the pulpit while taking written notes of the pastoral interactions with the congregation) to "active observer in the pew" (being actively involved in the worship services sitting in the pews while taking copious notes during the services). Recognizing that my presence had an effect on what I was studying, I reflected on my membership roles in my field notes and attempted to critique the impact that my choice of roles had on my data.

In this active insider role, I think that I gathered significant data because of closer interaction and better rapport with clergy as I participated in some aspects of the annual conference and congregations in my master status as "fellow pastor." During services, both pastors, on occasion, reflected aloud on the practice of pastoral leadership in their settings in a manner that I do not think they would have done if I was not present in these roles.

Notwithstanding the above explanation of my membership roles, I recognized the limitations of my active insider presence. Thus, in many instances I was able to supplement my direct observations with cassette recordings of public services. Some of these tapes were transcribed for further analysis. Extensive field notes of this period of participant observation were generated. In my field notes, I analyzed my membership role in the field and recorded my observations or recollections of experiences. Separate from my observations, I recorded my comments that included several categories of rudimentary analysis: reflecting on the relationship between my observations and my research questions; reframing of my questions during the course of field research; suggesting tentative connections between interpretations of my observations with theoretical concepts from the various streams of literature; and adjusting the directions of my research by articulating emerging questions to explore in subsequent times of observation, interviews, or document analysis.

Following this stage of gaining first-hand knowledge of these settings as a participant observer, I conducted taped semi-structured "active interviews" with lay leaders, the presiding elder, pastors, and the bishop. In using the term, "active interview" I am emphasizing the active social construction of meanings that take place between the person(s) interviewed and the interviewer.[9] The purpose of these interviews was to probe the meanings of experiences that I had observed, to ask them about things that I needed to understand, and to test out my emerging ideas.

My basic selection criterion for laity was that they be "wise" church leaders with attention to their ability to represent different perspectives of pastoral leadership. The persons selected spanned three generations of church membership. Because of the size of Christopher Temple and the pastor's leadership style, I solicited Rev. Harrison's assistance in the selection of persons who could ably represent the following perspectives: the pastor's wife who sees both the private and public dimensions of the pastor over time; a young adult who represented persons groomed through active participation in youth ministries; a matriarch who had done a lot of "kitchen work" down through the years; a leader of the men's ministry representing their efforts "to reclaim men for family, church, and community"; a church officer who worked closely with the pastor in carrying out the business of the church; and an associate minister who was selected to represent the pastor's interactions with ministerial staff.

Because of the smaller size of Isaiah-Matthews, it was easier to select active leaders of the congregation and arrange for an interview with them at the church or in their homes. In several instances, I experimented with interviewing multiple respondents at Isaiah-Matthews in one interview, a husband and wife, even when the spouse/partner may not have been very active. This different sampling strategy was chosen because I wanted to probe gender perspectives on pastoral leadership at Isaiah-Matthews. I conducted six interviews of church leaders at each of the churches.

In my selection of lay leaders, all of whom are in formal positions of church leadership, I acknowledge a potential bias in my data. Alternative perspectives of persons who stand outside of the leadership are not present in my taped interviews. The possibility exists that persons interviewed may follow a degree of "consensual knowledge"[10] as espoused by their pastor who in fact nominates them to formal positions of leadership. The potential bias in my taped interviews is offset to some degree by my conversations with youth of the church as well as the unsolicited comments of members as well as public officials (visiting Christopher Temple).

Though I began my study (originally titled, "Pastoral leadership in the Black Methodist Church") with the idea of choosing male and female clergy of the AME, AME Zion, and CME Church another comparative strategy, I decided to concentrate my clergy selections within the CME Church. Hence, interviews with the two CME pastors, their presiding elder, and their bishop allowed me to compare reflections from my direct observation with their insights. Interviews with AME and AME Zion ministers as well as the CME associate minister selected by Rev. Harrison were nonetheless helpful.

All of the interviews were transcribed. A copy of the transcript was sent to each respondent offering them the opportunity to edit the transcript or not use portions of the transcript in future publications. The nineteen taped interviews were coded using Ethnograph 5.08, a qualitative analysis software program. This computer program allowed me not only to code my data with respect to themes that I noticed in the interviews, but also assisted in multiple text management functions including attaching analytic memos to texts, building conceptual models of categories of codes, comparing and contrasting data from the two research sites, and selecting illustrative material for the story line that I created.

Though I obtained a number of congregational documents during the course of my field research (e.g., church bulletins, Bible study lessons, cassette tapes of selected worship services, literature available on racks, tables, or in the pews, as well as handout materials for church meetings), I created a list of documents not readily available to me after the close of my participant observation stage of research. The list of documents that I requested focused on the slice of congregational history relating to the pastoral tenure of Rev. Harrison and Dr. Evans with particular concentration on the current conference year.[11] These documents included church budgets, conference reports, conference minutes, church calendars, annual statistical reports, membership data, congregational histories, and a copy of Dr. Evans's doctor of ministry project.

Census data on the church community area and other secondary ecological studies of the communities in their metropolitan context were also reviewed. I completed my last interviews in August 2001. Thus, the period of my field research spanned more than a year, including my participation in the summer 2000 annual conference, my six months observing the pastors in the two conversations, my taped interviews, and gathering of congregational documents.

Writing

The goal of this research is to define and share practical wisdom that will be useful to pastors, lay leaders, and denominational leaders in their efforts to develop ministries that transform individuals and communities in a complex black urban context. In my writing, I have attempted to create a dialogue between the particular situations of leadership in my research sites and some of the larger questions that impact the praxis of pastoral leadership in the black church. My hope is that this will suggest transformative practices, principles, and processes for their own ministries. A story line was created for each research site placing my primary materials within selected frameworks, hopefully enabling my readers to see the familiar struggles of the black church in new and insightful ways. The story lines were created to advance my own emerging theories of transformation. In the tradition of grounded theory, these theories are offered in the form of thick descriptions as well as useful explanations.

I am aware of the fact that my representations of pastoral leadership are my own constructions of a complex social reality. Of this art Van Maanen writes:

> Ethnographic writing is anything but a straightforward, unproblematic descriptive or interpretive task based on an assumed Doctrine of Immaculate Perception. Rather, ethnographic writing of any kind is a complex matter, dependent on an uncountable number of strategic choices and active constructions (e.g. what details to include or omit; how to summarize and present data; what voice to select; what quotations to use).[12]

In my efforts to construct accurate and insightful ethnographic representations of pastoral leadership in the context of these faith communities, I have made strategic rhetorical choices to advance my arguments. Recognizing this problematic, the discerning reader is invited to judge the merits of my writing. If the product is deemed accurate, insightful, and useful, then my labor will not be in vain.

Appendix B: Clergy Interviews

Interview Number/ Pseudonym	Clergy Office (Denomination)	Age/ Gender	Education	Non-Church Occupation	Years in Traveling Ministry
C1 Rev. Benjamin Richards	Pastor (AME)	39/ Male	B.S., M.Div., Ph.D. Cand.	Seminary-Faculty	6
C2 Rev. Michael Linton	Pastor (AME Zion)	34/ Male	B.A., M.Div. in Progress	None	14
C3 Bishop James Norman	Bishop (AME Zion)	63/ Male	B.S., M.Ed., M.Div., D.Min.	None	35
C4 Rev. Walter Harrison	Pastor (CME)	52/ Male	B.A., M.Div., Hon. Doctorate	None	33
C5 Rev. Carl Gentry	Associate Minister (CME)	46/ Male	A.A., B.S., Masters Human Services/ Counseling	Banker	2
C6 Rev. Coleman Crider	Presiding Elder (CME)	70/ Male	B.S., Master of Theology	None	41
C7 Rev. Carol Evans	Pastor (CME)	55/ Female	B.A., M.Div., D.Min.	Director Social Services	7
C8 Bishop Isaiah Douglas	Bishop (CME)	70/ Male	B.S., Masters, Christian Ed., M.Div., Hon. Doctorate	None	44

Appendix C: Lay Leader Interviews

Interview Number/ Pseudonym	Church Membership Years as Methodist	Age/ Gender	Education	Occupation	Church Involvement
L1/ Mrs. Mary Duncan	Isaiah-Matthews/1	43/ Female	LPN/2 years of college	Administrative Assistant	Director of Christian Education
L2/[a] Mrs. Penny Aikens	Isaiah-Matthews/8	48/ Female	B.S., 2 years toward Masters	Registered Nurse	Steward Board; Missionary Society; Recording Secretary of Congregation
L3/[a] Mr. Bob Aikens	Isaiah-Matthews/50	50/ Male	B.S., Technical Institute	Self-Employed	Usher, Trustee
L4/ Mrs. Cynthia Walker-Simpson	Christopher Temple/29	29/ Female	B.S., Industrial Engineering; J.D.	Banker	*Former* Youth President, Youth Usher Board, Youth Choir, Youth Missionary; *Current* Chair, College Ministry; Member of Board of Christian Education
L5/ Mrs. Janice Parker	Christopher Temple/61	61/ Female	B.S., M.S., Advanced Courses	Retired Educator	Steward; Missionary; Board of Christian

Continued

Appendix Continued

Interview Number/ Pseudonym	Church Membership Years as Methodist	Age/ Gender	Education	Occupation	Church Involvement
					Education; One Church One School; Church Treasurer
L6/ Mrs. Cora Nolan	Christopher Temple/ 81	81/ Female	Tenth Grade	Housewife	Commission on Evangelism; Friendship Club; Prayer Group; Board of Christian Education; Stewardess; District Stewardess; Volunteer, One Church One School
L7/ Michael Evans	Isaiah-Matthews/7	33/ Male	B.S.	Technician	Chairman, Trustee Board; Audio-Visual Ministry
L8/ Mr. Guy Roberson	Christopher/ Temple/20	50/ Male	B.S.	General Contractor	President, Christian Methodist Men; Trustee; Choir Member
L9/[a] Ms. Mona Daniels	Isaiah-Matthews/ 9 months	49/ Female	Associates	Nursing Supervisor/ Legal Nurse Consultant	Steward, Missionary
L10/[a] Mr. Jack Ransom	Isaiah-Matthews/1	50/ Male	3 Years College, School	Computer Information Trade Services	Lay Leader, Trustee
L11/[a] Mrs. Wendy Sanders	Isaiah-Matthews/4	54/ Female	High School	Data Entry Operator	Chief Steward

Continued

Appendix Continued

Interview Number/ Pseudonym	Church Membership Years as Methodist	Age/ Gender	Education	Occupation	Church Involvement
L12/[a] Mr. Israel Sanders	Isaiah-Matthews/3	48/ Male	High School	Contractor	Trustee
L13/ Mrs. Constance Harrison	Christopher Temple	57/ Female	2 years of college	Business Administration/ Secretarial	*Former* Church Secretary of Pastors Wives; *Present* New Members Ministry, Consultant to Youth Department, Women's Ministry, Ministry of Encouragement, District Ministers' Spouses and Widows
L14/[a] Mr. Manford Billings	Isaiah-Matthews/ 80	80/ Male	1 year of college	Retired Janitor	*Former* Class Leader, Superintendent of Sunday School, Steward, Trustee *Presently* Class Leader
L15/[a] Mrs. Coretta Billings	Isaiah-Matthews/ 25	69/ Female	High School Graduate	Retired Machine Operator	*Former* Sunday School Teacher, Usher, Choir *Present* Stewardess

Note: [a] Some Interviews were conducted with male and female couples: L2 and L3, L9 and L10, L11 and L12, and L14 and L15 with the aim of stimulating conversation between the couple on the question of unique struggles of having a female pastor at Isaiah-Matthews.

Appendix D: Community Census Data

Community Areas of Christopher Temple: Middleton and Newton

Middleton[1]

Population

Total Population	37,275
White	157
Black or African American	36,648

Housing

Total Occupied Housing Units	15,717
Percent Owner Occupied Homes	6,481

Educational Attainment

Percent High School Graduate and Higher	77.9
Percent Bachelor's Degree and Higher	19.0

Employment

Unemployment Rate (% of Civilian Labor Force)	13.0
Mean Travel Time to Work (minutes)[2]	41.2

Poverty

Percent Families Living in Poverty	14.6

Income

Median Family Income	38,286

Newton

Population

Total Population	38,619
White	169
Black or African American	37,952

Housing

Total Occupied Housing Units	14,383
Percent Owner Occupied Homes	5,265

Continued

Appendix Continued

Educational attainment	
Percent High School Graduate and Higher	74.7
Percent Bachelor's Degree and Higher	12.4
Employment	
Unemployment Rate (% of Civilian Labor Force)	18.6
Mean Travel Time to Work (minutes)	43.3
Poverty	
Percent Families Living in Poverty	25.5
Income	
Median Family Income	31,951

Selected Neighborhood Characteristics Pioneer Park, Community Area of Isaiah-Matthews Census 2000 Data

Population	
Total Population	28,006
White	182
Black or African American[3]	27,502
Housing	
Total Occupied Housing Units	9,983
Percent Owner Occupied Homes	1,343
Educational Attainment	
Percent High School Graduate and Higher	61.4
Percent Bachelor's Degree and Higher	9.9
Employment	
Unemployment Rate (% of Civilian Labor Force)	24.4
Mean Travel Time to Work	37.4
Poverty	
Percent Families Living in Poverty[4]	43.8
Income	
Median Family Income	18,159

Notes

Introduction

1. The metaphor of "life support system" may evoke for some persons (reading through the lenses of their church experiences) the idea that financially strapped local churches have often been sustained by the generous infusion of denominational funds for expenses such as minimum pastor's salary and benefits, maintenance of aging buildings, and support of vital community ministries. In harsh economic times, denominations that do this have experienced dwindling resources for this kind of support. Denominational officials in Methodist polities have the power to close or merge struggling churches. In the case of the CME Church and other black-controlled Methodist denominations, there has never been long-term denominational support for crucial items such as minimum salary and health benefits. As a condition for my critical research into the strengths and weaknesses of the ministry of pastoral leaders working in their denominational systems, I agreed to use pseudonyms for the names of living leaders (clergy and laity) of the CME Church, the name of the annual conference, the names of the congregations, and the locations of the churches.
2. This delay was necessitated by my obtaining formal approval for my research to proceed at Christopher Temple and Isaiah-Matthews by the Northwestern University Institutional Review Board. My visit to the Tri-State Annual Conference though valuable from the standpoint of framing my questions was not a formal part of my research protocol.
3. Rick Warren, *The Purpose Driven Church: Growth Without Compromising Your Message and Mission* (Grand Rapids, MI: Zondervan Publishing House, 1995), 31.

I   The Quest for Transformative Pastoral Leadership in the Black Church

1. <http://www.tavistalks.com/CONTENT/Tavis Smiley Presents>
2. In my usage of the term, black church, I am following the operational definition of Lincoln and Mamiya. They write, "We use the term 'the Black Church' as do other scholars and much of the general public as a kind of sociological and

theological shorthand reference to the pluralism of black Christian churches in the United States. . . . In this study, however, while we recognize that there are predominantly black local churches in White denominations such as the United Methodist Church, the Episcopal Church, and the Roman Catholic Church, we chose to limit our operational definition of 'the Black Church' to those independent, historic, and totally black controlled denominations, which were founded after the Free African Society of 1787 and which constituted the core of black Christians." C. Eric Lincoln and Lawrence H. Mamiya, *The Black Church in the African American Experience* (Durham, NC: Duke University Press, 1990), 1.

3. Tavis Smiley Presents. Listed Panelists for the morning and afternoon sessions included the following: Michael Eric Dyson, Gardner Taylor, Floyd Flake, Eugene Rivers, Noel Jones, Paul Morton, Jeremiah Wright, Barbara King, Vashti McKenzie, James Cone, Cheryl Townsend Gilkes, Jacquelyn Grant, Marvin Winans, Cornel West, William Shaw, James Forbes, Cain Hope Felder, Jamal-Harrison Bryant, Carlton Pearson, Frederick Haynes, Johnnie Coleman, Marcia Dyson, Al Sharpton, Iva Carruthers, Carolyn Knight, and Charles Adams.

4. In this image of a community of "knowers," I am borrowing from an image of a "community of truth" explicated by Parker Palmer. He first describes what he calls "the objectivist myth" in which there is an "object" of knowledge that is grasped conceptually by "experts" who are better able to discern pure knowledge than "amateurs" who do not contribute to our understanding of truth because of their lack of training and subjective biases. In this view, truth flows from the experts qualified to grasp truth to amateurs who are only able to receive truth. Palmer rejects this model and proposes instead the image of a community of truth in which the subject, not the expert, is the center of our attention. "Knowers" in this community—who, in fact may be in communities separated by time, space, and disciplines—are willing to be guided by shared rules of observation and interpretation. In my study, the voice of those with limited formal schooling as well as of scholars is included in this "community of truth." Parker J. Palmer, *The Courage to Teach: Exploring the Inner Landscape of a Teacher's Life* (San Francisco: Jossey-Bass Publishers, 1998), 99–106.

5. Cheryl Townsend Gilkes, *"If It Wasn't for the Women . . ." Black Women's Experience and Womanist Culture in Church and Community* (Maryknoll, NY: Orbis Books, 2001), 1–6.

6. James MacGregor Burns, *Leadership* (New York: Harper and Row Publishers, 1978).

7. Robert M. Franklin, *Another Day's Journey: Black Churches Confronting the American Crisis* (Minneapolis: Fortress Press, 1997), 119–124.

8. W. E. Burghardt Du Bois, ed., *The Negro Church* (Atlanta: Atlanta University Press, 1903; reprint, New York: Octagon Books, Inc., 1968), 194.

9. C. Eric Lincoln argues that "the Negro Church" died during the turbulence of the 1960s and gave birth to the black church. The black church, then, is a term representing the full personhood of blacks and acceptance of the Christian responsibilities of being an instrument and not merely a symbol of the freedom of African Americans. E. Franklin Frazier, *The Negro Church in America*,

1963, new edition with C. Eric Lincoln, *The Black Church Since Frazier* (New York: Schocken Books, 1974), 103–110.

10. Lincoln and Mamiya, *The Black Church in the African American Experience*, 7–10.

11. Ibid., 274–308.

12. See especially sociological research of black church in the black community from the outset of the twentieth century to the present: W. E. B. Dubois, *The Negro Church* (1903); Benjamin Elijah Mays and Joseph William Nicholson, *The Negro's Church* (New York: Negro Universities Press, 1933). (Reprint, Greenwood, 1969); Aldon Morris, *The Origins of the Civil Rights Movement: Black Communities Organizing for Change* (New York: The Free Press, A Division of Macmillan, Inc., 1984); Lincoln and Mamiya, *The Black Church in the African American Experience* (1990); Cheryl Townsend Gilkes, "Plenty Good Room: Adaptation in a Changing Black Church," *The Annals of the American Academy, AAPSS*, 558, July 1998; Mary Pattillo-McCoy, "Church Culture as a Strategy of Action in the Black Community," *American Sociological Review*, vol. 63 (December 1998): 767–784; and Andrew Billingsley, *Mighty Like a River: The Black Church and Social Reform* (New York: Oxford University Press, 1999).

13. Lincoln and Mamiya, *The Black Church in the African American Experience*, 9–10.

14. W. E. Burghardt Du Bois, *The Gift of Black Folk: The Negroes in the Making of America* (Boston: The Stratford Co., 1924; reprint, New York: Johnson Reprint Corporation, 1968), 272.

15. Ibid., 260.

16. Ibid.

17. Ibid., 262–264.

18. Ibid., 270–272.

19. Ibid., 273.

20. Cheryl Townsend Gilkes speaking at a conference titled, "The Quest for Transformative Pastoral Leadership in the Black Church" sponsored by the Center for the Church and the Black Experience at Garrett-Evangelical Theological Seminary, Evanston, Illinois, February 21, 2004.

21. Gilkes, "*If It Wasn't for the Women . . .*," 4.

22. Ibid., 6–7.

23. Lincoln and Mamiya, *The Black Church in the African American Experience*, 12.

24. Lyle E. Schaller, *Discontinuity and Hope: Radical Change and the Path to the Future* (Nashville: Abingdon Press, 1999), 193–194.

25. Dale P. Andrews, *Practical Theology for Black Churches: Bridging Black Theology and African American Folk Religion* (Louisville: Westminster John Knox Press, 2002), 65.

26. James P. Martin, "Toward a Post-Critical Paradigm," *New Testament Studies*, vol. 33 (1987): 378, quoted in David Bosch, *Transforming Mission: Paradigm Shifts in Theology of Mission*, American Society of Missiology Series, No. 16 (Maryknoll, NY: Orbis Books, 1991), 189.

27. Bosch, *Transforming Mission*, 189.

28. Maria Harris, *Fashion Me a People: Curriculum in the Church* (Louisville: Westminster John Knox Press, 1989), 24.

29. Carlyle Fielding Stewart III, *The Empowerment Church: Speaking a New Language for Church Growth* (Nashville: Abingdon Press, 2001), 71–85.

30. Ibid., 87–103.

31. One way that clergy assert their power over and above the laity is by declaring, "God gives the vision to the pastor and not to the laity." I believe that discovering God's vision for the church requires both clergy and a group of laity, rooted in their relationship with God, to come together in a strategic vision planning process. The vision emerges out of dialogue with persons in the church and community. It articulates for a specific period in time, not what the church exists to do in general (a mission statement), but directions, strategies, and objectives that the church will pursue in the next three to five years. Even in the Methodist system of itinerant ministry, a vision should be written down so that the success of the vision is not predicated on that particular pastor continuing to serve the church. Stewart has a helpful discussion on developing and implementing a vision plan in an itinerant context. See Stewart, *Empowerment Church*, 75–80.

32. Thomas Edward Frank, *The Soul of the Congregation: An Invitation to Congregational Reflection* (Nashville: Abingdon Press, 2000), 23.

33. Frank argues that pastors and others set apart for ministry need to cultivate an "ethnographic disposition." This is not to say that they must be ethnographers, but that they cultivate a disciplined way of observation, description, exploration, and working so that they work by the light of "local knowledge" and discover "openings for ministry." Frank, *Soul of Congregation*, 169).

34. Scott J. Jones, *The Evangelistic Love of God and Neighbor: A Theology of Witness and Discipleship* (Nashville: Abingdon Press, 2003), 114–118.

35. James C. Logan, "The Evangelical Imperative: A Wesleyan Perspective" in *Theology and Evangelism in the Wesleyan Heritage* (Nashville: Kingswood Books, 1993), 15–33. See also the critical retrieval of Wesleyan fundamental traits of evangelism and practical spirituality in the work of the black United Methodist pastor, Carlyle Fielding Stewart III (Stewart, *Empowerment Church*, 47–55). According to Stewart, these fundamental traits are Bible literacy, conversion experiences, evangelical outreach, cultural fluency, spiritual discipline, and prophetic consciousness (Stewart, *Empowerment Church*, 48).

36. In my use of Thomas Groome's notion of shared Christian praxis, I am attempting to conceive of particular ways in which ethnography can be construed as an educational ministry in partnership with persons who are not merely research "subjects." Those persons who give consent to congregational research are individual agents operating with various capacities of freedom within their relationship to social structures. As Groome notes, the term "shared" denotes an approach "as one of mutuality, active participation, and dialogue with oneself, with others, with God, and with Story/Vision of Christian faith" (142). By working towards the ideal of an explicit hermeneutical dialogue, I attempt to do this in this study. In other instances, the interests of those agent-subjects must be explicitly included in the research relationship. Thomas H. Groome, *Sharing Faith: A Comprehensive Approach to Religious*

Education and Pastoral Ministry, The Way of Shared Praxis (New York: HarperCollins Publishers, 1991), 142.

37. In my use of the term, "praxis" I am drawing upon Groome's expansion of Aristotle's use of the term, which was limited to public political activity. Whereas Aristotle saw *theoria* (the contemplative life of speculative theory), *praxis* (the practical life of purposeful and reflective action), and *poiesis* (the productive imaginative life of creativity) as three separate ways of knowing and living, Groome subsumes all of these concepts under what he proposes is a more comprehensive way of understanding praxis. Thus, praxis is active, reflective, and creative, a way of engaging the world imaginatively, holding in dialectic unity theory and practice. Groome, *Sharing Faith*, 135–145. I was particularly conscious of this dialogue between theory and practice of ministry in my second appointment in which I was simultaneously engaged in Ph.D. courses in religion and theology. I believe that my engagement as a pastor provided a fertile set of experiences for theological reflection in the classroom. At the same time, I believe that my congregation benefited to some degree from theories from my studies that I tried to put into practice.

38. William J. Walls, *The African Methodist Episcopal Zion Church: Reality of the Black Church* (Charlotte, NC: A.M.E. Zion Publishing House, 1974), 111.

39. Ibid.

40. Franklin, *Another Day's Journey*, 62–67.

41. Acts 5: 38–39 NRSV.

42. Vashti M. McKenzie, *Not Without a Struggle: Leadership Development for African-American Women in Ministry* (Cleveland, OH: United Church Press, 1996).

43. In qualitative research, personal and professional experiences can be sources for research questions as well as for cultivating theoretical sensitivity to a topic. Anselm Strauss and Juliet Corbin, *Basics of Qualitative Research, Grounded Theory Procedures and Techniques* (Newbury Park: Sage Publications, 1990), 33–43.

44. Don S. Browning, "Congregational Studies as Practical Theology" in *American Congregations, Volume 2: New Perspectives in the Study of Congregations*, ed., James Wind and James W. Lewis (Chicago: The University of Chicago Press, 1994), 192–221.

45. In her argument that the contemporary black church is a product of the social movements of the 1960s, Gilkes theorizes that new pastors influenced by the civil rights movements and black power generation consciousness were capable of transforming traditional "silk stocking" churches and drawing many new members precisely because of their ability to transform their churches wisely applying the critical lessons of these social movements (Gilkes, "Plenty Good Room," 107). Morris argues that the black church has been a key institution for transmitting the protest tradition, the black community's response to a context of racial oppression. Utilizing Max Weber's theory of charismatic movements, he analyzes his interviews of civil rights leaders revealing qualities for effective pastoral leadership in the black church and the black community as well as the sources for that development. His analysis provides theories of the qualities, practices, aptitudes, and kinds

of education and preparation existing in transformative pastoral leadership in the black church (Morris, *Origins of the Civil Rights Movement*, 7–12).

46. Gilkes identifies a pattern of women, like Dr. Evans, who formerly functioned as "highly visible church workers who functioned as leaders of the female infrastructure that was the proverbial backbone of the church" discovering new callings as pastors independent of husbands (Gilkes, "Plenty Good Room," 112).

47. Through grounded research of Bethel AME Church in Baltimore led at the time by Rev. John Bryant, now elevated to the episcopacy, Lawrence Mamiya identifies what he calls the rise of a Neo-Pentecostal movement within the black Methodist churches. This movement reclaims the theological emphasis on the necessity of the work of the Holy Spirit and charismatic expression in worship combined with progressive social outreach. According to Bryant, this approach overcomes the typical emphasis on one side of the dialectic of a traditional Pentecostal tradition that has little or no involvement in the world and the traditional liberal churches which have many social ministries, yet are empty on Sunday mornings as their worship lacks emphasis on praise and the Holy Spirit. Lawrence Mamiya, "A Social History of the Bethel African Methodist Episcopal Church in Baltimore: The House of God and the Struggle for Freedom" in *American Congregations: Volume 1 Portraits of Twelve Religious Communities*, ed., James P. Wind and James W. Lewis (Chicago: The University of Chicago Press, 1994). From my perspective, people raised in Pentecostal traditions such as Dr. Evans are helping to foster this movement in black Methodism.

2   "God Did It": A Tale of a Male Pastor in a Transforming Traditional Church

1. Middleton is a fictional name for the middle-class black community area surrounding Christopher Temple. However, real census data for the community area is in appendix D: Community Census Data.

2. The classic religious and secular interests of black church find their roots in the Free African mutual aid societies of African Methodism, founded by Absalom Jones and Richard Allen in 1787. Gayraud S. Wilmore, *Black Religion and Black Radicalism: An Interpretation of the Religious History of African Americans*, 3rd. ed., rev. and enl. (Maryknoll, NY: Orbis Books, 1998), 108.

3. This black pastor is not alone in his belief that community economic development is a critical missional response for systemic disinvestments in racially segregated communities. According to the Hartford Institute for Religion Research, "African American churches were more than three times as likely (22% v 6% in other traditions) to name a local economic development group as a partner. While the idea of 'community development corporations' is getting a good deal of attention these days, it is the rare congregation that has taken on this sort of economic partnership." Hartford Institute for Religion Research, Hartford Seminary, Nancy T. Ammerman, project director, *Doing Good in Chicago: Congregations and Service Organizations Building the*

Community, A Research Report from the Organizing Religious Work Project, (Hartford: Hartford Institute for Religion Research, 2001), 16–17.

4. The One Church One School Program is a model of ministry adopted by the CME General Conference in 1994. A fact sheet on this program says: "The vision of One Church One School is that every school in America will be in partnership with one or more neighboring churches to improve the academic achievement, social behavior, and personal development of children and youth. . . . In 1992, Rev. Dr. Henry M. Williamson, Sr., the founder and National President, officially launched the One Church One School Partnership Program in Chicago Illinois and Gary, Indiana. Today, those cities have district wide initiatives and the OCOS network stretches across twenty states and forty cities, containing more than two hundred partnerships that impact thousands of students."

5. Othal Hawthorne Lakey, *The History of the Christian Methodist Episcopal Church*, rev. (Memphis, TN: The C.M.E. Publishing House, 1996), 286–295.

6. Ted A. Campbell, *Methodist Doctrine: The Essentials* (Nashville: Abingdon Press, 1999), 66–67.

7. Ibid., 67–68.

8. John Maxwell, *The 21 Most Powerful Minutes in a Leader's Day: Revitalize Your Spirit and Empower Your Leadership* (Nashville: Thomas Nelson Publishers, 2000), 299.

9. Luke 22:24–27.

10. Bishops, a higher degree of elders, also itinerate. In the CME Church, they are appointed by to their episcopal districts by their General Conference, the highest governing body, which meets every four years. Each episcopal district covers a geographical area comprised of the churches and pastors in that area. Currently, CME bishops are not appointed to the same district for more than eight consecutive years. Christian Methodist Episcopal Church, *The Book of Discipline of the Christian Methodist Episcopal Church* (Memphis, TN: The C.M.E. Publishing House, 1998), 115.

11. John H. Miller, Sr., *Trustees and Stewards: The Continuing Power Struggle* (Charlotte, NC: A.M.E. Zion Publishing House, 1973), ii–iii.

12. Laurent A. Daloz, *Mentor: Guiding the Journey of Adult Learners*, Second Edition of *Effective Teaching and Mentoring* (San Francisco: Jossey-Bass Publishers, 1999), 31.

13. A person called a "father in the ministry" may be the minister (usually the pastor) who was instrumental in helping someone discern his/her call to the preaching ministry. Furthermore, the "father in ministry" cares for or looks after the younger minister as a father might. Similarly, women pastors in ministry may be called, by young ministers, "a mother in the ministry."

14. One of the few exceptions of using the real name of this deceased national leader of the CME Church, whose reputation is not harmed by this reference.

15. K. Patricia Cross, Foreword in Daloz, *Mentor*, xi.

16. Daloz, *Mentor*, 20–22.

17. Of necessity, many CME preachers and other black preachers work at vocations other than their ministries. Devoting a portion of their time to preaching and other pastoral duties after fulfilling workday obligations, the

"Sunday Preacher" tradition has developed and remains, particularly in rural area appointments. Others, whose preaching gifts and leadership skills gave them opportunity of pastoring self-sustaining churches, formed a tradition of giving leadership to both the church and race. Lakey, *History of the Christian Methodist Episcopal Church*, 287–289.

18. Joseph A. Johnson, Jr., *The Soul of the Black Preacher* (Philadelphia: Pilgrim Press, 1971), 87–88.
19. Daloz, *Mentor*, 182–184.
20. Ibid., 184.
21. Gilkes, "Plenty Good Room," 107.
22. Lincoln and Mamiya, *The Black Church in the African American Experience*, 10–16. I agree with Lincoln that another dialectic is being introduced today, that of "race versus racelessness." In the past, one drop of African blood made a person "black" in this country; but with the rise of *The Tiger Woods Syndrome*, the child with a mixed racial–ethnic background does not define himself or herself as "black" based on the race of one parent. With growing racial and ethnic intermarriages, previously understood racial definitions, racial policies, and racial politics are threatened. C. Eric Lincoln, introduction to *Mighty Like A River*, xxiv.
23. Mary Pattillo-McCoy, "Church Culture as a Strategy of Action in the Black Community," 767–784.
24. Fredrick C. Harris, *Something Within: Religion in African-American Politics* (Ph.D. diss., Northwestern University, Evanston, 1994).
25. Vincent L. Wimbush, "The Bible and African Americans: An Outline of an Interpretive History" in *Stony the Road We Trod: African American Biblical Interpretation*, ed., Cain Hope Felder (Minneapolis: Fortress Press, 1991), 91.
26. Livingstone College is a liberal arts college founded by and supported by the AME Zion Church in Salisbury, North Carolina; Miles College is a college founded and supported by the C.M.E Church in Birmingham, Alabama; Lane College is a college founded by and supported by the CME Church in Jackson, Tennessee; Howard University, founded by the Freedman's Bureau in 1863, is a predominantly black university in Washington, DC; Spellman College, a black college for women in Atlanta, Georgia.
27. Cornel West, *Race Matters* (New York: Vantage Books, 1994), 56.

3 "God of a Second Chance": A Tale of a Female Pastor in a Transforming Merged Mission Church

1. Chicago Fact Book Consortium, *Local Community Fact Book Chicago Metropolitan Area 1990* (Chicago: Department of Sociology, University of Illinois at Chicago, 1990), 129.
2. This quality of knowing how to adapt one's speech depending on the context is not peculiar to black preachers, of course. Explaining the importance of noting such patterns while studying indigenous black communities,

Pattillo-McCoy notes that "code switching" is characteristic of the black middle class that has to navigate the different worlds that blacks and whites live in. Mary Pattillo-McCoy, *Black Picket Fences, Privilege and Peril among the Black Middle Class* (Chicago: The University of Chicago Press, 1999), 9.

3. Othal Hawthorne Lakey and Betty Beene Stephens, *God in My Mama's House: A Study of the Women's Movement in the C.M.E. Church* (Memphis, TN: The C.M.E. Publishing House, 1994), 44.

4. Ibid., 45–66.

5. Ibid., 60–66.

6. Ibid., 183.

7. Ibid.

8. Lakey, *History of the Christian Methodist Episcopal Church*, 663.

9. McKenzie asserts that despite evidence of the history of eighteenth- and nineteenth-century black women responding their call to ministry, the AME Church and other black denominational churches are just beginning to address sexism as a serious concern. Vashti M. McKenzie, *Not Without a Struggle*, xvi.

10. McKenzie, *Not Without a Struggle*, 71.

11. Ibid., 70.

12. Ibid., 71–72.

13. I Cori. 12: 7–11 is one key passage that persons use to explain their belief in and operation in the "supernatural gifts of the spirit." Others do not see the "word of knowledge" as knowledge that is revealed by the Spirit of God; the gift of knowledge is the fruit of one's research.

14. James Hopewell was one of the first researchers in congregational studies to emphasize congregational identity or culture in the service of practical theology. From his training in comparative religion, he studied congregations in the manner of an anthropologist discovering unique congregational cultures that he argued were identified by the structural logic of narrative. The editor, Barbara G. Wheeler writes in her foreword: "As congregations first come into being, Hopewell argued, they construct a narrative that accounts for their nascent identity. They attract to their fellowship those who want to participate in the local drama enacted there. They maintain their integrity against incursions by reiterating their distinct local story. And, they encounter the world by identifying similarities between its stories and their own." Barbara G. Wheeler, Editor's Foreword in *Congregation: Stories and Structures*, by James Hopewell (Philadelphia: Fortress Press, 1987), xii.

15. McKenzie, *Not Without a Struggle*, 35.

16. Russell Ackoff, "The Future of Operational Research Is Past," *Journal of Operational Research Society*, vol. 30, no. 2 (1979): 90–100, quoted in Jackson W. Carroll, "Leadership and the Study of the Congregation" in *Studying Congregations: A New Handbook*, ed., Ammerman et al. (Nashville: Abingdon Press, 1998), 169.

17. Jon R. Katzenbach and Douglas K. Smith, *The Wisdom of Teams: Creating the High-Performance Organization* (Boston: Harvard Business School Press, 1993), 138–139.

18. Mal. 3: 7–12.

19. The UMC utilizes local pastor–parish relations committees as a part of the appointment process. Congregational leaders profile the congregation and give input to the bishop's cabinet sharing what they feel the congregation requires in a pastor based on the direction of the church's ministry.

20. Presiding Elder Crider confirms that it would not be unusual that, at the discretion of a presiding bishop, this two-year college requirement be waived if "an equivalent is established provided it involves actual classroom experience acceptable to our church in doctrine and polity." *The Book of Discipline of the Christian Methodist Episcopal Church*, paragraph 420.2.

21. Ronald A. Heifetz, *Leadership Without Easy Answers* (Cambridge: The Belknap Press of Harvard University Press, 1994), 1–9.

22. McKenzie, *Not Without a Struggle*, 112.

23. Laurent A. Parks Daloz, Cheryl H. Keen, James P. Keen, and Sharon Daloz Parks, *Common Fire: Leading Lives of Commitment in a Complex World* (Boston: Beacon Press, 1996), 5–6.

24. Ibid., 190.

25. Ibid.

26. Ibid.

27. 2 Tim. 2: 3–6.

28. Daloz, Keen, Keen, and Parks indicate that people of color, especially African Americans, seemed to pay a heavier price for their commitment. Their follow-up interviews indicated a disproportionate number of persons suffering from strokes, cancer, and death since their earlier interviews. They indicate two possible reasons for this: suffering "less adequate health care" as disadvantaged minorities and what Katie Canon has called the "loneliness" and "pain" that comes from living as a bridge between the black community and larger society, constantly translating between them. Daloz, Keen, Keen, and Parks, *Common Fire*, 175.

29. Ibid., 174–177.

30. Ibid., 186.

31. The term, womanist, was first suggested by Alice Walker and is derived from how the word, "womanish," used in the black community. Walker writes: "Womanist, from womanish. (Opp. of 'girlish,' i.e., frivolous, irresponsible, not serious.) A black feminist or feminist of color. From the black folk expression of mothers to female children, 'You acting womanish,' i.e., like a woman. Usually referring to outrageous, audacious, courageous, or willful behavior. Wanting to know more and in greater depth that is consider 'good' for one. Interest in doing grown-up doings. Acting grown up. Being grown up. Interchangeable with another black folk expression: 'You trying to be grown.' Responsible. In charge. Serious." Alice Walker, *In Search of Our Mothers' Gardens* (San Diego: Harcourt Brace Janovich, 1983), xi.

32. McKenzie, *Not Without a Struggle*, 49–50.

33. Renita J. Weems, "Reading *Her Way* through the Struggle: African American Women and the Bible," in *Stony the Road We Trod: African American Biblical Interpretation*, ed., Cain Hope Felder (Minneapolis: Fortress Press, 1991), 57.

34. Ibid.

35. Ibid., 76–77.
36. Jacquelyn Grant, "Womanist Theology: Black Women's Experience as a Source for Doing Theology, with Special Reference to Christology" in *Black Theology, A Documentary History Volume Two: 1980–1992*, ed., James H. Cone and Gayraud S. Wilmore (Maryknoll, NY: Orbis Books, 1993), 278.

4   Emerging Strategies of Transformative Pastoral Leadership in the Black Church

1. Nancy Tatom Ammerman, *Congregation and Community* with Arthur E. Farnsley II and Tammy Adams, Penny Edgell Becker, Brenda Brasher, Thomas Clark, Joan Cunningham, Nancy Eiseland, Barbara Elwell, Michelle Hale, Diana Jones, Virginia Laffey, Stacey Nicholas, Marcia Robinson, Mary Beth Stevens, Daphne Wiggins, Connie Ziegler (New Brunswick, NJ: Rutgers University Press, 1997), 45.
2. Lowell W. Livezey, "The New Context of Urban Religion" in *Public Religion and Urban Transformation: Faith in the City*, ed., Lowell W. Livezey, 1–25. Religion, Race, and Ethnicity Series, ed., Peter J. Paris (New York: New York University Press, 2000), 18.
3. Livezey, "New Context of Urban Religion," 6–14.
4. Ibid., 6.
5. Ibid., 7–9.
6. Ibid., 9–12.
7. Ibid., 12–14.
8. Franklin, *Another Day's Journey*, 53–76.
9. Robert Michael Franklin, "The Safest Place on Earth: The Culture of Black Congregations" in *American Congregations Volume 2, New Perspectives in the Study of Congregations*, ed., James P. Wind and James W. Lewis (Chicago: The University of Chicago Press, 1994), 257–284.
10. Growing out of the Congregation in Changing Communities Project, a research effort funded by the Lilly Endowment and based at Emory University, Ammerman and Dudley outline seven common patterns of congregational response to cultural, economic, or social/structural changes in urban communities: (1) Many congregations attempt to "hold their own" repeating the same patterns and slowly dwindle. (2) Some congregations move deciding their gifts will be better used elsewhere. (3) A few congregations stare death in the face and, by establishing new ministries, experience resurrection. (4) A few congregations are far sighted enough to develop new ministries and integrate new members before their situations become critical. (5) Some found new congregations. (6) Some develop a niche that is less tied to a particular place but is more tied to the gifts, connections, and passions of their members. Christopher Temple would fit in this pattern of response. (7) Some congregations merge. This was the challenge given to Dr. Evans by Bishop Douglas. Carl S. Dudley and Nancy T. Ammerman, *Congregations in Transition: A Guide for Analyzing, Assessing, and Adapting in Changing*

Communities. Foreword by Loren B. Mead (San Francisco: Jossey-Bass Publishers, 2002), 6–8.

11. Ammerman explains the adaptation of congregations in their changing environments in terms of resources (e.g., human, financial, building, strength of pastoral and lay leadership, educational levels of pastor and leadership, morale of members with respect to congregation's future), structures of authority (e.g., creative partnership between the pastor and the members who recognize the legitimacy of pastoral leadership as well as the partnership between congregations and denominational authorities), and internal culture (e.g., the activities, artifacts, and accounts of congregational life). Ammerman argues that these factors explain more about how congregations change in their changing environments more than their biblical or theological beliefs. Ammerman with Farnsley and et al., *Congregation and Community*, 310–345.

12. *The Black Church in the African American Experience*, 129. Du Bois, *The Negro Church*; Mays and Nicholson, *The Negro's Church*; Frazier, *The Negro Church in America*; Lincoln, *The Black Church Since Frazier*; Morris, *The Origins of the Civil Rights Movement*; Lincoln and Mamiya, *The Black Church in the African American Experience*; Pattillo, "Church Culture as a Strategy of Action in the Black Community"; Billingsley, *Mighty Like a River*; Gilkes, "Plenty Good Room."

13. I did not have a document of pastoral salary in 1986, the year of Rev. Harrison's arrival. The 1989 and 1992 pastoral statistical reports indicated salaries of $27,000 and $28,000 respectively. Thus, the "starting salary" of about $25,000 per year (plus parsonage and expenses) assumes a very modest increase from 1986 to 1989. Of the 1,531 urban clergy in the Lincoln and Mamiya survey, only about 9.8% of the respondents said that they earned more than $25,000. Ibid., 127–128.

14. Lincoln and Mamiya, *The Black Church in the African American Experience*, 289–294.

15. Mozella Mitchell's study reported in Ibid., 301.

16. This low amount in the category of "pastor's salary and expenses" probably indicates that most if not all of this total was simply reimbursement for travel to mandatory church conferences.

17. This method of analysis is adapted from Strauss and Corbin's procedures of axial coding utilizing a coding paradigm involving the relationship between causal conditions, a phenomenon, context, intervening conditions, action/interaction strategies, and consequences. Transformative pastoral leadership in the black church is the central idea, or phenomenon, about which actions or interactions are related. Anselm Strauss and Juliet Corbin, *Basics of Qualitative Research*, 96–107.

18. Lincoln and Mamiya, *The Black Church in the African American Experience*, 77. This estimate of 3.5. million members of this, the largest of the black Pentecostal bodies, rivals the combined total of the three largest historic black Methodist denominations: the AME Church with a 1989 membership in the United States of 2.2 million (54), the AME Zion Church with a 1989 membership of 1.2 million members in the United States (58), and the CME Church with a 1989 membership of 900,000 in the United States (63). Out of the 9.4 million member United Methodist Church, 360,000 are black (67).

19. Stewart develops a similar list of "prevailing myths, assumptions, and realities preventing church growth in United Methodism" with his set of strategies of how churches can grow despite the attitudinal blockages to growth in their denominations (Stewart, *Empowerment Church*, 109–112).

20. Morgenthaler argues that in this postmodern context it is "time to get real." By this, she means that worship must nurture a real interactive encounter between seekers and the Divine. Sally Morgenthaler, *Worship Evangelism: Inviting Unbelievers into the Presence of God* (Grand Rapids, MI: Zondervan Publishing House, 1999).

21. Acts 2, especially Acts 2: 42–47.

22. David D. Daniels, "Ain't Gonna Let Nobody Turn Me 'Round: The Politics of Race and the New Black Middle Class Religion" in *Public Religion and Urban Transformation: Faith in the City*, ed., Lowell W. Livezey in Religion, Race, and Ethnicity Series, ed., Peter J. Paris (New York: New York University Press, 2000), 178.

23. Ibid., 181.

24. Ibid., 163–165.

25. One of the generalizations about embodying changes in congregations is gaining the support of the congregation's informal leaders, "gatekeepers," "matriarchs," and "patriarchs." Jackson Carroll provides a helpful list of general principles to smooth proposed changes. Ammerman et al., *Studying Congregations*, 188–189.

26. I am treating the three interrelated ministry ideas—evangelism, discipleship, and church growth—as one challenge for brevity. One could evangelize—proclaim the gospel of Jesus Christ with an aim of persuading persons to accept Jesus as Savior—without giving care to the consequent follow-up work of discipleship—the nurture, teaching, and training of persons to become responsible, obedient, reproducing disciples of Jesus. Furthermore, there are persons committed to ministries of discipleship that are not committed to church growth—a pragmatic set of strategies to grow churches regardless of external contexts that have grown out of the Fuller School of World Evangelism movement founded by Donald McGavran. Rev. Harrison may be regarded as one of the church growth leaders of the CME denomination, one of a handful of churches that are fast growing mega churches.

27. I have continually emphasized the theological response to changes in the world as a part of my concept of transformative pastoral leadership. However, I recognize that a critique of the church growth movement is its pragmatism. Believing that it is God's will for the church to grow, church growth leaders like Rev. Harrison set numerical goals for growth. The question of why some churches grow and some churches stagnate or decline in the same religious cultural environment is the central research question of church growth strategists. In the black religious environment, it is not unreasonable to assume that church growth leaders will study growing churches in their environment and adapt strategies that seem to bring more lost people to Christ and responsible membership in the church. The seminal work of the church growth addresses not only the theological consideration for church growth, but also searches for the causes of it, the sociological foundations for it, and suggests how one administers for church growth. Donald A. McGavran, *Understanding*

Church Growth, 3rd. ed., rev. and ed. by C. Peter Wagner (Grand Rapids, MI: Eerdman's Publishing Company, 1990). Another more contemporary researcher in the church growth movement is George G. Hunter III. The central question running through all of his writings is "how to reach and disciple significant numbers of pre-Christian secular people in a context in which the West, the historic bearer of the missionary message to other lands, has itself been 'lost.' " See e.g., George G. Hunter III, *A Church for the Unchurched* (Nashville: Abingdon Press, 1996).

28. Jones argues that a systemic approach to congregational evangelism involves correcting misconceptions about evangelism, emphasizing a missionary ecclesiology in the congregation, developing missionary leaders, both clergy and laity, analyzing the congregation as system, and enhancing the congregation's system of evangelism (Jones, *Evangelistic Love*, 185–205).

29. Taylor Branch, *Parting the Waters: America in the King Years 1954–63* (New York: Simon & Schuster, Inc., 1988), 3.

30. Ibid., 114.

31. Ibid., 114–115.

32. The matter of transformation in the thinking of the people regarding religious leadership in the black community remains a complex question given the sources of "traditional authority" in the black church. Max Weber's analysis of power and domination is particularly appropriate. In Weber's analysis, a particular case of "traditional authority" is patriarchal domination. Weber says that "the roots of patriarchal domination grow out of the master's authority over his household. In this structure of domination, "the master wields his power without restraint, at his own discretion and, above all, unencumbered by rules, insofar as it is not limited by tradition or by competing powers." Max Weber, *Economy and Society: An Outline of Interpretive Sociology*, Vols 1 and 2, ed., Guenther Roth and Claus Wittich (Berkeley: University of California Press, 1978), 1006–1007. Despite this strong tradition of preeminent ministerial authority, I think there are signs that ministers as well as laity are increasingly tired of pastors and bishops that act "as gods" or "masters." Greater accountability is being called for. A helpful resource that deals with crucial issues such as financial management, governing board relationships, insurance and legal matters, and responses to sexual abuse in the church is found in Paul Chaffee, *Accountable Leadership: A Resource Guide for Sustaining Legal, Financial, and Ethical Integrity in Today's Congregations*, rev. and exp. (San Francisco: Jossey-Bass Publishers, 1997).

33. Gilkes, "Plenty Good Room," 110–112.

34. Sid Buzzell, gen. ed., Kenneth Boa and Bill Perkins, ed., *The Leadership Bible: Leadership Principles from God's Word* (Grand Rapids, MI: Zondervan Publishing House, 1998), 89.

35. Burns, *Leadership*, 20.

36. Jackson W. Carroll in Ammerman et al., *Studying Congregations*, 1998, 181–183.

37. Wilmore notes that the black church has sustained the most brutal attacks by those once in it. In the 1920s and 1930s the black intelligentsia identified

black religion with ignorance and superstition. The social revolution of the 1960s provided critics with new opportunity to make the case that "blood sucking preachers and their churches" drained wealth from their communities and made no meaningful contribution to the struggle of black people. Wilmore, *Black Religion and Black Radicalism*, 201–202.

38. Lawrence Mamiya, "Black Church Congregational Studies Institute: Research Issues and Trends in African-American Religion," June 29, 1999.

39. Ibid., 203.

40. Lincoln and Mamiya, *The Black Church in the African American Experience*, 404.

41. Ibid., 13.

42. For example, the narrative in the seventy-fifth church history program closes with the statement: "The task is ever before us to be 'The Church Reaching and Teaching for Jesus,' as we carry out the 'Great Commission' in Matthews 28: 19–20. 'Go ye therefore, and teach all nations, baptizing them in the name of the Father, and of the Son, and of the Holy Ghost: Teaching them to observe all things, whatsoever I have commanded you: and lo, I am with you always, even unto the end of the world. Amen!' ".

43. In my review of one of the church budgets with the church administrator and former church treasurer, Mrs. Janice Parker, I questioned her about what the "benevolent" category included. "Benevolent" donations at Christopher Temple include contributions to "legitimate needs" such as utility payments, food, persons burned out, and the jobless. It was emphasized that discernment was used by the pastor and stewards who were appointed to make sure that money was not given just to "need to manage better" needs.

44. Balance sheet of the year 1999 prepared by the C.P.A. regularly employed by Isaiah-Matthews to do prepare an auditor's statement, balance sheet of assets and liabilities, and income and expense statement.

45. Dudley and Ammerman, *Congregations in Transition*, 7.

46. Grant, "Womanist Theology: Black Women's Experiences," 284–285.

47. Alice Walker, "In Search of Our Mothers' Gardens" in *Black Theology: A Documentary History Volume One: 1966–1979*, ed., James H. Cone and Gayraud S. Wilmore, 2nd ed. rev. (Maryknoll, NY: Orbis Books, 1993), 340.

48. Hartford Institute Religion Research, Nancy T. Ammerman, *Doing Good in Chicago*, 25.

49. The analytical study of process is elusive as one sees snapshots of the congregation at discrete times and places. Only in looking back on a process can you really see "growth, development, movement; or at the other extreme, the failure of growth, a sliding backward, stagnation" (Strauss and Corbin, *Basics of Qualitative Research*, 144).

50. Maria Harris.

51. Carl S. Dudley in Ammerman et al., *Studying Congregations*, 105–108.

52. Martin F. Saarinen, *The Life Cycle of a Congregation* (Washington DC: The Alban Institute, 1986).

53. Recognizing that some churches are insecure, low self-esteem churches that lack the confidence to develop a strategic plan for growth and development,

Hunter describes a model for turning around a church through a series of defining "breakthrough" projects. George G. Hunter III. *Leading and Managing a Growing Church* (Nashville: Abingdon Press, 2000), 110–136.

54. Linda J. Vogel, *Teaching and Learning in Communities of Faith: Empowering Adults Through Religious Education*, The Jossey-Bass Higher and Adult Education Series, ed., Alan B. Knox (San Francisco: Jossey-Bass Publishers, 1991), 1.

55. Mary Elizabeth Moore, *Education for Continuity and Change: A New Model for Christian Religious Education.* (Nashville: Abingdon Press, 1983), 176–178.

56. Ibid., 184.

57. Ronald Heifitz, *Leadership Without Easy Answers*, 64–66.

58. Alice Walker, *In Search of Our Mother's Gardens*, 340–341.

59. Dr. Evans's belief in the giftedness of every individual is shared by those who think that releasing individual capacities in marginalized communities is one of the steps to asset-based community development. See John P. Kretzmann and John L. McKnight, *Building Communities From the Inside Out: A Path Toward Finding and Mobilizing a Community's Assets.* (Evanston, IL: Institute for Policy Research Northwestern University, 1993).

60. For example, E. Stanley Ott, a white Presbyterian pastor, outlines shifts to transition from a traditional church to a transformational church, some of which are similar to the strategies explained in this chapter. His "shift from an unchanging worship format to a ministry of worship and music responsive to the variety of needs present in the congregation and in the community you are trying to reach" is similar to the strategy that I name as shifting from traditional worship to culturally affirming celebration. Ott's "shift from assuming discipleship to developing discipleship" corresponds well with the strategy that I name as shifting to intentional evangelism, discipleship, and church growth. Ott's three shifts concerning the practice of leadership (from a leader deploying ministry to a leader developing ministry, from a controlling leadership to a permission-giving leadership, and from a pastor-centered/officer-centered ministry to a shared ministry among pastors, officers, and congregation) correspond well with the shifts in the practice of leadership that I name as shift from pastor-centered leadership to shared transforming leadership. Ott's shift "from a primary emphasis on the communal life of the church to a balanced emphasis on the communal and missional life of the church" corresponds to the shift that I named a shift from a "members only orientation" to a "communal orientation." Ott's shifts regarding vision and expectation are seen in my naming of the building of a community of survival, wholeness, and healing. E. Stanley Ott, *Twelve Dynamic Shifts for Transforming Your Church* (Grand Rapids, MI: Eerdman's Publishing Company, 2002), 101–102. Dudley and Ammerman emphasize that congregations in transition must not only make programmatic changes, but they must also make the shift that I name "transforming attitudes and behaviors." New practices and habits of ministry must become ingrained in the new life of the congregation and assumed as normal if profound change is to occur (Dudley and Ammerman, *Congregation in Transition*, 145–173).

61. Ammerman with Farnsley et al., *Congregation and Community*, 45.
62. Ibid., 343.
63. Bosch, *Transforming Mission*, 23.

5   Independent Black Methodist Systems as Contexts of Transformative Pastoral Leadership

1. I do not claim that all of the issues and perspectives that are grounded in my analysis of pastoral leadership in the CME Church are applicable to the other major independent black Methodist denominations, the AME and AME Zion churches. They are three denominations that are independent of one another and thus have distinctive practices. However, my assumption is that, because of the nearly identical polity and doctrines of these denominations and their similar responses to the African American experience, this discussion addresses issues that affect all of these denominations. My interviews with Bishop Douglas of the CME Church, Bishop Norman of the AME Zion Church, and Rev. Benjamin Richards of the AME Church seemed to confirm this assumption.

2. Gilkes, "Plenty Good Room," 115–118.

3. Billingsley, *Mighty Like a River*, 89 and Obie Clayton, Jr., "The Church and Social Change: Accommodation, Moderation, or Protest" in *An American Dilemma Revisited: Race Relations in a Changing World*, ed., Obie Clayton, Jr. (New York: Russell Sage Foundation, 1996), 200–206. Though Clayton agrees, that in the post–civil rights movement years, the strategies of urban churches have been internal social services, he is particularly critical of traditional black Baptist and Methodist denominations that did not foresee the problems of urbanization and did not demonstrate the ability to plan strategically to provide aid to the needy. The Church of God in Christ and Nation of Islam are credited with greater attention to empowerment in the black community.

4. Billingsley poses the theory that when a community in severe and sustained crisis turns to the church for leadership, the black church tends to move from its purely privatistic orientation to its communal orientation "provided that the church, as an organization, is strong, stable, resourceful, and provided that the minister, as leader, is strong, charismatic, innovative, and community oriented." Billingsley, *Mighty Like a River*, 11.

5. Ammerman with Farnsley et al., *Congregation and Community*, 329–330.

6. Delores Carpenter conducted a 1999 national study of 324 black female and 448 male Master of Divinity graduates with special attention to the status of women in ministry. She reports that in the three graduating classes examined (classes of 1985, 1992, and 1999), nearly half of the women had switched denominations. Of these women who had switched denominations 24% indicated that they had done so for ordination reasons, 15% indicated that their switching was employment related, and 22% indicated that their switching was due to marriage-related matters. Delores C. Carpenter, "A Time For Honor: A Portrait of African American Clergywomen" in Alton B. Pollard, III and Love Henry Whelchel, Jr., ed. *"How Long This Road" Race, Religions,*

and the Legacy of C. Eric Lincoln, Black Religion/Womanist/Social Justice Series, ed. Dwight N. Hopkins and Linda E. Thomas (New York: Palgrave Macmillan, 2003), 148–149.

7. Bi-vocational pastors are also referred to as "tent-making" pastors because they are self-consciously following the example of the apostle Paul. Paul willingly relinquished his right to receive material support in exchange for his ministry (I Cor. 9) and supported himself through his trade of tent-making (Acts 18: 3). Like Paul, some twenty-first century "tent-makers" report greater freedom to focus on mission and ministry as a result of not having the stress of having to depend completely on the church for their salaries. Becky R. McMillan, "How Church Polity Affects Pastoral Salaries," in *Congregations* vol. 28, no. 5 (September/October 2002): 6–11.

8. The Lincoln and Mamiya study of black clergy of 2,150 churches consisted of 3.7% female clergy. They estimate that fewer than 5% of clergy in the historic black denominations are female. Among their findings was a strong relationship between the variable of denomination and attitudes of approval toward woman pastors. The three Baptist denominations and one Pentecostal denomination surveyed (Church of God in Christ) tended to be highly negative in their attitudes toward woman as pastors. The three Methodist denominations were strongly positive. Lincoln and Mamiya, *The Black Church in the African American Experience*, 291.

9. Ibid., 299–301.

10. Lakey and Stephens, *God in My Mama's House*, 44.

11. Sondra Higgins Matthaei, *Faith Matters: Faith Mentoring in the Faith Community* (Valley Forge, PA: Trinity Press International, 1996).

12. Ibid., 23.

13. Ibid., 11.

14. Ibid., 47.

15. Lincoln and Mamiya, *The Black Church in the African American Experience*, 297–298.

16. *The Book of Discipline of the Christian Methodist Episcopal Church*, paragraph 428.

17. Othal Hawthorne Lakey, *The History of the Christian Methodist Episcopal Church*, Revised (Memphis, TN: The C.M.E. Publishing House, 1996), 287–288.

18. The most recent law of the AME Zion Church on the subject of pastoral tenure says, "He/She (Bishops) shall allow a Preacher to remain in a Charge four consecutive years, provided in his/her judgment, it is best; but no longer, unless he/she is building a Church or Parsonage or engaged in paying off some heavy Church debt; he/she then may allow him/her to stay longer at his/her discretion." African Methodist Episcopal Zion Church, *The Doctrines and Discipline of the African Methodist Episcopal Zion Church*. Revised by the General Conference Greensboro, North Carolina July 26–August 4, 2000 (Charlotte, NC: A.M.E. Zion Publishing House, 2000), paragraph 242.

19. William Julius Wilson, *When Work Disappears: The World of the New Urban Poor* (New York: Vintage Books, 1996), 44.

20. Stewart, *Empowerment Churches*, 76.

21. Hab. 2:2.

22. Lincoln and Mamiya, *The Black Church in the African American Experience*, 307.
23. Carpenter, "A Time for Honor," 143–144.
24. The issue of benefits has not been a focus of this study. However, I agree with Lincoln and Mamiya (*The Black Church in the African American Experience*, 400–401) who identify improved benefits in the black denominations as a major issue. It will be a problem to attract and retain gifted and theologically trained clergy for full-time ministry without them feeling the security of health and pension benefits at the minimum. The CME Church has moved in this direction. Since 1986, they have required each local congregation to contribute 12% of the annual reported amount of the pastor's salary toward the retirement fund. *The Book of Discipline of the Christian Methodist Episcopal Church*, paragraph 1039–1041.
25. Preachers and Presenters included Dr. Harry Riggs, Dr. Dennis Proctor, Dr. Kevin Cosby, Rev. Marcus Cosby, Rev. Albert Tyson, Rev. W. Darin Moore, Dr. Susan Johnson-Cook, Rev. Otis Moss III, Dr. Bonnie Hines, Dr. E. Stanley Ott, Dr. Larry Murphy, Rev. Reginald Blount, Rev. Henrico White, Rev. Brenda Little, Bishop Henry Williamson, Sr., Dr. Hycel Taylor, Dr. Tracy Smith-Malone, Rev. Irene Taylor, and Dr. Essie Clark-George.
26. Palmer, *Courage to Teach*, 164.
27. Ibid., 166–171.
28. Ibid., 166.
29. Ibid., 172–175.
30. Ibid., 175–179.
31. Ibid., 166.
32. Ibid., 181.
33. Frazier, *Negro Church in America*, 48–49.
34. In an unpublished document, the plan of union of the AME Zion and CME churches (2000), one writer, Rev. Dr. James Samuels, urged a change in clergy attitudes from "magisterial to ministerial."
35. Nancy Bedford, lecturing at Garrett-Evangelical Theological Seminary.

Appendix A: Research Method

1. Ammerman, *Studying Congregations*.
2. Du Bois, *The Negro Church*; Mays and Nicholson, *The Negro's Church*; Frazier, *The Negro Church in America*; Lincoln, *The Black Church Since Frazier*; Lincoln and Mamiya, Morris, *The Origins of the Civil Rights Movement*; Lincoln and Mamiya, *The Black Church in the African American Experience*; Pattillo, "Church Culture as a Strategy of Action in the Black Community"; Billingsley, *Mighty Like a River*; Gilkes, "Plenty Good Room."
3. This four-step method, explained by James Poling in his September 31, 2001 lecture to a Methods of Research in Congregations class, is a later version of the six-step method for practical theology, which is published in an earlier text: James N. Poling and Donald E. Miller, *Foundations for a Practical Theology of Ministry* (Nashville: Abingdon Press, 1985), 62–99.

4. Wiley in Cone and Wilmore, "Black Theology, the Black Church, and the African-American Community."

5. Barney G. Glaser and Anselm L. Straus, *The Discovery of Grounded Theory: Strategies for Qualitative Research* (New York: Aldine De Gruyter, 1967). Strauss and Corbin, *Basics of Qualitative Research.*

6. Carlyle Fielding Stewart, *African American Church Growth: 12 Principles for Prophetic Ministry* (Nashville: Abingdon Press, 1994).

7. As a participating delegate of the General Conference of the AME Zion Church in 2000, I observed the politically charged debate of drafted legislation regarding "A Bill of Rights for Pastors in Charge." Pastor's rights as full-time ministers were extensively debated and weighed against the tradition of Episcopal authority. This legislation grew out of the claims of clergy drafting the legislation who stated that pastors have been dismissed from their employment without notice or statement of cause. In the form presented, this legislation was ultimately tabled by the conference of ministerial and lay delegates. Official Journal Forty Sixth Quadrennial Session General Conference of the African Methodist Episcopal Zion Church, pp. 78–79, 84–85, 862–864, 891–892.

8. Patricia Adler and Peter Adler, *Membership Roles in Field Research*, Qualitative Research Methods Series, vol. 6 (Newbury Park, CA: Sage Publications, Inc., 1987).

9. James A Holstein and Jaber F. Gubrium, *The Active Interview*, Qualitative Research Methods Series, vol. 37 (Thousand Oaks, CA: Sage Publications, Inc., 1995).

10. Ibid.

11. Methodist churches are influenced by the "conference year" that is marked by consecutive sessions of annual conference gatherings. This twelve-month conference year is very influential in local church life because congregations are mindful of pastors being appointed or reappointed on an annual basis; substantial financial assessments are paid to the denomination which is paid at various denominational gatherings during the conference year; membership and financial statistics are reported by pastors over the course of the conference year.

12. John Van Maanen, *Tales of the Field: On Writing Ethnography* (Chicago: The University of Chicago Press, 1988), 73.

Appendix D: Community Census Data

1. The pseudonym, Middleton was selected (1) to signify the predominantly black middle-class characteristics of the neighborhood around Christopher Temple and (2) to signify that Christopher Temple is near the boundary of two community areas that have significantly different employment, income, and poverty data. As a result of this, I have chosen to give the census data for Middleton and the adjoining community area of Newton, which contains new areas of poverty. Christopher Temple is actually in Middleton, the more prosperous of the two areas. However, its close proximity to Newton, which has a poverty rate nearly double that of Middleton, suggests the challenges

of the black middle-class neighborhood context, within which "the right and wrong paths are in easy reach of neighborhood youth." Mary Pattillo-McCoy, *Black Picket Fences*, 6. Tables DP-1 (Profile of General Demographic Characteristics 2000), DP-2 (Profile of Selected Social Characteristics 2000), and DP-3 (Profile of Selected Economic Characteristics 2000), Summary of General Demographic Characteristics for the City of Chicago and its seventy-seven Community Areas.

2. Though the unemployment rate of the Middleton (14.6%) is significantly lower than Pioneer Park (24.4%) (but higher than the citywide rate of 10.1%), the time to travel to work (41.2 minutes) is among the highest of all the neighborhoods of the city, a sign of the spatial dislocation in this community. Few people who live in the neighborhood can find work there. Also, it is likely that many who worship at Christopher Temple do not live in the neighborhood context of Middleton. This has implications, not only for the social cohesion of the community surrounding Christopher Temple, but also for the ability of Christopher Temple members to serve its community.

3. Only the population data for "white" and "black" is shown to demonstrate the continued high level of racial segregation in this neighborhood (98% black or African American). The definitions of "race" by the Census Bureau are self-identified social–political categories. Reflecting the growing complexity of racial and ethnic categories, the 2000 census included categories for "some other race" and "two or more races." Hence, the census bureau definition of race includes: "The concept of race as used by the Census Bureau reflects self-identification by people according to the race or races with which they most closely identify. These categories are socio-political constructs and should not be interpreted as being scientific or anthropological in nature. Furthermore, the race categories include both racial and national-origin groups. . . . The OMB requires five minimum race categories (American Indian and Alaska Native, Asian, black or African American, Native Hawaiian and Other Pacific Islander, and White) for race. The race categories are described below with a sixth category, 'Some other race,' added with OMB approval. In addition to the five race groups, the OMB also states that respondents should be offered the option of selecting one or more races."

4. The community description of chapter 3, Developing a New Congregation in a Redeveloping Community, utilizes census data in the *Local Community Fact Book Chicago Metropolitan Area 1990*. Though poverty and income data for 2000 was actually released in 2002, the high poverty rate of 43.8% in 2000 suggests that the community issues described in chapter 3, driven by the poverty of the community, have not significantly changed. As high-income families continue to move into the new homes being built, economic polarization between the higher income families and lower income families will increase.

Bibliography

Adler, Patricia and Peter Adler. *Membership Roles in Field Research*. Qualitative Research Methods Series, vol. 6. Newbury Park, CA: Sage Publications, Inc., 1987.

African Methodist Episcopal Zion Church. *The Doctrines and Disciplines of the African Methodist Episcopal Zion Church*. With an appendix. Revised by the General Conference Greensboro, North Carolina July 26–August 4, 2000. Charlotte, NC: A.M.E. Zion Publishing House, 2000.

Ammerman, Nancy T., Jackson W. Carroll, Carl S. Dudley, and William McKinney. *Studying Congregations: A New Handbook*. Nashville, TN: Abingdon Press, 1998.

Ammerman, Nancy Tatom with Arthur E. Farnsley II and Tammy Adams, Penny Edgell Becker, Brenda Brasher, Thomas Clark, Joan Cunningham, Nancy Eiseland, Barbara Elwell, Michelle Hale, Diana Jones, Virginia Laffey, Stacey Nicholas, Marcia Robinson, Mary Beth Sievens, Daphne Wiggins, Connie Ziegler. *Congregation and Community*. New Brunswick, NJ: Rutgers University Press, 1997.

Andrews, Dale P. *Practical Theology for Black Churches: Bridging Black Theology and African American Folk Religion*. Louisville: Westminster John Knox Press, 2002.

Arias, Mortimas and Alan Johnson. *The Great Commission: Biblical Models for Evangelism*. Nashville, TN: Abingdon Press, 1992.

Billingsley, Andrew. *Mighty Like a River: The Black Church and Social Reform*. With foreword by Lawrence N. Jones and introduction by C. Eric Lincoln. New York: Oxford University Press, 1999.

Bosch, David. *Transforming Mission: Paradigm Shifts in Theology of Mission*. American Society of Missiology Series, no. 16. Maryknoll, New York: Orbis Books, 1991.

Branch, Taylor. *Parting the Waters: America in the King Years 1954–63*. New York: Simon and Schuster, Inc., 1988.

Browning, Don S. "Congregational Studies as Practical Theology." In *American Congregations, Volume 2: New Perspectives in the Study of Congregations*. ed. James Wind and James W. Lewis, 192–221. Chicago, IL: The University of Chicago Press, 1994.

Brueggemann, Walter. *The Creative Word: Canon as a Model for Biblical Education*. Philadelphia, PA: Fortress Press, 1982.

Burns, James MacGregor. *Leadership*. New York: HarperCollins Publishers, Inc., 1978.

Buzell, Sid., gen. ed. and Kenneth Boa and Bill Perkins, eds., *The Leadership Bible: Leadership Principles from God's Word*. Grand Rapids, MI: Zondervan Publishing House, 1998.

Campbell, Ted A. *Methodist Doctrine: The Essentials*. Nashville, TN: Abingdon Press, 1999.

Carpenter, Delores C. "A Time for Honor: A Portrait of African American Clergywomen." In *"How Long This Road" Race, Religion, and the Legacy of C. Eric Lincoln*. ed. Alton B. Pollard, III and Love Henry Whelchel, Jr. in Black Religion/Womanist/Social Justice Series. ed. Dwight N. Hopkins and Linda E. Thomas, 141–159. New York: Palgrave Macmillan, 2003.

Chaffee, Paul. *Accountable Leadership: A Resource Guide for Sustaining Legal, Financial, and Ethical Integrity in Today's Congregations*. Revised and Expanded. San Francisco, CA: Jossey-Bass Publishers, 1997.

Chicago Fact Book Consortium. *Local Community Fact Book Chicago Metropolitan Area 1990*. Chicago, IL: Department of Sociology, University of Illinois at Chicago, 1990.

Christian Methodist Episcopal Church. *The Book of Discipline of the Christian Methodist Episcopal Church*. Memphis, TN: The C.M.E. Publishing House, 1998.

Clayton, Obie, Jr., "The Church and Social Change: Accommodation, Moderation, or Protest." In *An American Dilemma Revisited: Race Relations in a Changing World*. ed. Obie Clayton, Jr., 191–208. New York: Russell Sage Foundation, 1996.

Crain, Margaret Ann and Jack L. Seymour. "The Ethnographer as Minister: Ethnographic Research in Ministry." *Religious Education* (Summer 1996): 299–315.

Daloz, Laurent A. Parks, Cheryl H. Keen, James P. Keen, and Sharon Daloz Parks. *Common Fire: Leading Lives of Commitment in a Complex World*. Boston, MA: Beacon Press, 1996.

Daloz, Laurent A. *Mentor: Guiding the Journey of Adult Learners*, 2nd ed. of *Effective Teaching and Mentoring*. With a foreword by K. Patricia Cross. San Francisco, CA: Jossey-Bass Publishers, 1999.

Daniels, David D. "Ain't Gonna Let Nobody Turn Me, 'Round: The Politics of Race and the New Black Middle Class Religion." In *Public Religion and Urban Transformation: Faith in the City*. ed. Lowell W. Livezey in Religion, Race, and Ethnicity Series. ed. Peter J. Paris, 162–185. New York: New York University Press, 2000.

Du Bois, W. E. Burghardt, ed., *The Negro Church*. Atlanta: Atlanta University Press, 1903. Reprint, New York: Octagon Books, Inc., 1968.

———. *The Gift of Black Folk: The Negroes in the Making of America*. Boston, MA: The Stratford Co., 1924. Reprint, New York: Johnson Reprint Corporation, 1968.

Dudley, Carl S. and Nancy T. Ammerman. *Congregations in Transition: A Guide for Analyzing, Assessing, and Adapting in Changing Communities*. Foreword by Loren B. Mead. San Francisco, CA: Jossey-Bass Publishers, 2002.

Frank, Thomas Edward. *The Soul of the Congregation: An Invitation to Congregational Reflection*. Nashville, TN: Abingdon Press, 2000.

Franklin, Robert M. "The Safest Place on Earth: The Culture of Black Congregations." In *American Congregations Volume 2, New Perspectives in the Study of Congregations*. ed. James P. Wind and James W. Lewis, 257–284. Chicago, IL: The University of Chicago Press, 1994.

———. *Another Day's Journey: Black Churches Confronting the American Crisis*. Minneapolis: Fortress Press, 1997.

Frazier, E. Franklin. *The Negro Church in America*, 1963. New edition with C. Eric Lincoln, *The Black Church Since Frazier*. New York: Schocken Books, 1974.

Glaser, Barney G. and Anselm L. Strauss. *The Discovery of Grounded Theory: Strategies for Qualitative Research*. New York: Aldine De Gruyter, 1967.

Gilkes, Cheryl Townsend. "Plenty Good Room: Adaptation in a Changing Black Church." *The Annals of the American Academy*, AAPSS 558 (July 1998): 101–121.

———. *"If It Wasn't for the Women . . ." Black Women's Experience and Womanist Culture in Church and Community*. Maryknoll, NY: Orbis Books, 2001.

Grant, Jacquelyn. "Womanist Theology: Black Women's Experience as a Source for Doing Theology, With Special Reference to Christology." In *Black Theology, A Documentary History Volume Two: 1980–1992*. ed. James H. Cone and Gayraud S. Wilmore, 273–289. Maryknoll, NY: Orbis Books, 1993.

Groome, Thomas H. *Sharing Faith: A Comprehensive Approach to Religious Education and Pastoral Ministry, The Way of Shared Praxis*. New York: HarperCollins Publishers, Inc., 1991.

Hammersley, Martyn and Paul Atkinson, *Ethnography: Principles in Practice*, 2nd ed. New York: Routledge, 1995.

Harris, Fredrick C. *Something Within: Religion in African-American Politics*. Ph.D. diss., Northwestern University, Evanston, IL, 1994.

Harris, Maria. *Fashion Me a People: Curriculum in the Church*. Louisville, KY: Westminster John Knox Press, 1989.

Hartford Institute for Religion Research. Nancy T. Ammerman, project director. *Doing Good in Chicago: Congregations and Service Organizations Building the Community, A Research Report from the Organizing Religious Work Project*. Hartford, CT: Hartford Seminary, 2001.

Heifitz, Ronald A. *Leadership Without Easy Answers*. Cambridge, MA: The Belknap Press of Harvard University Press, 1994.

Higginbotham, Evelyn Brooks. *Righteous Discontent: The Woman's Movement in the Black Baptist Church 1880–1920*. Cambridge, MA: Harvard University Press, 1993.

Holstein, James A. and Jaber F. Gubrium. *The Active Interview*. Qualitative Research Methods Series, vol. 37. Thousand Oaks, CA: Sage Publications, Inc., 1995.

Hopewell, James. With editor's foreword by Barbara G. Wheeler. *Congregation: Stories and Structures*. Philadelphia, PA: Fortress Press, 1987.

Hunter, George G. III. *Church for the Unchurched*. Nashville, TN: Abingdon Press, 1996.

Hunter, George G. III. *Leading and Managing a Growing Church*. Nashville, TN: Abingdon Press, 2000.

Johnson, Joseph A., Jr. *The Soul of the Black Preacher*. Philadelphia, PA: Pilgrim Press, 1971.

Jones, Scott J. *The Evangelistic Love of God and Neighbor: A Theology of Witness and Discipleship*. Nashville, TN: Abingdon Press, 2003.

John P. Kretzmann and John L. McKnight, *Building Communities From the Inside Out: A Path Toward Finding and Mobilizing a Community's Assets*. Evanston, IL: Institute for Policy Research Northwestern University, 1993.

Katzenbach, Jon R. and Douglas K. Smith. *The Wisdom of Teams: Creating the High-Performance Organization*. Boston, MA: Harvard Business School Press, 1993.

Lakey, Othal Hawthorne. *The History of the Christian Methodist Episcopal Church* (Revised) Memphis, TN: The C.M.E. Publishing House, 1996.

Lakey, Othal Hawthorne and Betty Beene Stephens. *God in My Mama's House: A Study of the Women's Movement in the C.M.E. Church*. Memphis, TN: The C.M.E. Publishing House, 1994.

Lincoln, C. Eric and Lawrence H. Mamiya. *The Black Church in the African American Experience*. Durham, NC: Duke University Press, 1990.

Livezey, Lowell W. "The New Context of Urban Religion." In *Public Religion and Urban Transformation: Faith in the City*. ed. Lowell W. Livezey, in Religion, Race, and Ethnicity Series. ed. Peter J. Paris, 1–25. New York: New York University Press, 2000.

Logan, James C. "The Evangelical Imperative: A Wesleyan Perspective." In *Theology and Evangelism in the Wesleyan Heritage*. Nashville, TN: Kingswood Books, 1993, 15–33.

Mamiya, Lawrence. "Black Church Congregational Studies Institute: Research Issues and Trends in African-American Religion." June 29, 1999.

———. "A Social History of the Bethel African Methodist Episcopal Church in Baltimore: The House of God and the Struggle for Freedom." In *American Congregations: Volume 1 Portraits of Twelve Religious Communities*. ed. James P. Wind and James W. Lewis. Chicago, IL: The University of Chicago Press, 1994.

Martin, James P. "Toward a Post-Critical Paradigm." *New Testament Studies*. 33 (1987): 378.

Matthaei, Sondra Higgins. *Faith Matters: Faith Mentoring in the Faith Community* Valley Forge, PA: Trinity Press International, 1996.

Maxwell, John. *The 21 Most Powerful Minutes in a Leader's Day: Revitalize Your Spirit and Empower Your Leadership*. Nashville, TN: Thomas Nelson Publishers, 2000.

Mays, Benjamin Elijah and Joseph William Nicholson. *The Negro's Church*. New York: Negro Universities Press, 1933. (Reprint, Greenwood, 1969).

McGavran, Donald A. *Understanding Church Growth*, 3rd ed., rev. and ed. C. Peter Wagner. Grand Rapids, MI: William B. Eerdman's Publishing Company, 1990.

McKenzie, Vashti M. *Not Without a Struggle: Leadership Development for African-American Women in Ministry*. Cleveland, OH: United Church Press, 1996.

McMillan, Becky R. "How Church Polity Affects Pastoral Salaries." *Congregations.* 28.5 (September/October 2002): 6–11.

Mezirow, Jack. *Transformative Dimensions of Adult Learning.* San Francisco, CA: Jossey-Bass Publishers, 1991.

Miller, John H. Sr. *Trustees and Stewards: The Continuing Power Struggle.* Charlotte, NC: A.M.E. Zion Publishing House, 1973.

Moore, Mary Elizabeth. *Education for Continuity and Change: A New Model for Christian Religious Education.* Nashville, TN: Abingdon Press, 1983.

Morgenthaler, Sally. *Worship Evangelism: Inviting Unbelievers into the Presence of God.* Grand Rapids, MI: Zondervan Publishing House, 1999.

Morris, Aldon. *The Origins of the Civil Rights Movement: Black Communities Organizing for Change.* New York: The Free Press, A Division of Macmillan, Inc., 1984.

Ott, E. Stanley. *Twelve Dynamic Shifts for Transforming Your Church.* Grand Rapids, MI: William B. Eerdman's Publishing Company, 2002.

Palmer, Parker J. *The Courage to Teach: Exploring the Inner Landscape of a Teacher's Life.* San Francisco, CA: Jossey-Bass Publishers, 1998.

Pattillo-McCoy, Mary. *Black Picket Fences: Privilege and Peril Among the Black Middle Class.* Chicago, IL: The University of Chicago Press, 1999.

———. "Church Culture as a Strategy of Action in the Black Community." *American Sociological Review.* 63 (December 1998): 767–784.

Poling, James N. and Donald E. Miller. *Foundations for a Practical Theology of Ministry.* Nashville, TN: Abingdon Press, 1985.

Saarinen, Martin F. *The Life Cycle of a Congregation.* Washington DC: The Alban Institute, 1986.

Schaller, Lyle E. *Discontinuity and Hope: Radical Change and the Path to the Future.* Nashville, TN: Abingdon Press, 1999.

Stewart III, Carlyle Fielding. *African American Church Growth: 12 Principles for Prophetic Ministry.* Nashville, TN: Abingdon Press, 1994.

———. *The Empowerment Church: Speaking a New Language for Church Growth.* Nashville, TN: Abingdon Press, 2001.

Strauss, Anselm and Juliet Corbin. *Basics of Qualitative Research: Grounded Theory Procedures and Techniques.* Newbury Park, CA: Sage Publications, Inc., 1990.

Taylor, Steven J. and Robert Bogdan. *Introduction to Qualitative Research Methods: A Guidebook and Resource,* 3rd ed. New York: John Wiley & Sons, Inc., 1998.

Van Maanen, John. *Tales of the Field: On Writing Ethnography.* Chicago, IL: The University of Chicago Press, 1988.

Vogel, Linda J. *Teaching and Learning in Communities of Faith: Empowering Adults Through Religious Education.* The Jossey-Bass Higher and Adult Education Series. ed. Alan B. Knox. San Francisco, CA: Jossey-Bass Publishers, 1991.

Wachterhauser, Brice R. ed. *Hermeneutics and Modern Philosophy.* Albany: State of New York Press, 1986.

Walls, William J. *The African Methodist Episcopal Zion Church: Reality of the Black Church.* Charlotte, NC: A.M.E. Zion Publishing House, 1974.

Walker, Alice. *In Search of Our Mothers' Gardens*. San Diego: Harcourt Brace Janovich, 1983.

Warren, Rick. *The Purpose Driven Church: Growth Without Compromising Your Message and Mission*. Grand Rapids, MI: Zondervan Publishing House, 1995.

Weber, Max. *Economy and Society: An Outline of Interpretive Sociology*. ed. Guenther Roth and Claus Wittich. Berkeley, CA: University of California Press, 1978.

Weems, Renita J. "Reading *Her Way* through the Struggle: African American Women and the Bible." In *Stony the Road We Trod: African American Biblical Interpretation*. ed. Cain Hope Felder, 57–77. Minneapolis, MN: Fortress Press, 1991.

West, Cornel. *Race Matters*. New York: Vintage Books, 1994.

Wiley, Dennis W. "Black Theology, the Black Church, and the African-American Community." In *Black Theology: A Documentary History Volume II, 1980–1992*. ed. James H. Cone and Gayraud S. Wilmore, 127–138. Maryknoll, NY: Orbis Books, 1993.

Wilmore, Gayraud S. *Black Religion and Black Radicalism: An Interpretation of the Religious History of African Americans*, 3rd ed., rev. and enl. Maryknoll, NY: Orbis Books, 1998.

Wilson, William Julius. *When Work Disappears: The World of the New Urban Poor*. New York: Vintage Books, 1996.

Wimbush, Vincent L. "The Bible and African Americans: An Outline of an Interpretive History." In *Stony the Road We Trod: African American Biblical Interpretation*. ed. Cain Hope Felder, 81–97. Minneapolis, MN: Fortress Press, 1991.

Index